PRAISE FOR GET IT RIPE

jae offers practical advice and truly delicious recipes in her friendly, never-judgmental voice. This book is a breath of fresh, yummy air.

— Jessica Porter, author of *The Hip Chick's Guide to Macrobiotics*

Get It Ripe is awesome! Here is a book that tells us how eating luscious foods will make us healthy. jae pays homage to Eastern traditional understandings of the body and the most recent findings of Western nutritional science. Her enthusiasm for healthy eating is contagious. With her simple-to-follow and uncomplicated recipes, she creates dishes that will tempt vegans and omnivores alike. In this book, packed full of culinary tips for beginners and seasoned chefs, jae has gone well beyond the basics of vegan eating, affirming that we vegans never have to compromise on taste.

— Ruth Tal, owner of Fresh restaurants (Toronto) and author of *Juice for Life*, *Fresh at Home*, and *reFresh*

GET IT RIPE

A Fresh Take on Vegan Cooking & Living

jae steele

ARSENAL
PULP PRESS

VANCOUVER

ARSENAL PULP PRESS
200 – 341 Water Street
Vancouver, BC
Canada V6B 1B8
arsenalpulp.com

The publisher gratefully acknowledges the support of the Government of Canada through the Book Publishing Industry Development Program and the Government of British Columbia through the Book Publishing Tax Credit Program for its publishing activities.

The author and publisher assert that the information contained in this book is true and complete to the best of their knowledge, however it is intended as a reference volume only, and not as a medical manual. The information provided here is designed to help you make informed decisions about your health. It is not intended as a substitute for any treatment that has been prescribed by your doctor. If you have concerns regarding your health, we urge you to seek competent medical help.

Text and design by Electra Design Group
Cover photography by Kristin Sjaarda
Food photography by Roderick Chen
Food styling by Alison Lush
Illustrations by David Powell and Ann Powell
Author photograph by Michelle Clarke
Editing by Bethanne Grabham

Printed and bound in Canada

Library and Archives Canada Cataloguing in Publication:

Steele, Jae, 1980-

    Get it ripe : a fresh take on vegan cooking and living / Jae Steele.

Includes index.

ISBN 978-1-55152-234-0

    1. Vegan cookery. 2. Cookery (Natural foods) 3. Veganism.

I. Title.

TX837.S84 2008   641.5′636   C2008-901630-0

TABLE OF CONTENTS

To all the fine folks in whose kitchens I have cooked.

ACKNOWLEDGMENTS

I have been blessed with an impressively generous and skilled cheerleading squad. Meet the team I'd like to thank:

Team Captain: my mum, Nancy Steele, the wonder woman wearing a dozen hats. I'm not sure I will ever be able to truly thank you for your limitless support.

Assistant Captain: Elise Moser, my secret agent. What a blessing that you should have myriad skills that you were willing to offer to help get me through this process with a greater amount of ease. You've truly been the midwife in this adventure.

The Squad:

Ryan Johnston. You always want the best for me and give me so much. I am such a big fan of yours, and am so grateful for everything we share.

David Powell, who makes amazing meals that for years I was too picky to appreciate. And who provided most of the illustrations that line these pages.

Alison Lush, food-stylist extraordinaire. Thank you for your reliable support in so many areas, and for believing in this project since my very first zine.

Andrew Fair, my favorite cooking companion. You are wonderfully generous.

My dad and step-mum, Gerald and Alison Steele. I really appreciate your encouragement. Thank you for pouring roast beef gravy on the Spelt Sunflower Bread I bring to Sunday night dinners. And my little brothers, James and Charlie – enough with the teasing already! Maybe now you believe my food choices don't make me nuts?

Ann Powell, skilled illustrator and warm supporter.

Sharon and Harry Weisbaum. I am so blessed to have you two for all that you bring to my life.

Cheendana, who planted the seeds that helped to shift the way I looked at food and the natural world.

Michael Armstrong. You generously give support, and supply me with great organic (and often local) produce.

Michelle Clarke, who always licks the batter out of the bowl.

Daphne Gordon. You have been so generous with your time and space and thoughts.

Kristin Sjaarda and Roderick Chen – who made sessions with cameras such fun!

Caroline Dupont, one of my greatest health inspirations! I've got some deep appreciation for what you put out into the world and the time you've given me personally.

Maya Guruswami, who has offered a wealth of knowledge and enthusiastic support.

My chosen family, The Big Cedar Crew: especially Tim, Karla and Heather Holland, and Derek Pinto. You nourish me, and I am blessed to have lived and grown with you all.

Ann-Marie MacDonald and Alisa Palmer, as well as Isabel and Lora, who have one of my favorite kitchens, where many a recipe in this book was created! And thank you for your enthusiastic taste-testing.

Susan Baker, who has offered help with enthusiasm.

Howie Shia and Marco Crawley. I'm so glad I have you two to ask about the kind of techy things I'd rather know nothing about.

Anna Lee-Popham, Adrienne Connelly, Rebecca Singer, Eric Arner, Emily Bitting, Melina Claire, Bryn Rawlyk, Daniel Mongraw, Dan Olsen, Cathy Bouchard, Lindsay Shapiro, and Gayla Trail. Thank you all for the skills, recipes, and/or encouragement you brought to the table.

Bob Walberg and Omega Nutrition (*omeganutrition.com*), Eden Foods (*eden foods.com*) and Cocoa Camino (*cocoacamino .com*), who made very generous donations that allowed me to test these recipes with high-quality ingredients without breaking the bank! Enthusiastic, belly-warming thanks! Thanks also to La Maison d'Orphée (*maisonor phee.com*) and MaraNatha (*maranathanut butters.com*) for your support. I'm so glad your food products are becoming increasingly available.

The people who run the organic farms where I've gotten dirty: La Récolte d'Osiris, Osho Gardens, Stein Mountain Farm, Stowel Lake Farm, the Miller Family Farm, Alpha Farm, and the Sun Run Centre.

My recipe testers, many of whom I've never met, and especially Alisa Marrs Fleming who was so enthusiastically committed right down to the wire!

All the dedicated readers of my blog, *Domestic Affair* – especially those of you who offer encouragement and feedback in the comments!

And finally, to the fine folks at Arsenal Pulp Press – to Brian, Shyla, and especially Bethanne – a sweeter editor I couldn't ask for. I'm so thrilled that you've introduced me to this exciting world beyond zine making!

PREFACE

The book you hold here in your hot li'l hands is the product of almost a decade of self-education, formal education, work-exchanges on organic farms, family dinners with meat-eaters and wheat-eaters, and a whole lot of time in the kitchen – my kitchen, my parents' kitchen, kitchens I shared in co-op houses, my friends' kitchens, my friends' parents' kitchens, a vegan restaurant kitchen, and a vegan bakery.

In high school I quit eating meat, but I admired the commitment of my peers who were full-on vegans, bestowing them with a kind of rock-star status. It got personal a couple of years later, though, when I fell in love with someone who was vegan. He was charming, and passionate about wanting nothing to do with the consumption of animals – in the food he was eating or the belt that held up his pants. I wish I could boast that my conversion to more ethical eating habits had been based on political action, but in truth, that came later. The boy soon left to work for an animal rescue organization in California, but the veganism stuck, and it changed my life. Truth be told, when I started writing and collecting the information that came to be this book, I was writing it for me. After a twenty-year romance with dairy, I was doing my darndest to learn how to be vegan, and do it well.

The more I got into food – whether it was devouring cookbooks like trashy romance novels or studying holistic nutrition – the more I wanted to share what I was learning with others. I had been making zines – cut 'n' paste-style magazines – since high school and at first this seemed to be the perfect way to share what I was learning. It all started with a cookzine I called *Vegan Freegan*, then I published four issues of *Ripe*, then *Root* came along, and one simply titled *Cookie Zine*. I've made it my mission to make food that is satisfying for everyone, steering clear of bland, overcooked dishes or those with unappetizing flavor combinations that vegan cuisine can be in its least-inspired state. My most enthusiastic project has been to create vegan baked goods that don't taste stereotypically vegan. You know what I'm talking about – muffins that look like hockey pucks, or cake that isn't decadent enough for you to crave a second slice. And I want to make this kind of information available to the folks who wholeheartedly embrace all things DIY (do it yourself) – as in cooking with fresh whole food, from scratch, in your own kitchen – in a personal context that is more accessible than what is found in glossy food magazines.

Writing cookzines led to creating a food-based blog called *Domestic Affair* (*domestic affair.ca*). Online, my recipes are immediately available for scores of people to see. I swoon when I think of the thousands of cookzines and blog print-offs in kitchens around the world, pages spattered with squash soup or globs of peanut sauce. And it never ceases to thrill me that something I tried out in my kitchen one afternoon has been recreated by someone I don't even know for a road trip picnic or a kid's birthday party, all by way of a zine or blog. For me, this excitement is rooted in a sense of connectedness. Community action and grassroots efforts are important to me. I worry that we shell out tons of cash to faceless big businesses that churn out additive-packed meals, and then raise our eyebrows at organic broccoli selling for three dollars a pound at our local food co-op. By creating my cookzines, I hoped to encourage a food-positive movement that supports DIY cooking with whole foods instead of insta-meals from a box: food that really nourishes us, that we can build community around.

Now, with a couple hundred recipes in print, my handmade cookzines have become the building blocks for a full-fledged cookbook. I've taken the recipes that I've developed over the years, picked my favorites, seasoned them with more nutritional information, and now offer them to you in a palatable, perfect-bound cookbook.

As a holistic nutritionist, I of course believe that how we eat has a strong impact on how we feel and how our bodies function. Working with clients, I have found that when people need more calcium in their diets, a suggestion like "Eat quinoa" is not helpful enough. We need to know why eating whole foods is better than taking a supplement. We need

to know how to pronounce it (keen-wah) so we can ask for it in our local grocery or health food stores. And then we need to know what to do with it so that it doesn't just sit there in the pantry gathering dust or is prepared in a less than delicious way that leaves us uninspired to try it again. If we don't consider the nutritional factors of foods, we're not allowing foods to nourish us the way they were meant to, and we're certainly not getting the full spectrum of nutrients we need. If we want to "get it ripe," we need all the information to help us make the best choices for our body, mind, and spirit.

You can spark up a conversation about food with almost anyone. (My knowledge and opinions have served me well in many social situations, helping to avoid awkward silences.) Food – what with all the media buzz around considerations like organics, local foods, antioxidants, and omega-3s – is a hot topic these days, but it's also very personal for people. Dishes reminiscent of our childhoods are comforting for us. We celebrate with food all the time. We go out to eat, be it at a fancy restaurant or an inexpensive hole-in-the-wall, to experience exciting tastes, textures, and colors that differ from the day-to-day fare we have at home. But in this age of information and choice, we also have to consider where we should get our food (the farmers' market or the big box grocery chains?), and who we're supporting (local farmers or profit-driven agribusinesses?).

"Oh, I don't like vegan food," my yoga teacher said to me one summer evening as we were leaving class.

"No?" I teased. "Sweet potato soup with

coconut milk, or chai cake with cardamom frosting doesn't appeal to you?"

Anyone can, and should love food that just happens to be vegan, as long as it's prepared right. Vegan or not, we could all use the nutritional benefits of eating more vegetables, and have fun doing it. This book, full of food and health information and plant-based, whole-foods recipes, is not just for animal rights activist types or those who are allergic to dairy or intolerant to wheat, this book also is here to help uncover both the delectable goodness and health benefits of choosing foods that the earth naturally provides us. This vegan cookbook is for everyone.

GF, SF, NF & R
What the Symbols Mean

I have included the following symbols with my recipes for you to be able to easily spot which recipes can be complementary to any of your dietary requirements. Note that the symbols may not apply to any suggested substitutions, side dishes, or accompaniments.

GLUTEN-FREE (GF)
Indicates recipes that are safe for those with Celiac's Disease or others avoiding gluten. You must, however, check that the brand of non-dairy milk, tamari soy sauce, pasta, and/or vegetable stock called for in the recipe is gluten-free. I have not marked recipes containing oats as "gluten-free" because oats come from "contaminated sources" more often than not. For more detailed information, please refer to the Canadian Celiac Association: *celiac.ca*.

SOY-FREE (SF)
When this symbol is noted, you must, however, check that the brand of food, non-dairy milk, or margarine called for in the recipe is soy-free.

NIGHTSHADE-FREE (NF)
This means that recipes are free of tomatoes, potatoes, eggplants, and peppers (both bell and hot). For info on nightshades, check out The World's Healthiest Foods website (*whfoods.com/genpage .php?tname=george&dbid=62#answer*).

RAW/LIVING (R)
Recipes denoted as raw/living food recipes may not be completely 100% living ingredients; it's up to you to ensure all your ingredients are, in fact, raw. For example, you have to make sure any non-dairy milk, nut butter, soy sauce, miso, sweetener, cocoa, or carob powder called for would be raw.

CHAPTER

1

THE WAY WE EAT

Food Choices

We all arrive at our food choices from varied paths, learning food preferences and tastes from our experiences as kids, and then growing up and developing a new set of dietary habits and palates that may differ greatly from those of our parents.

I think it's fair to say that "vegetarian" is no longer a dirty or unusual word. Some people are the standard, lacto-ovo vegetarians – all that's nixed from their diets is the meat; dairy and eggs are okay. Some who keep dairy in and eggs out of their diets are lacto-vegetarians, and those who avoid dairy but not eggs are – you guessed it – ovo-vegetarians.

And some folks, vegetarian or not, later step it up a notch or shimmy to the left, choosing to eat, or live, as macrobioticists, raw foodists, slow foodists, bioregionalists, locavores, organitarians, or freegans. (My pal Ryan identifies as an "opportunivore," being perfectly satisfied with animal-free meals, but wouldn't turn up his nose if you slid a plate of beef carpaccio in front of him.) We all make our own choices that best suit who we are and our lifestyles in the end, but as this is a vegan cookbook, let's start with what it means to be vegan.

As you may already know, vegans take popular vegetarianism a step further by omitting all animal byproducts – this includes dairy (milk, cheese, yogurt, cream, ice cream, whey, etc.), eggs, and often honey (as it's an insect product). Veganism extends beyond food to consumerism, affecting the rest of your life. Living a vegan lifestyle means eschewing leather products (e.g., belts, shoes, purses, and car interiors), as well as fur, wool, feathers, beeswax, film (which contains gelatin), and other products, like cosmetics and pharmaceuticals, that are animal-based or have been tested on animals. As a vegan, you make your own decision about where on the scale of veganism you stand.

WHY GO VEGAN?

As I've nestled my way into the vegan community, I've noticed that there are some key reasons why people opt for a more plant-based diet. Politics is a biggie – maybe you saw a gory documentary from PETA or Farm Sanctuary, or a graphic pamphlet from the Animal Liberation Front. Maybe you have a deep concern for the way we humans relate to the environment and want to reduce our footprint on the earth. Perhaps you cut out dairy and eggs from your diet for health reasons – you may be lactose intolerant or eggs may give you a rash. You may have come to a spiritual realization that a plant-based diet has a higher energetic vibration, or agree with

Buddhist monk Thich Nhat Hanh, who suggests that when you drink the milk of a cow that has suffered in a factory farm, you're pouring that cow's suffering into a glass and gulping it down.

There are lots of reasons to choose Veganism.

BUT IS VEGANISM HEALTHY?

It all depends on how you approach it. While choosing to be vegan means that you will cut some unhealthy things from your diet (vegans, for example, consume considerably less "bad cholesterol" than the average North American), there is also nothing, by definition, inherently healthy about veganism. The high school and university students trying to subsist on peanut butter on toast and pasta with tomato sauce, which are technically vegan, will tell you that. And if something like Reese's Peanut Butter Puffs cereal, with its refined sugars, artificial flavors, and preservatives, is also technically vegan, can we really claim that a vegan diet will automatically keep us healthy? Clearly the answer is no.

Unless you understand something about nutrition, you won't be able to make healthy choices as a vegan, or for that matter, as someone following any diet. So, the chapters on digestion and how your food turns into you (chapter three), and the section on the energetic properties of food (pages 27–32) are all included in this book to help you begin to make healthy decisions about what you eat.

HIDDEN MESSAGES: READ THE LABELS

It's important to check product labels. There are a number of ingredients in store-bought, packaged goods that don't appear to be animal-derived, but they can be. **Gelatin** *is a good example of something that vegetarians often forget to omit, but there's no denying that it's extracted from the collagen inside the connective tissues of animals. When folks become vegan, though, gelatin usually takes a top spot on the nix list. Other animal-derived ingredients to look for:*

Casein: *a milk protein; often found (oddly enough) in soy or rice "cheese."*

Lactic acid: *a byproduct of both animal and plant metabolism, so it's not always unvegan; found in some fermented foods and body care products.*

Lard: *fat, often from pigs; found in some baked goods (especially in pie crusts from traditional bakeries), French fries, and cosmetics.*

Rennet: *an enzyme from cows' stomachs; often found in cheese.*

Tallow: *beef fat; found in some wax products (wax paper, crayons), cosmetics, and even, until recently, in Peek Freans and Jos. Louis desserts.*

Whey: *a serum from dairy products (the clear liquid that floats on top of unstirred yogurt); found in some nutritional supplements, margarines, and some baked goods.*

Scrutinizing ingredient lists can be exhausting – just do the best you can. And for more resources, contact a related vegan or animal-rights organization like PETA or consult the cookbook How It All Vegan! *or* The Vegan Sourcebook.

MAKING THE SWITCH

Switching to a plant-based diet and crossing things off the list of what you eat may actually open doors to other foods you'd never thought you'd enjoy. That's what happened for me. I went vegan at the age of twenty and began discovering everything I'd been missing in the first two decades of my life: quinoa, squash, flax seeds, tahini, kale, non-wheat flours, tempeh, beets, dates, adzuki beans, nutritional yeast, cilantro, pumpkin seeds.… I must have figured that I didn't need to try these foods because I had cheese.

I grew up eating a lot of dairy. Looking back, I can say that it was not the best food to have as a mainstay. Even if you're not vegan, dairy products should not be your main protein source. Cheese, for example, is generally high in fat and not easily digested. To the folks who say, "But I could never give up cheese!" I say, "You can, and you will – if you want to."

I didn't really miss cheese after becoming vegan, and as my taste buds changed, so did my mind-set. At first I spent a lot of time finding substitutions for my favorite meals – I could make the best macaroni and "cheese" with nutritional yeast sauce (see page 158); shepherd's pie using grated tofu and mushrooms; "whipped cream" by whirling up soy-milk, sugar, and oil in the blender. Finding substitutes for your favorite foods can be a good way to start. But as time goes by, you may find you don't need to "substitute" any more.

There are some people who think vegans have lower standards for taste or culinary enjoyment, but the recipes in this book should help refute that myth – like me, you may even find your traditional Scottish relatives exclaiming that the chocolate birthday cake you baked for your little brother is "decadent!" and "delicious!"

SUBSTITUTIONS

Here are some simple substitutions that can make switching to a vegan diet easier:

DAIRY: use **non-dairy milks**, **silken tofu**, **nuts**, and **seeds** (including butters like tahini), and **coconut milk**. Human breast milk is amazing – we should all be lucky enough to start off our lives on a pure diet of the stuff. Cow's milk (or sheep's or goat's), on the other hand, is meant for baby cows (or sheep or goats). Not humans. We are the only species to consume another mammal's milk, or any milk, for that matter, after infancy.

There are many comparable "milks" around these days made from beans, grains, and nuts, but not all non-dairy milks are created equal; some milks are better for certain recipes. (Check those labels – some non-dairy milks get their "creeminess" from oil.) Health education specialist Annemarie Colbin suggests that we crave dairy when we need nurturing, but that it should be avoided if you suffer from congestion (colds, allergies, sinus infections) or reproductive system issues (as you're ingesting the byproduct of another species' reproductive process).

EGGS: researching the practices of egg farming factories can be disturbing enough to immediately turn you off eggs. They are relatively easy to omit from your diet; if brunch is a big part of your life, start enjoying "scrambled" **tofu** (page 123) and tofu quiches. In baking, there are a number of egg-replacing options, including **applesauce**, **mashed ripe banana**, **ground flax seeds**, **silken tofu**, and **powdered egg-replacer** (see page 101).

MEAT/PROTEIN: soy is a complete protein, so **tempeh** and **tofu** (and even some of the higher quality "faux meats") are good sources of protein, as long as you can digest them comfortably. And, if your body can tolerate wheat, there are also "meaty" high-protein wheat gluten products, like **seitan**, available. **Chickpeas** (garbanzo beans) are also complete proteins, and **legumes** (beans and lentils) that are eaten **with** a **whole grain** provide all the essential amino acids and only a tiny bit of fat. **Nuts** are a fine protein source, but they are high in fat. Though they provide healthy fats, too much fat in your diet can cause problems, most obviously regarding weight and circulation.

SUGAR: if sugar is part of your diet (and hopefully only in moderation), research how the brand you buy has been refined, as refining conventional sugar sometimes involves a process that filters the sugar through charcoal that is made from animal bones. **Organic sugar** is not processed this way. Substitute also with **fruit** (like dates!), **maple syrup**, **molasses**, **barley malt**, **agave nectar**, **brown rice syrup**, and **stevia**. It is also important to consider the labor conditions under which the sugar was farmed (more on that on page 103).

When I first became vegan I enthusiastically pored over vegan cookbooks and cookzines. After a while, I started to read about other types of healthy diets. Macrobiotic resources gave me practical ideas for including min-

THE GREAT SOY DEBATE

There are plenty of arguments for and against soybeans. On the pro side, they're a good source of protein and have phytoestrogenic properties that, for example, fight breast cancer. On the con side, some people find soy difficult to digest, and many become intolerant to it because it's used so often as a meat, dairy, and egg substitute. If you are unsure of your soy tolerance level, observe how you feel after eating the stuff; a reaction may vary depending on how the soy was processed – tempeh and tamari soy sauce may be fine, while soymilk and tofu may stir up a lot of gas. If you don't digest soy products well, limit your intake or eliminate soy altogether from your diet. If your body is happy to digest it, always buy organic brands to avoid consuming genetically modified (GM) soybeans, which, currently in Canada and the US, are not required to be labeled as such. To avoid over-consumption of soy, use a variety of non-dairy milks, like rice or almond milk or diluted coconut milk. And consider the ways of the raw foodists, who use nuts and seeds to make their foods "creemy."

eral-rich sea vegetables in my diet. Raw food cookbooks gave me the inspiration to use nuts and seeds to make things "creamy." The lesson here, I guess, is that a narrow view of your food options can keep you from being as healthy and happy an eater (and person) as you could be. Open up to the possibilities! Experiment to discover what suits you best; and no matter what your other dietary beliefs are, if you want to be healthy and eat plant-based meals, there are many options in this book to guide you to nutritional nirvana.

RAW RAW SIS-BOOM-BAH!

In warmer months, increasing the amount of raw food in our diet can be a great way to boost our overall feeling of good health. One of the things that make spring and summer in northern climates so exciting is the arrival of fresh, local produce at our community farmers' markets, food co-ops, and health-food stores. We no longer require the warming soups and stews from the frosty months before; we can now begin to enjoy more raw foods that are closer to the form in which Mother Nature offers them.

Raw foods, also known as living foods, are whole and unrefined – with minimal or no processing. The benefits of a raw approach to eating relate to enzymes and nutrient availability. Consider a can of soft, greyish-looking peas that contain 5% of the nutrients of the same measurement of fresh green peas; the more a food is cooked, the less useful it becomes for our bodies. As a food is refined, or processed, the energetic value, or "life-force," is diminished. Raw foods also contain digestive enzymes that aid in assimilating the nutrition of what you eat. On principle, living foods should not be heated above 110°F (45°C); the temperature at which enzymes start to die. Those who are more committed to raw food preparation will use a dehydrator to make crackers, cookies, pie crusts, and fruit leathers – a process that can take up to twenty-four hours.

To become an exclusive "raw foodist," you've got to be committed; the awareness of eating this way has increased in recent years, with raw-food restaurants in urban areas enjoying huge success, but once you go completely raw, easily accessible, prepared meals will become a thing of the past. What's required in becoming a raw foodist is an interest in re-learning how to eat (something that also goes for anyone switching to an alternative diet), creativity (energy once put into sautéing or baking now goes into blending, chopping, and sprouting), and time for planning and preparing meals. This is not just a diet approach; it is a lifestyle change and requires a strong sense of whole health – body, mind, and spirit – for one to be really successful.

If you're interested in the healthful benefits of living foods but can't see yourself becoming a complete convert, consider reaping the benefits of a diet that is seasonally raw (e.g., summer months produce a large amount of fresh produce that can be enjoyed uncooked), or be "raw" one day a week or one meal a day, or, at least, eat something raw at every meal – your body will be happy you did.

Sprouted legumes, seeds, and grains are a living food and highly nutritious (see page 95). Sprouted quinoa, for example, is a complete protein. Natural raw sweeteners include fruit (both fresh and dried – dates are especially good), fresh fruit juices, and raw agave nectar (maple syrup can be listed as "raw" in recipes, but it doesn't technically count, as it is pasteurized). Green superfoods, like spirulina and chlorella, are also excellent raw food sources.

Tasty raw breakfasts might include a fruit smoothie or some living cereal: sprouted grains with ground flax seeds, a dash of cinnamon, and raw almond milk (page 107). For lunch, get creative with beautiful salads that feature grated beets and carrots, sliced cucumber, bell peppers, wedges of avocado and tomato, bean sprouts, and raw sunflower, pumpkin, or sesame seeds. For dinner, living foods can be added to a cooked food main dish, like a soup or stew served in a bowl on a bed of fresh baby spinach, or a lightly cooked stir-fry with lots of fresh sprouts. And don't worry about missing dessert – blending avocado with fresh coconut milk, cocoa powder, and agave nectar makes a decadent mousse (page 241).

My favorite resources for living foods can be found in the Resource List, starting on page 256.

Getting a greater taste for raw can expose us to a whole new dimension of health. Three cheers for raw foods!

VEGAN'S GUIDE TO EATING OUT

Nowadays, more and more restaurants are vegetarian and/or offering a wider selection of vegan menu items; many major cities even have restaurants that are dedicated solely to vegan or raw food fare. But there will be many times that you will want to join your meat-eating loved ones at one of their restaurants. On these occasions, you may feel like picky Sally Albright from the movie *When Harry Met Sally*, ordering everything "on the side," but here are some tips to help you (and others at the table) enjoy the dining experience – just be sure to lay on the charm with the serving staff when ordering!

• First, be up front with your server: tell her or him that you are vegan and ask what is available for someone who doesn't eat any animal products. (You may find you need to say you're allergic to dairy and eggs – instead of just making a political choice – in order for

MAKING THE MOOOVE AWAY FROM DAIRY: SUBSTITUTIONS

Milk: non-dairy beverages or "milks": soymilk, rice milk, almond milk, oat milk, and diluted coconut milk (as it's too high in fat to use straight up).

Cream: rich, non-dairy beverages like coconut milk (if appropriate) or soymilk. In lieu of whipped cream as a dessert topping, try Cashew Creem (page 219).

Buttermilk or clabbered (cultured) milk: soymilk + apple cider vinegar or lemon juice (1 cup: 1 tsp–1 tbsp, depending on recipe).

Butter: as a spread: nut butters, non-hydrogenated dairy-free (no whey) margarine, or preferably Earth Balance Organic Buttery Spread or Margarine, which is made with non-GM (genetically-modified), expeller-pressed oils. Ideally, I'd like to use a product that's organic, does not contain soybean oil (which is low-quality stuff), and has less salt, but I have yet to find one on the market. For cooking and baking: oil (use 7/8 cup oil for each 1 cup butter called for in a recipe); also, coconut oil (often solid at room temperature, so you may need to soften it first) or margarine (see above) can be used.

Yogurt: there are a variety of non-dairy yogurts (most are made of soy) available. The selection is greater in the US than in Canada.

Cream cheese & sour cream: there are some vegan brands of cream cheese and sour cream on the market, but be sure to check the labels, as some contain junky ingredients like conventional (likely GM) corn and soybean oil.

Ricotta: see the tofu "Ricotta" recipe on page 199; note that it can also be made with nuts, such as cashews.

them to take you seriously.)

• If the soups are made with a vegetable broth, they are a good choice, especially those made with legumes (split peas or lentil soups).

• Be specific, and ask with a smile, "There's no dairy in that pea soup?" or "Is this soup

made with vegetable broth?"
- Look for the simple dishes. You can have the roasted vegetables from any entrée; just ask to "hold the chicken, please."
- Salads are often fine choices, but ask for the dressing or olive oil and vinegar on the side. If they serve rye breads, choose them over white. Ask for olive oil to moisten them.
- Skip desserts made with white sugar whenever possible.

Some restaurants are easier than others
- Japanese restaurants will have vegetarian sushi and miso soup (ensure it isn't made with bonito fish powder), and avoid tempura which can be fried with "bad" oils. Some establishments even offer brown rice; just ask.
- In Chinese restaurants, ask which dishes are made with fresh veggies; broccoli is usually served fresh. Keep the white rice to a minimum, and eat more bean sprouts instead.
- Vietnamese restaurants will have some vegetarian offerings. My favorite makes tasty veggie spring rolls (although they are fried).
- Fish sauce is used commonly in Chinese, Thai, and Vietnamese restaurants; be sure to ask.
- Indian restaurants usually have many veggie choices. Dal (lentils) and chana (chickpeas/garbanzo beans) are good protein sources. Remember, ghee is clarified butter, so ask what dishes are made without it. And avoid naan (flat bread), which is typically made with refined wheat flour; papadums (made with chickpea, lentil, or rice flour) are a good alternative. Also, do your best to avoid white rice and dishes that are super-oily. I like to order take-out Indian food and serve it at home with fresh spinach, lightly steamed broccoli and cauliflower, and steamed organic grains.
- In Italian restaurants, order soups and steamed veggies and salads, with dressing on the side, and they are likely to have olive oil and balsamic vinegar for your bread or salad.

Dining out right: being a happy eater is part of good nutrition
- Appreciate the benefits of eating with friends and family, being social and laughing, to create "good energy" in the environment in which you are eating your food.
- Resist speaking negatively about others' food choices or what's available; even if your choices are slim, stay positive (it is better for your digestion) and don't make anyone else uncomfortable (emotions can run high when it comes to food).
- Compliment the restaurant staff or party host on the nutritious and tasty menu items.
- Unless you dine out often, eating a few less nutritious meals won't kill you, so don't be hard on yourself; choose the best foods that are available, and then have a good time.

TRAVELIN' RIPE
I don't like to be away from home without the foods that help me feel balanced. Sadly, fresh vegan foods are rarely available at truck stops, airport gift shops, or small-town restaurants (funny, but soda pop always is!). Over time, I've learned from the snail and carry what I need on my back – on a recent trip to Scotland I carried one backpack of clothes and another of food. It was embarrassing for

my sixteen-year-old brother (and traveling companion), but I was never in a panic at mealtime.

Consider packing some of these essentials for your next vacation:

- Filtered water
- Apples and/or other fruit (fresh and dried) and vegetables that travel well
- Raw nuts and seeds
- Non-dairy milk (drink-box size)
- "Nutrition" bars (protein-based energy bars)
- Packets of miso broth
- Herbal tea bags
- Spirulina or chlorella (blue-green algae) capsules or tablets
- Probiotics (brands that do not need to be refrigerated)
- Immune-boosting tinctures and teas (like astragalus, echinacea, and ginger); vitamins C and B-complex

Also, *happycow.com* is a great resource for traveling vegans, vegetarians, and raw foodists, as it includes restaurant and natural foods store guides.

So, wherever you place yourself on the vegan spectrum, or even if you subscribe to a totally different diet, learning about food and how to eat in a healthy way is probably one of the most important things you can do. After all, as a spiritual teacher I know says, "All you have in this life is your body and your mind. You should really take care of them."

CHAPTER

2

EAT RIPE

A Manifesto for a Vegan
Whole Foods Diet

With all the different diets that people swear by these days, how do you know what are the best choices for you? It's all about trial and error, my friend. It takes patience to find your groove. And even then, once you've found your rhythm, who's to say what will stick with you a year or two down the road?

In my humble opinion, healthy eating requires a conscious and open approach.

DON'T BEAT YOURSELF UP

One of the worst things you can do is beat yourself up for eating "bad" food; a close second is policing others for their food choices, and sometimes the two go hand in hand. True, we need to make informed choices – with the amount of information out in the world these days there's no excuse not to – but we should also allow ourselves to be human. One of my favorite affirmations is from Louise L. Hay's book *You Can Heal Your Life*: **"The point of power exists in the present moment."**

In other words, you can choose right this second to make the best choice for yourself – if you want to eat healthier right now, you can choose to eat a juicy apple or drink refreshing filtered water, and pass on the bag of potato chips. Don't beat yourself up for things that happened in the past, even an hour ago, because they're in the past! And it would taint the pleasurable memory if you saturated it with guilt.

I don't think anyone is deliberately eating their way through nutrient-lacking food toward poor health. I think people have lots on their minds, or they don't know how to access the information they need, or they don't know what information is actually true or best for them. My goal as a nutritionist has never been to get anyone to give up meat or convert to a vegan diet. What I am rooting for when it comes to food is that everyone make conscious and informed decisions on a regular basis.

LISTEN TO YOUR BODY

I have had conversations about eating habits with people who'd say, "Oh, I've tried to give up meat, but my body just needs it. I crave it." Okay, I wouldn't argue with that. (Wanna know what I will fight them on? Read the "ethical meat-eating" note.) I want to respect everyone's intuitive notion of what's best for them (just like I want more conventional eaters to respect my decision to be vegan and stop challenging me "for argument's sake"). It's taken me years to get my mind to quiet itself

ETHICAL MEAT-EATING

I do take a firm stand on the quality of animal products people consume. Some folks may crave meat, but I don't think anyone's body ever tells them to go out and eat a chicken that's been de-beaked, or a pig that's been pumped with antibiotics because there's over-crowding at the factory farm. While I'm not overly militant about it, I do feel very strongly that if you're going to eat animal bodies or products that come from animals (i.e. dairy, eggs), you should make the effort to get them from more ethical sources. Look for products from organic, biodynamic, local, and/or small or family-run farms – and resist being ushered onto the conveyor belt of convenience, putting your hard-earned cash toward unethical factory-farmed products.

enough so I can hear what my body was saying. Does my body want that entire bowl of rice at a restaurant or am I eating because I don't want to waste food? Does my body want another piece of cake at a dinner party, or does my mind want it because it's there and tasty; do I really need the "nutrients" it has to offer? Take a breath and make your decisions with a level head.

Whew, now that I've had my say, let's talk about what your diet should entail.

THE RIPE REVOLUTION FOOD GUIDE

I'm not a huge fan of the Canada Food Guide (the government-supported guide for nutritional health for Canadians). While it was recently updated to include more foods like quinoa, flat bread, and tofu, it just doesn't say enough about the quality of the foods consumed. Canned vegetables and fruits pale in comparison to fresh produce, hands down. When it comes to grains, there is not enough emphasis in the guide on whole grains and non-glutinous grains, and the recommended daily intake is more than most people need. And don't even get me started on the fact that dairy products get a category all to themselves! What about those of us who don't eat dairy – or an acknowledgment that many of us are lactose intolerant?

Also, people often assume that because eggs and meat and nuts are listed as protein sources in the guide, those are the only sources of protein. All foods are complicated combinations of nutrients, both macro and micro, and it helps if we have more of an understanding of what this means for our bodies. Legumes, for example, are generally 9% pro-

tein and 64% water, 23% carbohydrates, 3% fiber, and >1% fat; or nuts, which are about 20% protein and 50% fat, 18% carbs, 11% fiber, and 1% water. Most people think of eggs as a good protein source, but here's how eggs break down: 13% protein and 75% water, 11% fat, and 1% carbs. Eggs have an equal amount of fat and protein. Nuts have a 1:2.5 ratio of protein to fat. Legumes have an 18:1 ratio of protein to fat, but they also have a 2.5:1 ratio of carbohydrates to protein.

It may seem complicated, but making the right food choices is simpler than you might think.

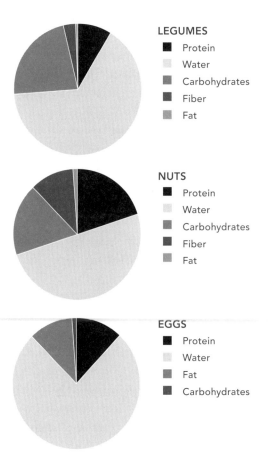

LEGUMES
■ Protein
░ Water
▓ Carbohydrates
■ Fiber
▒ Fat

NUTS
■ Protein
░ Water
▓ Carbohydrates
■ Fiber
▒ Fat

EGGS
■ Protein
░ Water
▓ Fat
■ Carbohydrates

Look for a diet that creates a wholesome, nutrient-packed picture. Refer to the food guide below and try to include something from each area in your diet each day. Variety is the key. Many of us are creatures of habit, but try not to eat the same things all the time. Vary the colors, vary your choices, and have fun with your food!

(This information that follows comes from my training as a holistic nutritionist. I want to especially thank my teacher and friend, Caroline Dupont, for her wise take on health and nutrition.)

Vegetables & fruits
• Vegetables and fruit should make up *at least* 50% of your daily consumption, if not closer to 75% – when you sit down to a meal, at least half of the food on your plate should be vegetables.
• Fruits and vegetables supply so many important micro-nutrients. They are also good sources of carbohydrates.
• To ensure you consume adequate digestive enzymes, eat fresh, raw vegetables and fruit every day, and I'm not talking about a token slice of cucumber or tomato, I'm talking about colorful and luscious salads! See the section on raw foods on pages 18 and salad recipes that begin on page 146.
• Fruit should be fresh and ripe, harvested locally, and organically produced as much as possible. Fruit consumption should increase in the summer, when there is an abundance of fresh and local produce. In the winter, eat fruits that store well, like apples.
• Include sea vegetables, like nori, arame, or wakame, for their impressive mineral content.

• Eat about 3 cups raw and 2 cups cooked vegetables, and 2–6 pieces of fruit a day.

Whole grains
• Whole grains provide micronutrients and complex carbohydrates; in combination with legumes, they complete the "amino acid picture" for building new proteins in our body. They are generally low in fat.
• Prioritize non-glutinous grains like quinoa, millet, brown and wild rices, buckwheat, and amaranth.
• Include grains other than wheat: spelt, kamut, oats, rye, and barley.
• The more "whole" (unprocessed) the grain, the better – flour products should be kept to a minimum.
• If you're on a living food (raw food) diet, you might eat sprouted grains or eliminate this category.
• Eat 1–2 cups cooked grains a day.

Protein
• Eating protein will make you feel grounded and satiated.
• Protein builds muscle mass and should be eaten within forty minutes of exercising.
• Legumes (beans and lentils) should be your major source of protein. They contain many essential amino acids that build protein, and combined with the essential amino acids supplied by whole grains, you will have all the protein you need.
• Work up to eating 1 cup cooked legumes a day.
• Sprouts are complete proteins; they have

impressive "life-force" energy. Eat sprouts as often as you can (on salads, in smoothies), about ½ cup a day.

• Nuts and seeds have protein. But they should not be your main source of protein, otherwise you will have too much fat in your diet. Consuming 2–3 tbsp nuts and seeds (including nut/seed butter) a day is fine.

• Protein powders are tasty (or tastily disguised) in smoothies, and they travel well. Protein powders should only be used as a supplemental protein; check label for serving suggestion; and ensure the product is vegan – featuring hemp, rice, or soy – and does not include whey (see page 15).

Fats

• Along with nuts and seeds, olive oil and flax seed oil, as well as small quantities of coconut oil or sunflower oil, should be your main sources of fat.

• Essential Fatty Acids (EFAs) are found in high quantities in flax and hemp seed oils. Have some every day (drizzled over salads or steamed vegetables are ideal ways to consume them); make sure you store them in the fridge.

• Sunflower oil is ideal for baking, although it has more saturated fat than canola (which has the least), but canola oil is often over-sprayed with pesticides and is a GMO (genetically modified organism); *if* you're going to buy canola, ensure it's organic.

• Organic nut butters are good sources of fat. Try using them instead of oil in salad dressing.

• Use organic coconut oil sparingly. It is a highly saturated fat (see page 68).

Snacks

In order to keep blood sugar levels balanced throughout the day, it's beneficial to eat more smaller meals, rather than to eat three big meals a day.

If you're feeling snacky, have healthful op-

MY DAILY DIET GENERALLY INCLUDES:

• *2–3-L filtered water (including lemon water first thing in the morning [page 105] and 1–4 cups herbal tea depending on the time of year)*

• *3–6 pieces fresh fruit*

• *1 fresh, colorful salad (about 3 cups veggies), with dressing that includes cold-pressed flax seed oil*

• *2 cups cooked vegetables (steamed, roasted, or in soup) – often including something from the Brassica family (e.g., broccoli, Brussels sprouts, cabbage, cauliflower, kale)*

• *1 cup cooked legumes (often in salad or soup)*

• *1 cup whole grains (steamed, or in the form of rice cakes, cereal, or whole-grain toast)*

• *2 tbsp flax seeds, freshly ground (in fiber drink, or sprinkled on cereal or rice cake with nut butter)*

• *up to ¼ cup raw nuts/seeds, or 2 tbsp raw nut/seed butter (e.g., almond butter or tahini)*

• *… and a few nibbles of dark chocolate (70 or 85% cocoa, organic, fair trade; or a handful of raw cacao nibs)*

Of course, this diet changes, depending on the season, my schedule, how I'm feeling, or if I'm away from home. And I'm not saying that this diet would be ideal for you – it's what I've figured out works for me based on years of education, as well a lifetime of trial and error.

tions on hand, in the kitchen, or in your bag to keep the junk food at bay. Some snack options include:

- Fruit
- Chopped veggies with hummus or another dip
- Carrots and a handful of almonds
- Fruit smoothie (possibly made with greens powder, ground flax seeds, or non-dairy protein powder)
- Rice cake (or other gluten-free cracker) with hummus, or with nut butter, molasses and ground flax seeds
- Homemade muffin or granola bar
- Good-quality trail mix (e.g., raw organic nuts, seeds, and dried fruit; even some goji berries and cacao nibs)
- Cereal with non-dairy milk, ground flax seeds, and cinnamon

Treats

It's a funny how we "reward" ourselves: "It's going to be a hard day today. I need to start with a chocolate croissant," or, "I managed to eat a salad today – I'll celebrate with pie!" Understanding what is a truly rewarding treat is something I had to learn when I started to pay attention to how food really affected my body and sense of well-being. Try substituting chocolate-chip cookies with freshly pressed juices from a local juice bar, a magazine or book, a DVD rental, or even a massage – of course, treats like those can be expensive, so be creative – find a special book from the library or take time out of your schedule to go for a walk with a friend. There are, admittedly, certain foods that are best left for special occasions (you'll find many in the sweets chapters [nineteen and twenty]), but it's good to experience all the options that are available for pampering ourselves.

ENERGETIC PROPERTIES OF FOOD

Scientists continue to study the effects of food on the body, and are often making new findings about the benefits of eating whole foods, all the time. Ancient Eastern healing practices like traditional Chinese medicine and Ayurveda (from India) observed the effects certain foods had on the body and drew conclusions about what people should eat. Some people feel that you need

SERVING SIZES

Many resources will talk about "servings" – a measurement that is typically ½–1 cup, depending on the food – ½ cup is about the size of a deck of cards or a hockey puck. Of course, the serving size depends on your size (e.g., if you're 5'2", 6'4", or growing a baby) and your activity level.

FOR THE MOUTHS OF BABES

One day I will write a book about nutrition for kids because I think it is such a fascinating topic. The way we're fed when we're children has a lot to do with the food habits – good and bad – that we develop as adults. I am a "breast is best" advocate for infant nutrition. There are, however, organic formula options making their way into the market, which is exciting for those who can't breastfeed. Also, young bodies need clean food sources as much as possible; introducing wheat, sugar, and dairy should be done as late as possible (if at all) – wait until your child is at least two years of age. Children can indeed be successfully raised on vegetarian and vegan diets! For more information on nutrition, I've listed a number of great, holistically focused books in the resource section (see page 256).

to choose one approach or the other (i.e. Western or Eastern medicine), but, in my opinion, it's beneficial to be aware of all approaches.

As Annemarie Colbin explains in *Food and Healing*, foods have energetic properties that are arranged into four categories to make up what she calls the "Table of Opposites." Most healthful diets around the world balance all four (foods related to these properties are listed later in this section):

• *Warming/Cooling*: food's temperature-related energy provided for body functioning.
• *Expansive/Contractive*: food which creates a "high" or "light" feeling; or sense of being grounded.
• *Acidifying/Alkalinizing*: food's effect on the body's pH level.
• *Build-up/Break-down*: food that helps to build muscle and bone; or cleanse and detoxify.

This way of looking at foods is based on the idea that our bodies do best when they are balanced. Some situations or things that we do naturally lead to imbalances, like strenuous exercise on a hot summer day, giving a speech in front of a huge audience, going on a long road trip, or getting wasted on a Friday night. If we understand what is happening in our body at these times, we can use food to help return us to a more balanced state. If your body is too warm or too cold, cooling or warming foods will help (i.e. eat warming food in winter, cooling food in summer). If you feel weakened, building foods are required. If you have ingested too many toxins or wastes (i.e. junk food), foods that will help break them down and eliminate them from the body are needed. If you feel too jittery or scattered, contractive foods can help; too sluggish, try expansive foods. Too many acid-forming sweets consumed, you can balance yourself with fruits and vegetables which metabolize with an alkalinizing effect.

Our bodies seem to have an innate knowledge of how to balance themselves, but many of us have lost touch with it; I hope this section will help you get back in touch. And while some of us might do this intuitively, it is a skill to create a better balance in our daily diets. We need to learn to build satisfying meals and understand how to nourish our bodies appropriately for various conditions and in various seasons.

Discussions of "energy" can sound kind of kooky to some. The concept of energetic properties can't always be substantiated in a "scientific proof" kind of way, but sometimes you've got to be willing to just go with it, use your inner wisdom, and see if you can draw any parallels to what exists in nature. I talk more about "eating locally" in chapter four, but when I say you should "eat with the seasons," I'm asking you to include the produce in your diet that naturally grows in your climate at the particular time of year; stone fruits and melons are amazing in the summer and keep you feeling cool, but come fall and winter, squash, onions, potatoes, and sweet potatoes can make you feel warm and grounded (it's not surprising that these foods can be stored best over the winter months – nature designed them that way).

Warming & cooling

Our bodies have an ideal temperature at which they want to operate; it is a constant balance of warming up and cooling down our bodies according to their reaction to food, physical and mental activity, and the environment. As Annemarie Colbin points out, "life needs warmth to unfold"; whereas, in a cold environment, life slows down – think of hibernating animals, or how the ripening process slows when food is stored in the refrigerator. Warming foods stimulate us, elevating our core energy to the surface of our bodies. Some foods do this too quickly – like cayenne pepper – which creates heat inside us immediately, but then, in a flash, it quickly disappears, and as a result, our bodies become colder. Foods like ginger root, parsnips, and oats provide steadier, slow-burning warmth that better sustains us.

In general:*
- Plants that take longer to grow (roots – carrots, parsnip, ginseng; or cabbage) are more warming than those that grow quickly (like lettuce, radish, summer squash, and cucumber), which are cooling.
- Chemically-fertilized foods, which are stimulated to grow quickly, are often more cooling. This goes for most conventional fruit and vegetables (see chapter four)
- Any food preparation – like grating or cooking (steaming, baking, roasting, frying) – will "warm up" a food. Therefore, raw (living) food is more cooling than cooked food; and, cooked food eaten cold will reduce its warming properties.
- Hot (as in temperature and spice) foods provide additional heat and are often seen to support metabolic activity even more, which is important during the cooling season of winter.
- Food-preparation methods that involve more cooking time, sustained temperatures, and greater pressure and dryness, impart more warming qualities to food. For instance, foods are "warmer" when cooked at a low heat for a long time than when they are cooked quickly at a high temperature.
- The heat source also affects the warming quality of the food. I can't say I'd ever go out of my way to cook over a straw fire (said to be the "warmest" heat source) when it's forty below outside, but gas stoves do offer more "warming" heat than electric; microwaves don't offer any benefits to our food at all. Paul Pitchford, author of *Healing with Whole Foods*, says that microwaves diminish a food's *qi*, or vital energy.
- Chewing food well, along with helping to ease digestion, creates warmth.
- Food color is also a factor: blue, green, or purple foods tend to be more cooling than similar foods that are red, orange, or yellow (so yes, a green apple, is more cooling than a red apple).

Warming
- Fruit & veg: avocado, cabbage, cherries, coconut, garlic, ginger root, potatoes, root

* This section is for informational purposes only. If you are concerned about changing your eating habits in relation to balancing your energetic body, consult a registered traditional Chinese medicine or holistic health practitioner, who will properly assess your body's individual needs.

MORE WAYS TO KEEP WARM

• Keep moving, build muscle mass (muscle keeps you warmer than fat).

• Warm baths – but finish off with a cool shower to close your pores so you don't lose too much heat.

• End showers on cold (again, to close up your pores).

• Skin brushing (see page 251).

• Bundle up.

• Manifest emotional warmth – don't hibernate from your friends!

• Spend more time in your kitchen.

vegetables, sweet potatoes, tomato sauce, winter squash; any fruit or veg eaten in cooked (or dried) form is more warming than eaten in uncooked, raw form (cooling).

• Grains: barley, cornmeal, kasha (toasted buckwheat), oats, quinoa, wild rice.
• Legumes: kidney beans, lentils, tempeh.
• Nuts & seeds.
• Fat & oil.
• Herbs & spices: basil, bay leaf, black pepper, caraway, cinnamon, cloves, coriander seed, cumin, oregano, thyme.
• Other: chocolate, coffee, kudzu, miso, salt (retains heat), vanilla, vinegar; animal products (if you eat 'em).

Cooling*

• Fruit & veg: alfalfa, apple, berries, bok choy, borage, broccoli, Chinese cabbage, cilantro, citrus fruit, corn (on cob), cucumber, dandelion leaves and root, eggplant, raw fruit, kiwi, lemon, lettuce, lychee, pineapple, plum, radish, rhubarb, sour cherry, sprouts, summer squash, tomato, tropical fruit (some exceptions), watermelon; seaweed, spirulina and other wild blue-green algae; any fruit & veg eaten in raw form is more cooling than in cooked form (warming).

• Grains: amaranth, bulgur, millet.
• Legumes: mung beans, soybeans, tofu.
• Others: peppermint, green tea; alcohol is warming in the short term, but depletes your energy in the long run (cooling).

Expansive & contractive

This category relates to the orientation of the energy in your body. Expansive foods cause an "airy" feeling, feet feel light on the earth, as energy is moving upward and outward from the inner core of the body. Eating expansive foods can cause a feeling of high energy and well-being, and promote spiritual and intellectual alertness, but an overabundance can lead to a feeling of "spaciness," or lack of grounding. Contractive foods, on the other hand, have a grounding effect, as energy is moving inward and downward, making you feel solid, rooted, and connected to the earth.

Various factors influence whether a food is expansive or contractive. Foods that grow upward (plants) tend to be expansive; those that grow downward (roots), contractive. Flavor is another determinant: spicy or sweet foods tend to be expansive; bitter or salty, contractive. Speed of growth is also important: you guessed it – fast is expansive; slow, contractive. If foods grow in a hot climate they are expansive; cold, they are contractive. Watery or moist foods tend to be expansive; dry and dense food, contractive. Obviously, you can have a mixture of all these elements in a food, and how they are mixed with other foods determines their expansive or contractive effect

* In winter, it's best to avoid iced drinks, ice cream, meals only consisting of cooling foods.

on your body. A spicy, watery plant that grows quickly in a hot climate would be most expansive, and a bitter, dense root that grows slowly in a cold climate, most contractive. So, if you are feeling spacey, see how you feel after you eat some root vegetables; if you need some intellectual energy, try some spicy greens.

Build-up & break-down

Food's ability to build and repair our bodies is well known. We need macro and micro nutrients to build our muscles and bones and to repair cells. Proteins, fats, carbohydrates, and water have great "building-up" elements. Foods that build up our stores also tend to be warming, contractive, and acid-forming. Eating only "building" foods can lead to an enlarged body mass, so it is important to stay balanced with foods which aid the break-down (and elimination) process. Minerals, vitamins, fiber, and water are food elements that help the body break down, cleanse, detoxify, and remove wastes. Foods that provide these break-down elements are vegetables (including sea vegetables), fruit, and water, which are also detoxifying and tend to be alkalinizing and expansive.

Acid-forming & alkalinizing

These energetic properties refer to food's effect on your body's pH level, after metabolism; not whether they are acidic or alkaline in themselves. The pH of our blood plasma needs to remain between 7.35 and 7.45 for us to be healthy. Our bodies automatically adjust our pH levels through a whole variety of mechanisms. We can help this process by eating in a balanced way so that those mecha-

nisms can do their work. Since a more acidic environment encourages the growth of disease, our diet should be primarily made up of alkaline foods, like vegetables and fruit (especially ripe and organic) – if you're into numbers, it'd be safe to say about 80%.

Acidic foods in a whole foods diet: grains (millet is the least acidic), nuts, seeds, legumes (except when sprouted), as well as animal products (if you eat 'em).

It's easier to become overly acidic than overly alkaline. When this occurs, our bodies draw minerals out of our cells. Signs of a body that's too acidic include fatigue, headache, inflammation, slower thinking, and feelings of depression; there may also be problems with weakened nails and teeth.

When you are consuming too many acidic foods, you may crave alkaline foods that will balance you out – just pay attention to your body.

Building a balanced plate

A general list of our foods' energetic components and benefits.

Fruit
Cooling, expansive, break-down, alkalinizing; encourages or supports self-development, spirituality, sense of connection and artistic ability.

Vegetables
Leaves & sprouts: cooling, break-down, expansive, alkalinizing; helps us open up and feel alive.

Nightshades (eggplants, tomatoes, potatoes & bell peppers): Cooling (mostly), ex-

THE BEST MEALS ARE BALANCED

As well as eating an abundance of vegetables, whole grains, and good protein-sources, the best meals also provide a variety of colors, texture (crunchy, soft, chewy), flavor (sweet, sour, bitter, salty, astringent), and orientation of growth (sprouts, leaves, shoots; things that grow along or close to the ground; and, of course, roots). I kept this in mind when designing the menus; see page 253.

pansive, breakdown (except potatoes), alkalinizing.

Roots: warming (when cooked), contractive, breakdown (moderate), alkalinizing; helps us feel grounded and establishes sense of identity.

Sea vegetables: cooling, contractive, both build-up and break-down, alkalinizing.

Herbs & spices
Can be warming or cooling, usually expansive and alkalinizing; stimulates metabolism.

Grains
Warming, contractive, build-up, acid-forming; helps foster a holistic worldview.

Legumes (beans & lentils)
Warming, contractive, build-up, acid-forming; creates grounded feelings, brings us down to earth.

Fats & oils
Warming, expansive, build-up, acid-forming; makes us warm and friendly (with the right amount; too little fat or oil makes us joyless and cool; too much makes us dull).

GETTIN' IT RIPE, FROM A TO Z

This book focuses on how to "get it ripe," having a holistic approach to nourishing your body. The focus is on consuming the highest quality foods – those that are plant-based, locally-grown, organic, and whole (unrefined). The shorter the time between when something is harvested and when it is eaten, the more nutrition it offers – a gardener who has enjoyed sun-warmed tomatoes fresh off the vine from her own plot of land (or planter on her balcony) will tell you that.

These essential notes will help you move toward a healthier lifestyle.

Apples: I'm sure you've heard that an apple a day keeps the doctor away. Fresh fruit is a great source of water, natural sugars,

vitamins, and fiber. Enjoy a few pieces of fruit every day, including locally-grown organic apples.

B12: an important vitamin for promoting good energy levels and healthy nervous system function. Be sure to top-up your B12 regularly by including sprouts, tempeh, nori, spirulina, and nutritional yeast in your diet. If you opt to take a supplement, a sublingual tablet (placed under the tongue) is best.

Community Supported Agriculture. Also known as CSA, this food box program supports relationships between consumers and local farmers that last an entire growing season, or all-year round. It's a super way to familiarize yourself with seasonal and locally-grown foods, and to cut out the cost of the grocery store middleperson. (For more info, see page 73.)

Detox regularly. We live in a world in which, sadly, we are exposed to toxic substances on a regular basis. Toxins are not always easily eliminated from the body, so it's wise to detox to stay healthy. Detoxing is as simple as drinking lemon water in the morning, eating more fiber, improving the quality of your food (e.g., buying fresh and organic), or manifesting more positive thoughts and actions (as negativity is toxic to our health too!). Consider doing a more thorough detox regime once or twice a year, see chapter twenty-one for more info.

Essential Fatty Acids, or EFAs, are crucial anti-inflammatories. Also known as omega-3 and omega-6, they're "essential" because our bodies can't make them on their own. Get your daily dose from a couple of teaspoons of flax or hemp seed oil drizzled over raw or cooked veggies.

Flax seeds. Speaking of EFAs, flax seeds are a superfood. In fact, their species name, *Linum usitatissimum*, actually means "most useful." They provide fiber and are rich in the anti-inflammatory omega-3 fat alpha linolenic acid. Flax seeds also have anticarcinogenic properties that help reduce the risk of certain cancers (like breast cancer). Store flax seeds in the freezer, and grind 'em fresh for each use for optimum nutrient absorption. Add to smoothies, or sprinkle on top of cereal or rice cakes with nut butter; blended with water, flax seeds also make a great egg-replacer in baking (see page 101).

Glass jars are safer than plastic for storing food because they're "non-reactive" (see page 77). You can salvage and sterilize the wider-mouthed jars from your recycling bin, but Mason jars, available from your local hardware or grocery stores, lined up along your kitchen counter or in your pantry, are pretty attractive, not to mention inexpensive!

Happiness is a key component to good health. Scientific studies tell us this all the time, but you don't need a scientist to tell you that – its effects are all around us every day. You could eat the most nutrient-dense foods in the world, but if you're walking around with a dark cloud over your head, you're not really all that healthy, are you?

Iron is crucial for good energy levels and a healthy immune system. Dried fruit, blackstrap molasses, lentils, spinach, parsley, Swiss chard, sesame and pumpkin seeds, kidney beans, and soybeans are excellent sources.

Jump on a trampoline to get your heart and your lymphatic system going. I'm not kidding – I have a mini trampoline (and they're not too expensive) that I roll out of my closet a couple times a week for a good half-hour bounce. If your ceilings are too short, ensure you get other cardio exercise – like running, biking, *Jane Fonda's Workout Challenge* … something that really gets you sweating – at least twice a week.

Kick your addictions to sugar, coffee, and smokes. They're stimulants that send you into "fight or flight" mode, putting your body under acute stress response every time you ingest them. If you are smoking, or even if you're in a high state of emotional or mental stress, your body is oxidizing (as if you were a rusting car) at a faster rate. You'll need to actively fight those free-radicals with good amounts of antioxidants (e.g., blueberries, pomegranates, high-quality chocolate, and vitamins A, C, and E; see pages 45–51).

Love your liver! Sitting humbly under your ribcage on the right side of your abdomen, your liver does about 400 things for you, including filtering drugs, alcohol, excess hormones, and bacteria. It also produces necessary cholesterol and proteins. In traditional Chinese medicine, anger is the emotion linked to the liver, so if you find your temper's bubbling up, you may need to give this organ some extra love.

Magnesium is just as important as calcium, its popular co-factor mineral (meaning, they work together). It helps to relax smooth (non-striated) muscles, making it a useful mineral to treat cramps and headaches, and to improve circulation. Leafy greens, navy beans, almonds, and sesame seeds are excellent sources; magnesium's even found in high-quality dark chocolate (fancy that, something many women crave during their period contains something their bodies actually need to ease cramps!).

Nutrient-dense foods have a high ratio of micronutrients (vitamins and minerals) to calories. Vegetables and fruits are nutrient-dense; refined foods and those with added sugars and saturated fats are considered nutrient-poor or empty-calorie foods.

Organic foods ought to be a priority for greater health – that is, your health and that of the environment. Eating organic means that you are avoiding synthetic fertilizer- and pesticide-residues, and irradiated, genetically modified foods that are grown in continuously depleted soil. At a minimum, ensure that the main foods that you eat are organic. (See also the Dirty Dozen and the Clean Thirteen on page 62.)

Potlucks are a great way to trade food ideas, whether you're new to veganism, or just bored with your day-to-day fare.

Quinoa is the superstar of grains. With more protein and calcium than the same volume of cow's milk, we should all be eating this gluten-free grain more often. Found in yellow or red varieties, enjoy quinoa steamed with veggies, sprouted in soups, as a breakfast cereal or in muffins.

Raw or living foods offer us enzymes that die off when cooked. Try to eat something raw at every meal to help ease digestion. Some health advocates recommend an average of 50% of your daily diet be raw. Even if we don't want to immerse ourselves completely in a raw foods diet, living foods resources have a lot to offer anyone interested in whole foods. See page 18 for more info.

Slow down at mealtime. Let your brain and your body unwind: your meal will be more enjoyable and easier to digest.

Tell the Food Police to mind their own business. Sticking to a health or food plan that feels best for you is hard enough as it is;

you certainly don't need anyone else looking over your shoulder and telling you what you're doing wrong. If I had a nickel for every time a non-vegan told me at a restaurant or party what I can and can't eat (and another nickel for every time they were wrong)…. Vegans can also be guilty of policing other vegans.

Un-learn whatever you've heard about animal products being essential for adequate sources of protein, calcium, and iron. Deficiencies can exist in any diet that's not varied enough. A whole-food, plant-based diet can give yer bod what it needs!

Vegetables – of course! Be sure they make up at least 50% of your daily diet. Get 'em fresh, local, and organic as often as you can. Enjoy in all sorts of ways: raw, steamed, roasted, or stewed.

Water is life. You need the stuff for your body to function properly. Aim for 2–3 liters each day. Try and find a cleaner source than straight-up tap water. Ideally, acquire de-chlorinating shower and tub filters too. Oh, and you might watch how much water you use – 'cause you don't want to waste the stuff. See page 69 for more info.

XXX. You know it's true – good health is sexy. Whole-food-eating vegans do taste better.

Yoga and other restorative exercise (like Tai Chi, Qigong, and Pilates) can have an impressive impact on the quality of your life. It

can improve digestion and circulation, and promote a more Zen state of mind.

Zzzzzz. Be sure to get adequate sleep. Eight hours is optimal. It helps to sleep in a dark room.

Now you have the essential tools for a nourishing diet and lifestyle. If this seems like a lot of work, think about it this way: the first thing you need to do is to be gentle with yourself, make change as slowly as you want, and listen to your body as you go. Pick the easiest changes to make first. After a while, you'll know when to add more. Even if you start with just eating more fruits and vegetables, you will have taken a big step to better health. If you add different fruits and vegetables each week, you will begin to give your body access to all the super things nature provides to keep us healthy. As you start to notice how much better you feel, you may just be motivated to learn more and make even bigger changes. Your body will thank you for it.

FRUIT & VEGETABLE CHECKLIST

As mentioned throughout this book, fruit and vegetables are an excellent source of water, fiber, energy-rich carbohydrates, and many vitamins and minerals. They have an alkalinizing effect on your body, which protects your body from cell damage.

Below, note the fruits and vegetables you like. How many of them do you actually eat? Bring this list to the grocery store, and pick up something new.

Fantastic fruit

- ☐ Apple
- ☐ Apricot
- ☐ Asian pear
- ☐ Avocado
- ☐ Banana
- ☐ Blackberries
- ☐ Blueberries
- ☐ Cantaloupe

- ☐ Honeydew
- ☐ Kiwi fruit
- ☐ Lemon / Lime
- ☐ Lychee
- ☐ Mango
- ☐ Nectarine
- ☐ Orange
- ☐ Papaya
- ☐ Peach
- ☐ Pear
- ☐ Persimmon
- ☐ Pineapple
- ☐ Plum
- ☐ Pomegranate
- ☐ Pomelo
- ☐ Raspberries
- ☐ Rhubarb
- ☐ Star fruit
- ☐ Strawberries
- ☐ Tangerine
- ☐ Watermelon

Keep in mind that heating, and even cutting fruit with a knife, destroys both vitamin C and live enzymes that support a healthy immune system.

- ☐ Cherries
- ☐ Currants
- ☐ Figs
- ☐ Grapefruit
- ☐ Grapes
- ☐ Guava

Valuable vegetables

- ☐ Artichoke
- ☐ Aruqula (rocket)
- ☐ Asian greens
- ☐ Asparagus
- ☐ Beans (green, yellow)
- ☐ Beets
- ☐ Beet greens
- ☐ Bok choy
- ☐ Broccoli
- ☐ Brussels sprouts
- ☐ Cabbage
- ☐ Carrots
- ☐ Cauliflower
- ☐ Celery
- ☐ Celery root
- ☐ Collard greens
- ☐ Corn
- ☐ Cucumber
- ☐ Dandelion greens
- ☐ Eggplant
- ☐ Endive
- ☐ Fennel bulb (anise)
- ☐ Garlic
- ☐ Herbs, fresh (parsley, cilantro, basil, dill weed,…)
- ☐ Jerusalem artichoke (sunchoke)
- ☐ Kale
- ☐ Leeks
- ☐ Lettuce (Romaine, mixed greens)

- ☐ Mushrooms
- ☐ Mustard greens
- ☐ Okra
- ☐ Onions
- ☐ Parsnip
- ☐ Peas
- ☐ Peppers, bell
- ☐ Peppers, hot
- ☐ Potato
- ☐ Radishes
- ☐ Rapini
- ☐ Snow peas
- ☐ Spinach
- ☐ Sprouts
- ☐ Squash
- ☐ Sweet potato (yellow & orange-fleshed)
- ☐ Swiss chard
- ☐ Tomato
- ☐ Turnip (rutabaga)
- ☐ Turnip greens
- ☐ Zucchini

Like fruit, raw vegetables provide vitamins and live enzymes. Cooked vegetables maintain some vitamins as well as minerals; many are excellent sources of calcium, magnesium, and iron. Enjoy your veggies raw, steamed, baked, roasted, grilled, or in soup.

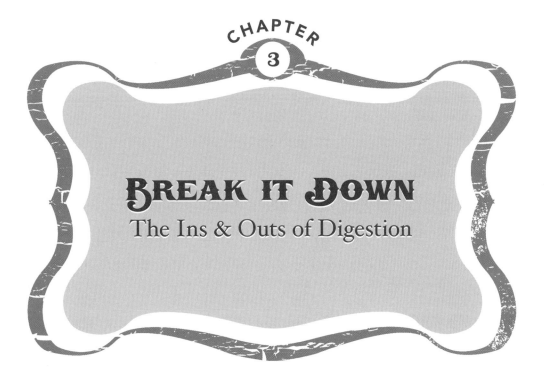

CHAPTER

3

BREAK IT DOWN

The Ins & Outs of Digestion

It amazes me how many years of my life I was eating without any understanding of what happened to my food after I swallowed it. Turns out, 40% of our body's energy is directed toward digestion. Yup, it's that much – so it makes sense that we should try to understand a process that requires so much energy.

Let's take a close look at this process that occurs in our bodies every day. To make it easier to understand, we'll follow the path of a good healthy snack, say, a carrot stick dipped in hummus. (If you'd like to have a more interactive experience, grab a carrot from the fridge, whip up a hummus recipe from chapter fourteen, and chew along as you read.)

First, let's consider the nutrients that this snack supplies. Nutrients are any substances in food that the body uses to maintain and repair itself, and promote normal growth.

There are three types of major nutrients, called *macronutrients*, which can be thought of as the building blocks that the digestive system works with: carbohydrates, fats (or lipids), and proteins. Then there are *micronutrients*: vitamins, minerals, and accessory nutrients (other substances, like omega-3s, that are good for us). And of course there's water, which makes up 60% of the volume of food we eat, and is also considered an important nutrient. In our bodies, water's major job is to act as a solvent. All the chemical reactions in our bodies need water.

When you eat a carrot stick and hummus, you receive an assortment of these major and minor nutrients. In the chart below, "yes" indicates that a significant amount of that nutrient is contained in the food.

Even before you put food in your mouth, the process of digestion has started. As soon

CARROT & HUMMUS NUTRIENT CONTENT

Food		Macronutrients			Fiber	Micronutrients
		Carbs	Good Fats	Protein		
carrot		yes	a bit	a bit	yes	yes (including antioxidants)
hummus	chickpeas (garbanzo beans)	yes	a bit	yes	yes	yes
	olive oil	no	yes	no	no	yes
	lemon juice	insignificant	no	insignificant	insignificant	yes
	garlic	a bit	insignificant	a bit	a bit	yes
	sesame seeds (tahini)	a bit	yes	yes	yes	yes

as you see, smell, or even think about food, your mouth starts to water, or more accurately, a greater amount of saliva is produced, and the digestive juices are activated in your stomach, pancreas, liver, gallbladder, and small intestine to prepare your entire digestive system for what's to come.

FROM MOUTH TO STOMACH

When you take a bite of that hummus-coated carrot and start to chew, the food is broken into smaller particles and mixed with saliva. The more you chew (breaking the food down mechanically), the easier the digestion process is on the rest of your system and more nutrients can be extracted from your food later on. Saliva contains amylase, an enzyme that begins to break down the carbohydrates in the food you are chewing. When you swallow, the carrot-hummus mixture is propelled down your esophagus and into your stomach.

THE STOMACH

Your stomach's main job is to turn the carrot into soft mush that is ready for your small in-

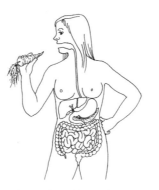

testine, where it continues to break down. (The hummus doesn't require as much work as it is already the consistency needed for your small intestine to work with.) Your stomach has three layers of muscles to churn the food and mix it with its acid and digestive enzymes. It is here that protein digestion begins.

A normal meal (as long as it's not too high in fat) spends about 4 hours in the stomach. The same meal will spend 3–6 hours in the small intestine, where nutrients are extracted, and up to 12 hours in the large intestine, where water is removed and your stool is formed.

CHEWING GUM: NOT SUCH A GREAT IDEA

When you chew gum, you activate your digestive juices though there's no food coming. This can cause you to feel hungry and can deplete the concentration of digestive juices that your body needs when food is later ingested.

ANTACIDS: WHY THEY'RE A PROBLEM

Sometimes stomach acid travels up into the esophagus which, lacking the protective mucus coating of the stomach lining, can cause heartburn or indigestion. Many people take antacids for this problem, but that's not such a great idea. Antacids decrease the amount of acid in your stomach, and it's crucial to have enough acid to break down your food efficiently. The uncomfortable feeling in the belly after eating can actually be from food sitting there too long due to low stomach acid. Rather than take an antacid (note that some brands contain aluminum), it's best to support the digestive system by preventing heartburn and indigestion (see page 52). Protect the healthy mucus layer in your stomach from bacteria by eating foods with choline, which is found in cauliflower and lettuce, as well as lecithin, found in soybeans (and eggs if you eat 'em). Green tea, cinnamon, the carotenoids found in vegetables, and vitamin C can protect the stomach from the particular bacteria which destroys the mucus lining. And forget about taking antacids as a calcium supplement – you're better off eating more white beans and greens.

- *Excessive gas, burping, or belching*
- *Painful bloating*
- *Heartburn, acid-reflux*
- *Nausea*
- *Heavy-feeling, sleepy after eating*
- *Bad breath*
- *Food allergies or intolerances*
- *Excess weight*
- *Undigested food in stool*

Eventually, the protein in the hummus is broken down into amino acids that can be absorbed and used by the body to build new proteins depending on your body's needs. Over the course of the next several hours, small quantities of carrot and hummus, now a creamy mush (eww, sorry – let's call it by its technical name, "chyme"), is pushed into your small intestine, where the greatest amount of nutrient absorption occurs.

THE SMALL INTESTINE

When food reaches your small intestine, it is flooded with digestive juices from your pancreas, liver, and the small intestine itself. These secretions contain enzymes that finish the process of digesting the proteins, break down complex sugars into simple sugars, and digest the fats. Bile from your liver breaks large fat molecules into smaller ones that can be absorbed. As the chyme travels through an impressive 23 ft (7 m) of small intestine, it is completely broken down into nutrients that are absorbed into the blood to be used for energy and to repair the body. These products of digestion travel through tiny blood vessels in your intestinal "villi" (little finger-like projections) and then through a vein to the liver. Your liver filters all the blood draining the digestive track.

As molecules formerly known as carrot and hummus reach the end of their journey through your small intestine, the water and certain fibers that can't be digested pass into your large intestine.

THE LARGE INTESTINE

There are no digestive enzymes in your large intestine, but the bacteria that live there metabolize some of the few remaining nutrients in the chyme. (Gas is a byproduct of this phenomenon, unfortunately.) Bacteria in your large intestine also make vitamin K and some B vitamins.

The job of your large intestine is to absorb these vitamins, some ions, and any remaining excess water. Your large intestine, or colon, will experience slow-moving waves of contractions 3–4 times a day. These contractions force fecal matter toward your rectum. Fiber in your diet increases the strength of the contractions and softens the stools. A healthy digestive tract should produce at least one, if not 2 or 3, relatively soft stools a day. When these involuntary contractions of the colon occur, a message is sent to your brain. Your brain then sends a message to your external voluntary sphincter, telling it whether or not it is appropriate to release itself.

So that's what happens to that tasty carrot and hummus once they're inside of you, providing all sorts of nutrients to give you energy and help you rebuild your body cells. What follows is a closer look at those macro- and micronutrients that will help you understand why you should eat certain foods and avoid others.

MACRONUTRIENTS

Again, the three categories of macronutrients are: carbohydrates, proteins, and fats.

Carbohydrates

There are three types of carbs: monosaccharides, disaccharides, and polysaccharides. The digestive process breaks down all carbohydrates into simple sugars (monosaccharides).

There are many important monosaccharides in the body, but the most important one is glucose, which is also known as *blood sugar* and is the universal food for your cells. Other simple sugars include fructose (found in fruit) and galactose (found in sugar beets and dairy), both of which are converted to glucose to be used as energy.

The next group of carbohydrates is the double sugars, or *disaccharides*, composed of two sugars that have bonded together. Sucrose, which is cane sugar, and lactose, found in milk, are disaccharides. Disaccharides also have to be broken down into simple sugars to be digested and absorbed by the blood.

The last group of carbohydrates is *polysaccharides*, "many sugars," which is a molecule made of many linked simple sugars. Starch and glycogen are polysaccharides – starch is the storage polysaccharide formed by plants (mainly found in grain products and root vegetables). Take that carrot: its carbohydrates are made up of starch polysaccharides. In the digestion process, all the linked sugars in the carrot are broken down into simple sugars in order to be used by the body. This process is completed in the small intestine.

PROBIOTICS

The sad fact is, many of us walk around with an excess of "bad" bacteria and not enough good bacteria in our intestines – we call this "dysbiosis." If you are prone to yeast or fungal infections, you might consider taking a probiotic supplement to increase good bacteria in your body. Here's how this works: say you have been eating a lot of sugar, are taking antibiotics, under stress, or just not treating your body well. The micro-flora in your digestive tract are therefore probably unbalanced. In order to return the good bacteria into your system, you might take a probiotic supplement with Lactobacilli acidophilus *and* Bifidobacterium longum. *There are some probiotics present in raw foods, and particularly in foods like yogurt (dairy and non-dairy varieties) and unpasteurized sauerkraut, but it's likely your best bet is to supplement for at least 1–2 weeks. The most effective supplements will have at least 1 billion organisms per capsule (look for a dairy-free formula in veggie caps) and be stored in the refrigerated section of your health food store. They come in capsule, liquid, powder, or tablet form and you should take them shortly after a meal. (At this time, the alkalinity of the food buffers the acidity of the stomach so that fewer of the good bacteria are destroyed.) Claims for probiotics include improving your digestion, killing off harmful bacteria and yeast, and producing B vitamins and vitamin K. Along with supporting healthy digestive functioning, probiotics are said to promote immune system functioning and lower cholesterol.*

What the body does when we eat carbs
When sugar is absorbed into the blood, the pancreas secretes insulin, which allows the transport of glucose from blood into cells. It can then be used immediately for energy or stored for later use. When all the glucose has been taken out of the blood, the pancreas stops producing insulin.

TAKE CARE OF YOUR PANCREAS

Staying healthy is important to treat your pancreas well. Don't put huge amounts of simple sugars into your system. *This doesn't mean you can never enjoy anything sweet, just be moderate in your consumption. If eating chocolate, have a little bit at a time. On the other hand, a snack of carrot and hummus is very gentle on the pancreas. (Complex carbohydrates take longer to digest so glucose enters the blood stream more slowly.) The starch in the carrot is a complex sugar and will therefore slowly break down into simple sugars, and the proteins and fats in the hummus slow down the rate at which these simple sugars are digested as well. As a result, your blood sugar levels will remain fairly stable.*

Excessive consumption of simple sugars causes stress for the pancreas. It is believed that diets very high in simple sugars can lead to type-2 diabetes, which is becoming epidemic in North America. This disease is caused when the pancreas cannot produce enough insulin to deal with the glucose that has been absorbed by the blood.

Proteins

For vegetarians and vegans, it is especially important to know something about proteins, which make up over 50% of the organic matter in our bodies and are the nutrients with the most diverse functions. Amino acids are the building blocks of proteins. As an adult human, your body can produce all but nine of the twenty-two amino acids it needs to build new proteins. Therefore, you have to eat foods with those missing amino acids, called "essential amino acids." Some foods that are not available to vegans (like eggs and chicken) contain all essential amino acids. Most vegetables do not contain all nine.

So, to get all amino acids needed to build new proteins we need to combine sources that have different essential amino acids. Both rice and legumes (lentils and beans) are limited in their amino acid content. For example, rice does not have the amino acid "lysine" and legumes are missing "methionine." If rice and legumes are eaten together, however, your body has access to all the amino acids it needs to build any new protein required. If you are consuming a varied plant-based diet that has a healthy number of calories, you are most likely meeting your protein needs, but it is good to include some grain and legumes (or fresh sprouts or greens) on a daily basis. Also, chickpeas (garbanzo beans) are a complete protein. Sprouted grains are another option because they contain some lysine. (For sprouting directions, see page 95.)

Fats

A healthy amount of fat in our bodies gives us attractive curves, but on a more functional level, fats provide cushioning for our organs. Along with other functions, fats can be burned to provide energy. Fatty tissue helps regulate our body temperature.

Saturated or unsaturated fat?
It's important to have a balance of unsaturated and saturated fats in our body. With unsaturated fats, it is also important to eat a healthy balance of monounsaturated and polyunsaturated (like omega-6 and omega-3, which we call "essential fatty acids"). The chemistry of all this is complicated, so I am simplifying it so you can make good choices without your brain starting to hurt.

It all has to do with hydrogen atoms.

Saturated fats are "stable," in that they are made up of molecules that hold all the hydrogen that they are capable of holding. Hydrogen atoms tend to be inert, do not interact with other molecules in the body, stabilize cell membranes, and are not easily damaged. Saturated fats are solid at room temperature.

Unsaturated fats have missing hydrogen atoms on their molecular chains. They are less stable and more easily damaged by light or heat. Since these fats are fragile, some need to be stored in dark bottles or in the fridge, and some, like flax and hemp seed oil, should not be heated. They are essential for providing flexibility in the cell membranes and provide other essential bodily services.

The type of fat we eat determines the type of fat we store. The average North American diet is too high in saturated fats. As most of these are animal fats, this is not too much of a problem for vegans to avoid. However, coconut oil is over 85% saturated fat and should not be used in excess. It is also recommended that our consumption of omega-3 to omega-6 polyunsaturated fats be about 1:2 or 1:4, rather than the usual proportion of 1:10 or 1:20 that most people eat. The chart on the previous page shows omega-3s appear at a much lower percentage than omega-6s in almost every oil but flax seed. That's why using flax seed oil in salad dressings (or anywhere else you'd pour it, like on popcorn with nutritional yeast!) is such a good idea.

TYPES OF FAT IN FOODS

Over 50% saturated fat	Over 50% mono-unsaturated fats	Over 50% total polyunsaturated fats		
			Omega-3 percentage of total fat	Omega-6 percentage of total fat
coconut oil palm oil butter	almond oil avocado canola oil cashew nuts macadamia nuts olive oil	flax seed oil	54%	13%
		grapeseed oil	trace	70%
		pumpkin seed oil	5–15%	43%
		safflower oil	trace	74%
		sesame oil	trace	43%
		sunflower oil	trace	69%
		walnut oil	3–5%	53%
		wheat germ oil	7%	55%

Source: Staying Healthy with Nutrition *by Elson Haas*

MICRONUTRIENTS

There are myriad micronutrients and, as you can imagine, they do many great things for our bodies. It seems that every day we read about some new scientific finding that reveals how the micronutrients in a particular food protect us from cancer or promote mental health. It makes sense that the foods we eat should be good for us because we and our plant foods have evolved together for millions of years. A

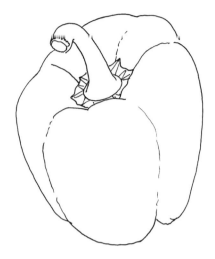

varied diet of whole foods is the best way to consume these nutrients because that's the way that nature provided them for us.

TRANS FATS – THE REALLY BAD GUYS

Because unsaturated fats are so delicate, they do not have a long shelf life when used in processed food. To make them more stable, a "hydrogenation" process is sometimes used to supply them with missing hydrogen atoms. This process removes some of the delicate unsaturated fatty acids and converts others to trans fats, which have been shown to increase blood cholesterol and LDL cholesterol ("bad cholesterol"), leading to hardening of the arteries and other problems. Trans fats have been identified as a major contributor to coronary heart disease; not only do they increase levels of LDL but they also lower levels of HDL ("good cholesterol"). Avoid those trans fats!

Recently at the recommendation of the National Academy of Sciences, both the US and Canadian governments have been introducing laws that regulate the amount of trans fats permitted in products meant for human consumption. As a result, companies, like Crisco, whose products were about to be banned, started working hard to remove the trans fats. Crisco now claims its shortening is essentially trans-fat free and many of the big restaurant chains now say they are not using trans fats for cooking.

MICRONUTRIENT TABLE

Nutrient	Function	Sources	Additional notes
vitamin A (carotenoids- alpha & beta retinol)	antioxidant (neutralizes free radicals); necessary for normal immune function; membrane protection (for skin, stomach, etc.); helps reproductive system function properly	yellow & orange fruits & vegetables (e.g., apricots, cantaloupe, carrots, cherries, mango, papaya, peaches, sweet potatoes, bell peppers); cilantro, green beans, leafy greens, Swiss chard, tomatoes, watermelon, winter squash	carotenoids are converted to vitamin A in the intestines; increases absorption when consumed with zinc
alpha-linolenic acid	*see* omega-3		
alpha-lipoic acid (ALA)	known as a "universal antioxidant"; co-factor of vital, energy-producing reactions; binds heavy metals; reduces blood glucose levels; decreases insulin resistance; inhibits nerve & tissue damage	broccoli, potatoes, spinach, tomatoes	
vitamin B1 (thiamine)	maintains energy supplies; coordinates nerve & muscle activity; supports heart function; supports hydrochloric acid production	black beans, Brussels sprouts, cantaloupe, eggplant, green peas, mushrooms, Romaine lettuce, spinach, sunflower seeds, tomatoes	
vitamin B2 (riboflavin)	used for cellular energy production	brewer's yeast, legumes, millet, nori & other sea vegetables, sunflower seeds, wild rice; small amounts in asparagus, broccoli, collards, spinach	
vitamin B3 (niacin)	helps lower "bad cholesterol" (LDL); stabilizes blood sugar; stimulates circulation; involved in bile synthesis; hydrochloric acid production; needed to produce enzymes that supply energy to cells	almonds, asparagus, avocado, cantaloupe, collard greens, cremini (brown) mushrooms, dark rye, peanuts, spelt	

MICRONUTRIENT TABLE (con't.)

Nutrient	Function	Sources	Additional notes
vitamin B5 (pantothenic acid)	supports healthy adrenal gland function – the "anti-stress" vitamin; supports adrenal glands in increasing production of cortisone & other hormones which help counteract stress & enhance metabolism (helps turn carbohydrates and fats into usable energy)	avocado, brewer's yeast, broccoli, cantaloupe, cauliflower, green peas, mushrooms, peanuts, sunflower seeds, sweet potatoes, turnip greens	
vitamin B6 (pyridoxine)	formation of red blood cells; contributes to healthy cardiovascular & nervous system function	avocado, banana, cabbage, cantaloupe, cauliflower, coconut, mung bean sprouts, peanuts, prunes, sweet potatoes, walnuts, watermelon, wild rice	depletes with use of birth control pill
vitamin B12	critical for healthy nervous system function & good energy levels; supports production of red blood cells & prevents anemia	brewer's yeast, nori, spirulina, sprouts, tempeh	don't forget about these foods!
vitamin B-complex	*see* vitamins B1, B2, B3, B5, B6, B12 & folic acid	B-complex is a formulated supplement	
beta carotene	*see* vitamin A		is a precursor to vitamin A: fat must be consumed at the same time as beta carotene-rich foods in order to ensure vitamin A absorption
bioflavonoids	enhances vitamin C absorption; helps maintain capillary health	citrus, grapes, tea (green, black & white)	
boron	hormone regulation, particularly related to bone health	apples, grapes, leafy greens, legumes, nuts, pears	
vitamin C (ascorbic acid)	antioxidant, attacks free radicals in body's fluids & cells; prevents or slows rate of disease & aging; collagen formation; used in high amounts by adrenal glands, particularly in times of stress; supports liver detoxification	beets, broccoli, Brussels sprouts, cantaloupe, cauliflower, collard greens, grapefruit, guava, kale, papaya, parsley, strawberries	enhances iron absorption

MICRONUTRIENT TABLE (con't.)

Nutrient	Function	Sources	Additional notes
calcium	vital in muscle contraction; maintains healthy, strong bones; supports nerve function	basil, black turtle beans, black-eyed peas, blackstrap molasses, bok choy, collard greens, kale, navy beans, rhubarb, shepherd's purse, soybeans, spinach, white beans	in supplement form, calcium citrate has an absorption rate of 80%; (calcium carbonate is 60%); suggested consumption with magnesium is a 2:1 calcium to magnesium ratio; vitamin D & fat are needed for absorption
carotenoids	*see vitamin A*		
choline	aids liver & gallbladder function – promotes bile flow; important for nervous system health	brewer's yeast, some leafy greens, peanuts, wheat germ	
chromium	helps maintain normal blood sugar & insulin levels; important in fat & cholesterol synthesis	onions, Romaine lettuce, tomatoes	found in GTF (glucose tolerance factor) supplements
coenzyme Q10	aids in converting food energy into energy for body; anti-oxidant (neutralizes free radicals)	germ of whole grains	generally produced in sufficient supply by young healthy bodies; may need to be supplemented for elderly or sick people
copper	helps body utilize iron; reduces tissue damage caused by free radicals; maintains bone & tissue health; helps produce melanin; supports normal thyroid gland function; preserves myelin sheath that surrounds & protects nerves; supports phase-I liver detoxification; supports enzyme function	asparagus, beets, blackstrap molasses, chard, cremini (brown) mushrooms, kale, mustard greens, sesame seeds, spinach, summer squash, turnip greens	vitamin C, iron & manganese inhibit copper absorption; oral contraceptives increase absorption of copper
vitamin D	regulates calcium, metabolism & normal calcification of bones	regular exposure to sunshine (some say 20 min/day, depending on skin pigmentation); "enriched" foods (like non-dairy milks)	best utilized with vitamin A

MICRONUTRIENT TABLE (con't.)

Nutrient	Function	Sources	Additional notes
vitamin E (tocopherol)	antioxidant (neutralizes free radicals)	avocado, grapes, kiwi, nectarine, peach, wheat germ oil	may be used as a preservative
essential fatty acids (EFAs)	*see* omega-3 & omega-6	evening primrose oil, flax seed (oil), hemp seed (oil), olive oil, pumpkin seeds	
folic acid (folacin)	promotes bile flow; acts in formation of your genetic coding (RNA & DNA); aids in production of red blood cells; reduces risk of heart disease & stroke; in pregnant women, prevents neural problems for developing fetuses	asparagus, avocado, beets, black-eyed peas, broccoli, cantaloupe, buckwheat, green peas, leafy greens (beet greens, kale, Romaine lettuce, raw spinach); lima beans, oranges	
gamma-linolenic acid (GLA) *(see also* omega-6*)*	possibly anti-inflammatory; useful in treatment of eczema & skin irritations	blackcurrant oil, borage oil, evening primrose oil, spirulina	
glutamine	maintains intestinal tract health; helps body produce glutathione (a key antioxidant nutrient); ensures proper acid-base balance; helps maintain muscle mass	beans, beets, cabbage	is commonly made inside the body by converting glutamic acid (an amino acid; niacin is needed)
iodine	helps ensure proper thyroid gland functioning	kelp & other sea vegetables, strawberries	iodized salt is not a particularly useful source

MICRONUTRIENT TABLE (con't.)

Nutrient	Function	Sources	Additional notes
iron	essential carrier of oxygen throughout body; maintains immune system health; aids production of energy	chickpeas (garbanzo beans), dried fruit, kidney beans, lentils, molasses, navy beans, parsley, pumpkin seeds, sesame seeds, soybeans, spinach, Swiss chard, thyme, tofu, turmeric	vitamin C, copper, cobalt & manganese increase absorption; proper stomach acid secretion is necessary for absorption
vitamin K	allows blood to clot normally	asparagus, Brussels sprouts, carrots, green peas, green string beans, polyunsaturated oils (like safflower oil), red bell peppers, spinach, strawberries, Swiss chard, tomatoes	
linoleic acid	*see* omega-3		
lycopene	powerful antioxidant	apricots, guava, papaya, pink grapefruit, tomatoes, watermelon	member of carotenoid family of phyto-chemicals; natural pigment responsible for deep red color of several fruits, most notably tomatoes
magnesium	aids absorption of calcium; releases energy from muscle storage; regulates body temperature; relaxes muscles & calms nervous system; supports liver detoxification	almonds, artichoke, black beans, broccoli, chocolate, lima beans, molasses, navy beans, okra, plantain, pumpkin seeds, sesame seeds, spinach, sunflower seeds, Swiss chard	
manganese	keeps bones strong & healthy; helps body synthesize fatty acid & cholesterol; maintains normal blood sugar levels; promotes optimal function of thyroid gland; maintains nerve health; protects cells from free-radical damage	almonds, banana, beets, brown rice, chard, collard greens, chickpeas (garbanzo beans), kale, maple syrup, mustard greens, oats, pecans, pineapple, raspberries, Romaine lettuce, tempeh, spelt	

MICRONUTRIENT TABLE (con't.)

Nutrient	Function	Sources	Additional notes
methionine	promotes bile flow; important in detoxification	almonds, potato	
molybdenum	as a part of three enzyme systems, it plays a role in uric acid formation; iron utilization; carbohydrate metabolism; sulfite detoxification	chickpeas (garbanzo beans), green beans, lentils, lima beans, potatoes, spinach	
omega-3 (alpha-lino-lenic acid)	reduces inflammation (see also essential fatty acids)	flax seed (oil)	
omega-6 (linoleic acid)	anti-inflammatory or pro-inflammatory (see also essential fatty acids)	blackcurrant oil, borage oil, evening primrose oil	
phosphorous	needed for bone & teeth formation	nuts, seeds	
potassium	helps muscle & nerve function (regulates heart rhythm); maintains proper electrolyte & acid-base balance; helps lower risk of high blood pressure	asparagus, avocado, bananas, beets, cantaloupe, lentils, lima beans, papaya, spinach, Swiss chard, winter squash	
selenium	protects cells from free-radical damage; enables thyroid to produce thyroid hormone; helps lower risk of joint inflammation; supports glutathione metabolism	asparagus, barley, blackstrap molasses, garlic, mushrooms (button, shiitake), oats, rye, sunflower seeds, tofu	iron & copper deficiencies appear to increase risk of selenium deficiency
silicon	promotes tissue firmness & strength of arteries, tendons, skin, connective tissues & eyes	avocado, cucumber, dandelion, dark leafy greens, horsetail (herb), lettuce, onion, strawberries	
sodium	helps regulate fluid balance inside & outside cells (along with potassium); involved in production of hydrochloric acid in stomach; used for transport of amino acids from gut to blood	artichoke, beets, celery, carrots, kelp & other sea vegetables (almost all foods contain some sodium, particularly in form of sodium chloride)	

MICRONUTRIENT TABLE (con't.)

Nutrient	Function	Sources	Additional notes
sulfur	involved in enzyme reactions & protein synthesis; important for brain function; supports phase-II liver detoxification	Brussels sprouts, cabbage, garlic, kale, legumes, lettuce, onions, some nuts, raspberries, turnips	
tryptophan	supports serotonin & thus aids in production of nervous system messengers, especially those related to relaxation, restfulness & sleep; small amount is converted into niacin (vitamin B3)	avocado, beets, cashews, leafy greens, cremini (brown) mushrooms, oats, soybeans & other legumes	an essential amino acid; vitamin B6 is necessary for conversion to both niacin (vitamin B3) & serotonin; vitamin C, folic acid & magnesium also needed for optimum absorption
zinc	supports phase I & II liver detoxification; increases vitamin A absorption (therefore protects mucous membranes); helps balance blood sugar; stabilizes metabolic rate; supports immune function; improves sense of smell & taste	avocado, buckwheat, coconut, green peas, mung beans (sprouts or cooked beans), mushrooms, pumpkin seeds, sesame seeds, spinach	

TIPS FOR GOOD DIGESTION

Develop a sense for when you should eat.
This is a challenging skill to learn – listening to your body. If you're feeling out of sorts, it's worth considering whether you should eat or not. If you feel tense, your body may not be open to digesting food. If you feel jittery and unstable, some whole foods may be needed to help ground you. And if you're not sure what your body is saying, take a breath, consult your wise mind, and ask yourself, "What's best for me in this moment?"

Take your time when eating. Slow down, enjoy it. Chew really well. Don't prepare the next bite on your fork until you've thoroughly chewed and swallowed the one you've got in your mouth. Avoid eating on the run or when you're stressed. Do your best to eat in a quiet atmosphere, or at least try to quiet your mind, no matter where you are.

Eat simply. It's less complicated for the digestive system to deal with only a few types of foods at once. There's no need to eat every kind of food at every meal. If you eat a balanced diet over the whole day, or even over a few days, you should be fine. Try it and see.

Avoid drinking liquids with meals, especially anything cold. Digestion works best in a warm environment; if you drink something cold (like ice water), the digestive system has to warm up again and this slows the process. About half a cup of liquid (like warm water or herb tea) with your meal is fine, but don't dilute your stomach juices with more than that — instead, drink a big glass of filtered water at least an hour before or after your meal.

Practice food combining. I was first introduced to food combining in high school when I turned to a Suzanne Somers diet book to fit into a dress for a friend's prom. The diet promised that if I didn't put cheese on my spaghetti, I could eat as much as I wanted and still lose weight. (In the end, I gave up before my weight changed, but that's beside the point.) Food combining gets a lot of attention in the world of holistic health, but the jury is out on this one. There is an ongoing controversy between the conventional scientific community, which says that nothing has been scientifically proven, and the holistic health community, which claims that it makes sense and works. Some folks swear by food combining for weight loss, ease of digestion, detoxification, and dealing with dysbiosis. The basic theory of food combining is that only certain foods should be eaten together because they require different enzymes to digest, and some foods (like fruit) should always be eaten on their own, as foods that digest quickly should not be eaten after foods that digest slowly because this can lead to fermentation of the food while it sits in your stomach. Fermentation leads to acidity in your body and prevents detoxification on a cellular level.

This said, most vegetarian foods are actually a combination of proteins, carbohydrates, and fats which our bodies can digest. The best thing to do is listen to your own body — I know I feel best when I eat fruit first thing in the morning, then wait a bit before eating other grains, carbs, proteins, and fats. If I eat fresh fruits with other foods, I get bloated — that's just me. There's no definitive answer, though, so just pay attention to how your food affects you.

Consider your enzyme intake. Enzymes cause the chemical reactions in the body. The pancreas secretes digestive enzymes during digestion. Food enzymes are present in raw food and are often destroyed during cooking. When you eat cooked food, your body has to work harder to produce the enzymes necessary for digestion. Whether you're a raw foodist or not, it's beneficial to eat some raw foods at every meal to access their enzymes. In some cases, you may not be producing all the digestive enzymes needed to fully digest your food — there are digestive enzyme supplements that may help. If you think you may need a supplement, consult a health practitioner, and be sure to use a supplement from a non-animal source (as some come from animal pancreas).

Don't stuff yourself. Eating four or five smaller meals in a day is probably better than two or three large ones – stuffing yourself with an oversized meal means your digestive system has to do lots of work all at once and you will likely feel bloated and tired as your body directs energy to processing all that food. Aim to finish your meal when you feel 80% full.

Keep a diet diary. It's not always easy to pin down which foods we might have an intolerance to. But by keeping a record of what you ate, when you ate it, and how you feel (physically and emotionally) – even just for four or five days – you may get a better sense of what's going on, and what foods you might try to avoid.

KEEP IT MOVING

It's important to have one to three bowel movements a day. Your large intestine needs to eliminate what's moved through your body so that toxins are not reabsorbed. There are many ways to help keep yourself regular; but if constipation is a chronic problem for you, consider consulting a holistic health practitioner.

• Eat a high-fiber, low-fat diet, including lots of vegetables and some seeds (like freshly-ground flax and unhulled sesame).

• Eat fewer refined carbohydrates (white flour and sugar products), caffeine, potatoes, and animal products – they contribute to constipation. Go for whole foods.

• Avoid overeating – this will burden your system and make it sluggish.

• Drink a glass of warm filtered water with the juice of ¼–½ a lemon first thing each morning (see Good Morning Elixir, page 105).

• Keep well hydrated by drinking ample amounts of clean water between meals – aim for one glass per hour.

• Exercise daily, even if it's just two 15-minute brisk walks – it's a great way to stimulate your bowels and get things moving.

• Wear loose clothes around your waist to allow your digestive system the room it needs to do its work.

• Massage your abdomen: start at the lower right side of your belly, massage up to the bottom of your rib cage, then across your upper abdomen and down the left side, massaging in a clockwise circle around your navel.

• Eat whole foods that are naturally laxative, like prunes (reconstituted if possible), apples, figs, pears, grapes, cherries, melon, and spinach.

• Place hot applications (like a hot water bottle) on your abdomen.

• Train your bowels: try to move them at the same time each morning after a meal or after drinking warm water. Relax and wait. Pay attention to your body – resist the urge to read! It may be easier to go if you are in more of a squatting position – try putting your feet up on a footstool, or while on the toilet, slowly twist your body to one side and hold for a few counts, and then to the other side (and hold) to give your ascending and descending colon a gentle squeeze.

• Practice deep breathing. Let everyday activities like flicking a light switch or stopping at a red light be cues to take a full inhalation and exhalation.

IF YOU'RE UNWELL

If you have an illness – whether it's a 24-hour bug or chronic migraines, diabetes, or even cancer – your diet should be the first place to look to start you on your road to wellness. Along with this guide, it is important to consult a holistic health practitioner who may be able to help you start a healing regime.

CHAPTER 4

WHEN A PEACH AIN'T JUST A PEACH

Organic, Local & Other
Food Quality Considerations

The way we see it, eating vegetables is good. Eating organic vegetables – better. Eating organic family-farmed vegetables from someone you know, or someone you feel connected with – best.

— Jonathan Steinberg, organic farmer, Route 1 Farms, California

By now, I'm sure you've noticed that I'm encouraging you to eat organic and locally-grown food whenever possible. Buying things with the QAI (Quality Assurance International) seal or a label stating the food is from Quebec (the province where I live) is second nature to me now. It's not always what I end up buying, but it's always my first choice.

I remember the first time I knowingly ate something that was certified organic. It was in the early 90s and my mum served steamed broccoli one evening, cheerfully exclaiming, "I got this from the health food store. It's *organic!*" I willingly dug in, but a few mouthfuls later I realized that many of the florets were populated by small, round, grey bugs. Horrified, I pushed the plate away, and for a couple of years, all I thought of was bugs when I thought of organic food.

When I reflect on it now, I can see just how little I considered where my food came from. I knew where we bought it – I liked shopping trips of any kind, even to the "big box" supermarkets. But I didn't truly think about the field where the broccoli and bugs were a natural part of the food system, or consider that synthetic chemical insecticides were probably on my conventionally-grown broccoli any other night of the week. (And, I also didn't know about the trick of soaking produce in cold salted water to get the bugs off.)

THE BIG O: WHAT MAKES A FOOD ORGANIC?

If I'm advocating that you eat organically-grown foods as often as possible, it's important to know what makes them different from conventionally-grown foods, and why they are a better choice.

Although there are slightly different definitions of "organic" in the countries that have certification processes for farmers who want to produce "organic" foods, they all mean basically the same thing: *Organic agriculture promotes the health of the soil, plants, animals, and people who consume them by natural, sustainable, and environmentally friendly means.*

In Canada, each province has several agencies that develop standards and certify farms. In 1999, the federal government created a national standard for organic produce, and in 2006, legislation (the Canada Agricultural Products Act) set standards for those certifying organic products that would be sold interprovincially and internationally.

This logo was created for foods that are certified under these federal regulations: A similar certification process, the rules of which were established by the

WHEN SHOPPING FOR ORGANICS, REMEMBER:
• *The food you eat most often should be organic.*
• *Just because something's organic doesn't mean it's good for you – e.g., "organic" cookies made with white flour and sugar or "organic" salad dressing made with soybean oil (a highly refined byproduct of soy that is difficult to digest).*

United States Agriculture Department, exists in the US (where many of Canada's organics originate); they also have their own logo.

CAN WE TRUST THAT CERTIFIED ORGANICS ARE SAFE?

Since people expect to pay more for organic food, which often comes from small operators, many "mega-farmers" have lobbied to lower the standards for organic certification so they can meet them and then charge more for their produce. Thanks to counter-lobbying from organizations like the Canadian Organic Growers (cog.ca) and the US-based Organic Consumers Association (organicconsumers.org), standards are generally kept high. The battle continues, however, and recent changes have been made in the US that allow non-organic additives in some foods that will still carry the USDA organic label.

MYTH #1: ORGANICALLY-GROWN FOOD IS WEIRD & CONVENTIONALLY-GROWN FOOD IS NORMAL

When did fruits & vegetables start becoming dangerous for our health?

My grandparents grew up eating organic food. I'm sure yours did too. Until World War

II, most food grown on North American farms would qualify as "organic." Actually, most food grown on the planet from the time that agriculture began (about 11,000 years ago) until World War II was what we now call "organic." Farmers worked with nature, saving seeds that produced the most productive plants and the best tasting fruits and vegetables, and using natural fertilizers (like animal manure) and pest control methods (like companion planting). In the days when farms were small, before mega-farming corporations and factory farming of animals, the land and livestock were more humanely treated. Not to say that everything was perfect; there were droughts and famines and some people argue we were healthier when we ate the varied diets of hunter-gatherers who came before farmers. Sustainable farming practices began to deteriorate worldwide at the time of the Industrial Revolution and when European colonizers replaced local sustainable agriculture with monoculture plantations, producing products like rubber for manufacturers in Europe. Local farmers who subsisted on the land became workers who had to buy imported foods. But even then, the foods that were available to buy, if you could afford them, were free of chemical toxins.

During and after World War II, scientists developed new uses for petroleum-based products, some of which were turned into fertilizers and pesticides. It was presumed that the newly developed fertilizers and pesticides would increase world food production and end world hunger. However, the so-called "Green Revolution" of the 1940s to 60s was not the success people had hoped it would be. If more food could be produced with fewer insects and other pests, wouldn't that be a good thing? Well, if that was all that was happening it might be, but those pesticides poisoned the ground water and the land, and everyone who ate the products of that land.

With the "Green Revolution," sustainable agriculture worldwide took another hit. Farmers growing food were encouraged to plant one single crop rather than a traditional variety. Since single-crop, or monoculture, farming leads to an increase in insects that affect that crop (because of the decreased biodiversity, which helps provide natural protection), more pesticides needed to be used. Agricultural workers began to suffer from exposure to these toxins and pesticide-resistant species of organisms began to develop faster than pesticides could be made to deal with them. The "Green Revolution" actually destroyed sustainable farming in many of the poorer countries that had been convinced to try it.

In the 1970s, scientists thought that the solution for world food problems might lie in modifying the genes of the food plants. Genes could be implanted so that the new improved plant would be resistant to pests, or produce more per acre, have a longer shelf life, or look more appetizing. Farming was becoming big business, and profits began to outweigh safety as a regulator of food-producing innovations. Food companies (like Monsanto) hired their own scientists to create genetically modified seeds, which became patented and "owned" by these companies. Farmers who used the patented seeds were then not allowed to save their seeds. Each year, they were obligated to buy new ones

from the large companies, who also produced particular fertilizers and pesticides that farmers needed to use with the seeds.

These new foods, chemically fertilized and "pesticided," and possibly genetically modified or irradiated, are what we now call the "conventional" food products on our grocery shelves.

MYTH #2: ORGANICS AREN'T ANY HEALTHIER FOR YOU THAN CONVENTIONAL FOODS

A few years ago, an article published in *The New York Times* asked if organic food is more nutritious. As someone with even a basic understanding of conventional vs. organic farming practices will know, that question may not be the most important one to ask when considering whether or not to switch to consuming organically-grown food.

Conventional foods often contain toxins. The negative health implications of consuming pesticide residue on conventional

IN CANADA, ORGANIC FARMERS ARE NOT ALLOWED TO USE:
- *Synthetic pesticides, including fungicides, insecticides, rodenticides, defoliants, desiccants & wood preservatives*
- *Synthetic fertilizers*
- *Materials & products produced from genetic engineering*
- *Sewage sludge*
- *Synthetic growth regulators (hormones)*
- *Synthetic veterinary drugs, including antibiotics & parasiticides*
- *Irradiation*
- *Synthetic processing substances, aids & ingredients; additions to food including sulphates, nitrates & nitrites*
- *Equipment, packaging materials & storage containers; bins that contain a synthetic fungicide, preservative, or fumigant*
- *Genetically modified organisms (GMOs)*
(Source: Canadian Organic Growers cog.ca)

The safety of GMOs (genetically modified organisms) is hotly debated and the dangers are still not fully understood. Many areas in North America have banned their production and countries in Europe have banned their import. To date, Canada does not have a law that requires foods that have GMOs be identified as such. That means that unless you are buying organically grown vegetables, you may not know if they have been genetically modified.

produce have been extensively documented. The consumption of *organochlorines* found in pesticides has been associated with organ damage, cancers, immune deficiencies, and hormone imbalances in animals and humans who consume them. When pregnant or lactating women consume the residues of organochlorine pollutants from the fertilizers and pesticides that are found on conventional foods, it has health implications for their developing fetuses and breastfeeding infants. Pesticides and synthetic fertilizers used in conventional farming remain in the food and pollute the environment, entering the water supply and working their way up the food chain. Because our planet is a closed ecosystem, there is nowhere on earth that has not been affected by these harmful chemicals.

Conventional farming requires that more and more of these lab-produced fertilizers and pesticides be produced. Organically-grown foods, on the other hand, are fertilized with composted livestock manure and organic wastes. Pests are controlled through biological control

(e.g., using biodegradable sprays or pheromone traps) or are mechanically removed (e.g., simple hand-picking or vacuuming). These techniques do not add dangerous human-made chemicals to our environment. To me, this is reason enough to walk right past the aisles of conventionally-grown produce and to choose organically-grown produce instead.

But let's get back to the original debate about nutrients. The article cites studies that seem to indicate that organically-grown foods are more nutritious. Various "experts" give their opinions on the validity of these studies and most feel that, though the variables are hard to control, further studies will probably support the contention that organic foods are more nutritious. The only "expert" who questioned this in the article works for an organization that receives funds from major chemical-producing companies like Monsanto. It would be surprising if someone whose work is funded, even partially, by large chemical companies would be unbiased in his opinions about organic foods.

Some environmental benefits associated with organic farming were a surprise even to the organic farmers. Who would have guessed that organic farming would produce equivalent yields to those of conventional farming while using significantly less fossil fuel to do so? Conventional monoculture mega-farming causes degradation of the topsoil that is supposed to supply plants with most of their nutrients; with organic farming, topsoil is preserved. Organic crops retain more carbon in the soil, reducing carbon dioxide in the atmosphere, and consequently, reducing global warming. Plants grown organically have been shown to be less likely to be hurt by drought and flooding, two phenomena that global warming is known to cause. As writer Barbara Kingsolver notes in *Animal, Vegetable, Miracle*, foods raised organically have had to fight their own battles with pests and have thus developed more antioxidants that become available to us when we eat them. Antioxidants are important for preventing diseases in our bodies like cancer.

While officially the jury may still be out about the nutritional value of organic vs. conventional, it seems clear to me that the only really healthy choice for individuals and the planet is to choose food grown as "organically" as possible.

MYTH #3: ORGANICS ARE TOO EXPENSIVE

This is a tricky one to argue. Organic produce can be up to twice the price of conventional produce, and if you're feeling strapped for cash this is certainly a consideration. There are a variety of reasons for price tags on organics:

• Organic farming is more labor-intensive – when extra hands are needed on a farm to produce food, the price of food naturally goes up. One fall, I worked on a farm on Salt Spring Island off the west coast of Canada with an organic strawberry u-pick operation. The strawberry season was over by the time I'd arrived, but there was still lots of work to be done in the berry patch. Once a week, everyone living on the property would put in a good morning's work, weeding and pruning the strawberry field. It was a job that seemed to take forever, and what struck me was the quantity of chemicals that conven-

IRRADIATION: LOOKS CAN BE DECEIVING

Another fairly recent agricultural treatment, irradiation, subjects foods to low levels of radiation emitted from a nuclear source to destroy bacteria and insects, giving foods a longer shelf life and decreasing the risk of their carrying disease-causing pathogens. Pro-irradiation folks argue that irradiated foods need fewer toxic chemicals to preserve them during shipping and storage. However, the long-term safety of eating irradiated foods has not been established. The World Health Organization (WHO) and various government bodies in the US and Canada claim that irradiated foods are completely safe and are as nutritious as non-irradiated food. But food safety advocates who have studied the research upon which the WHO and others based their decision claim it is flawed, and their research that painted this different, darker picture of irradiation was disregarded. There is concern that eating irradiated foods can affect cell growth and damage chromosomes, and they also may not be as nutrient-rich because vitamins and enzymes (and the food's essential "life-force") has been destroyed. In addition, foods that can sit on the shelves longer, looking "fresh," lose their vitamin content daily and thus will be much less nutritious by the time they are consumed. There is pressure in the US to remove the present requirement to label irradiated foods, but various consumer health organizations are resisting this change. More info: greenlivingnow.com/column/irradiation.htm.

EASY WAYS FOR EVERYONE TO EAT LOCAL

• *Stock up on seasonal summer produce like peaches, strawberries, and tomatoes. Preserve them by freezing, canning, or drying to enjoy them throughout the year.*

• *Prepare food at home more often (i.e. avoid buying processed, pre-packaged products) – your food won't have to travel from the farm to the processing plant before it hits the grocery store.*

tional farmers would need to put in their fields in order to have the same effect. Conventionally-grown strawberries are at the top of the Dirty Dozen list (page 62) for highly sprayed produce, and I can certainly see why.

• Organics don't benefit from many of the food subsidies in Canada given to conventional farmers (this is something about which you could lobby your politicians) or the same economies of scale. Most organic farmers are too small to qualify for the perks available to conventional farmers who can grow enough to supply the large supermarket chains.

• Conventional food can be considered cheaper only if you don't factor in the health costs that may arise from eating it, or the cost to society from growing or raising it (i.e. soil erosion, flooding, and desertification).

Although organics may seem to be expensive in the short term, they may turn out to be the least expensive and the healthiest way for us to put food on the table in the long run. I think the solution to expensive organics lies in convincing governments that organic farming needs support. By providing organic farmers with sufficient subsidies, governments can ensure that organic farmers could sell their produce more cheaply, within the same realm of affordability as the conventional stuff.

IF YOU COULD ONLY PICK LOCAL OR ORGANIC, WHAT WOULD YOU CHOOSE?

The peach story on page 62 reminds me of the choice that we often face as we become more aware of the environmental effects of burning fossil fuels. Should I buy that organic peach from 5,000 km away or the lightly sprayed one that was grown locally? Or, living in Montreal, should I eat organic berries in January, knowing that they must have come from another hemisphere? Eventually, the answers will have to be no, but it is going to be really hard to convince those of us who have grown up with a year-round supply of asparagus and bananas.

• The relatively cheap prices for out-of-season foods originating from great distances do not reflect their true cost. The hidden costs include those that each citizen will have to pay to cover the results of global warming after the devastating storms, or to transport water to areas of drought caused by climate change.

• Some foods are shipped thousands of miles for processing to take advantage of cheap labor. Purchasing local helps to support the local economy – another point with which to lobby your politicians. (On this note, the less the food that you purchase is processed, the less it's had to travel around. Another vote for whole foods!)

• Also, often local farmers cannot produce enough to supply the large supermarket chains. Your best option is to join a CSA (Community Supported Agriculture) program (see page 73) or shop at farmers' markets.

• Local small-scale farmers, unlike large

monoculture farmers, will often produce several different crops and some of these may not be available in the larger supermarkets, including heritage, or heirloom, varieties.

• Eating locally can be a fascinating challenge (read *The 100-Mile Diet*), and the rewards for your health (fresh local foods are more nutritious, containing more vitamins and digestive enzymes) *and* the health of the planet (doing your bit to slow global warming) will give you a virtuous glow.

On the other hand, local hothouse tomatoes grown in the winter may actually have a larger carbon footprint than tomatoes grown in a sunny climate at that time of the year. The factors are complex. The next section may give you some idea of the pros and cons and help you make your food-buying decisions.

PRODUCE PROS & CONS

Conventional vegetables grown far away

Pros: farmers may have used less fossil fuel-based fertilizer than local farmers; used local sun, not heated greenhouses
Cons: more fossil fuel used for transport; soil is degraded; ground water contaminated; may be picked unripe to ripen in containers; affecting taste and vitamin content; contains toxic chemicals

Local conventionally-grown vegetables

Pros: less fossil fuels used for transport; picked ripe – better taste and more nutritious; supports local farmers

Cons: sprayed with toxic pesticides; ground water contaminated; soil is degraded

Local organically-grown vegetables

Pros: no toxins or chemical fertilizers used; less fossil fuels used for transport; maintains soil vitality; picked ripe – better taste and more nutritious; supports local farmers
Cons: often not readily available; higher price

Organic vegetables grown far away

Pros: no toxins or chemical fertilizers; maintains soil vitality
Cons: more fossil fuels used for transport; higher price; not as fresh

"Local Food Plus" vegetables

Pros: fewer toxins and chemical fertilizers used; maintains soil vitality; supports local farmers; increases availability of safer food; less fossil fuels used for transport
Cons: not completely organic; may be more expensive than conventional

COUNTING YOUR CARBON FOOTPRINT

Research indicates that 85–98% of CO_2 emissions caused by conventional farming are due to the fossil fuel use at the farm, processor, and retailer. Transportation to markets accounts for between 2–15% of those emissions. Clearly, it is a complicated phenomenon, and determining the carbon footprint may be hard for you and me, as the consumers. Luckily, CarbonCounted (carboncounted.com), a nonprofit organization, offers a tool that companies and farmers can use to determine the carbon footprint of the products they're selling. CarbonCounted advocates for both businesses and consumers to ask for carbon footprint information and make eco-sensitive decisions about what we buy.

THE DIRTY DOZEN & CLEAN THIRTEEN

The US-based nonprofit organization Environmental Working Group (*ewg.org*) has developed a list of common fruits and vegetables ranked according to the amount of pesticide residue consumed when you eat them. Peaches, which carry the heaviest load, are given a ranking of "100" and onions, which have the lowest load, are given a "1." The list (see below) was based on tests by the US Department of Agriculture and the Food and Drug Administration.

DIRTY DOZEN (produce that should be "organic priorities," in order of pesticide load):

1 | Peaches (100)
2 | Apples (96)
3 | Bell peppers (86)
4 | Celery (85)
5 | Nectarines (84)
6 | Strawberries (83)
7 | Cherries (75)
8 | Lettuce (69)
9 | Imported grapes (68)
10 | Pears (65)
11 | Spinach (60)
12 | Potatoes (58)

CLEAN THIRTEEN (conventional produce that is least contaminated [though possible genetic-modification and irradiation isn't accounted for/factored in]):

1 | Onions (1)
2 | Avocados (1)
3 | Sweet corn – frozen (2)
4 | Pineapples (7)
5 | Mangoes (9)
6 | Sweet peas – frozen (11)
7 | Asparagus (11)
8 | Kiwi (14)
9 | Bananas (16)
10 | Cabbages (17)
11 | Broccoli (18)
12 | Eggplants (19)
13 | Papayas (21)

(Source: Environmental Working Group, Washington, DC – *foodnews.org*)

SOME FARMERS DON'T OPT FOR ORGANIC DESIGNATION

Farmers who produce healthy food in an environmentally-sensitive way and choose not to apply for organic certification may do this because of the complexity and financial costs of being certified. Instead, they rely on support from local people who know and respect their farming practices. A farmer in Ontario's Niagara region from whom I get my peaches chooses to be "almost organic." Peaches are particularly susceptible to pests and conventionally-grown ones are often sprayed over and over during the growing season, but this farmer produces a crop of luscious fruit which he only sprays with pesticide once, when the trees are in flower, before the peaches have even begun to form, making these peaches a safer bet than those in conventional farms from the same area.

Since there is more demand for healthy, sustainable food than can be filled by certified organic farmers, it's important that we know where on the scale of safe and environmentally-sensitive our non-certified food falls. Recognizing this, the Ontario organization Local Food Plus has begun certifying green-friendly farmers who are trying to be ecologically aware but may not yet qualify for organic certification. Their website, localflavourplus.ca, offers lists of these farmers and their products. Foods with this certification are beginning to appear in grocery and restaurant chains in the area.

CHAPTER
5

YOUR PANTRY

Essential Ingredients

For me, there's something really satisfying about a well-stocked pantry. It allows for more creativity in my kitchen and variety in my diet In this chapter, I identify what I consider to be the essentials of a whole-foods kitchen. Keeping these things on hand should make preparation of the recipes in this book a snap (see chapter six for information on where to purchase pantry essentials).

VEGETABLES

A vegetable is any edible part of a plant – stems, roots, tubers, buds, bulbs, immature or mature flowers, berries, seeds, and leaves. This can technically include fruits, grains, and legumes; however, in common usage, we refer to them separately because of their unique nutritional properties.

In addition to providing a plethora of vitamins and minerals necessary for our continued health, vegetables are an excellent source of fiber, which absorbs water and provides the bulk that we need for digestion, as well as carbohydrates (e.g., potatoes and sweet potatoes).

Be sure to buy garlic that is firm. Don't buy garlic that has sprouted because when it's that old it becomes hard to digest. I never recommend purchasing prepared garlic (peeled cloves stored in oil or water, or made into a paste) because it quickly loses its vitality and never tastes as good.

Allium genus: garlic, green onions, leeks, onions; also chives, garlic scapes, shallots, wild leeks – this veg group is highly nutritious, offering a savory dimension to any dish, and some have been shown to lower blood pressure, improve circulation, and increase absorption of vitamins and minerals.

Brassica genus (a.k.a. crucifers): broccoli, Brussels sprouts, cabbage, cauliflower, collard greens, kale; also broccoflower (Romanesco) Rapini – known for being high in calcium, vitamin C, folic acid, riboflavin, and iron; some are high in potassium and zinc.

Asian greens (also crucifers): bok choy, Chinese broccoli (gai lan), mustard greens – also offer micronutrients and variety for a Western diet.

Lettuces: green leaf, mizuna, red leaf, Romaine – excellent sources of vitamins A and C, folate, manganese & chromium; very good source of dietary fiber, vitamins B1 and B2, potassium, molybdenum, iron, and phosphorous.

Greens must be stored in a sealed container or plastic bag in the fridge to keep them from wilting. And be sure to not store them wet, or they'll get slimy – fast.

Deep greens: spinach, Swiss chard – tend to be high in iron, vitamin A and chlorophyll. (Spinach has lots of calcium, but also oxalic acid which blocks calcium absorption – if steamed, calcium will be more available.)

Mushrooms: cremini (brown), oyster, Portobello, shiitake, white button – phytonutrients in mushrooms have been found to have cancer fighting properties.

Nightshades: bell peppers, chili peppers, eggplant, potatoes, tomatoes – proven to lower risk

of some cancers (protecting against free radicals), promote lung health, and reduce risk of cardiovascular disease; some contain phytonutrients, which have antioxidant activity. (This group is avoided in the macrobiotic diet and can be aggravating for some people; particularly those with arthritis.)

Root vegetables & tubers: beets, carrots, celery root, Jerusalem artichoke (sunchoke), parsnip, rutabaga/turnip, and sweet potatoes/yams – high in vitamins and minerals; are mostly complex carbohydrates, so they provide energy and make us feel full and grounded.

Shoots & stems: artichokes, asparagus, celery, fennel bulb – high in vitamins and minerals, but with far fewer calories than roots & tubers.

Sea vegetables (a.k.a. seaweed, macroalgae): agar-agar, arame, dulse, hijiki, kelp/kombu, nori, wakame – help to regulate blood cholesterol and remove heavy metals and radioactive elements from body; high in protein and vitamins A, C, E, B1, B2, B6, B12; contain more minerals than any other food. Add soaked arame to salads and Asian-seasoned noodle dishes; shake dulse flakes into salads and soups; add wakame to miso soup and cook legumes with a piece of kombu to boost mineral content and ease digestion.

Microalgae: chlorella, spirulina – high in protein, vitamins, minerals, and nucleic acids. These deep green powders are amazingly good for us, containing a whole gamut of nutrients. Chlorella and spirulina are better sources of protein, beta-carotene, and nucleic acids than any other food.

When it comes to fresh produce, strive to do as Europeans do: buy only enough produce for the next couple of days (with the exceptions of root vegetables, which can be stored for longer in the pantry, and fresh spinach, which may be stored in the fridge for up to a week).

FRUIT

Apples, bananas, berries (blueberries, cranberries, raspberries, strawberries), citrus (grapefruit, lemons, limes, oranges), dates, figs, grapes, kiwi, mango, melons (cantaloupe, honeydew, muskmelon, watermelon), papaya, pear, pineapple, stone fruit (apricots, cherries, nectarines, peaches, plums); also try Asian pears, kumquats, lychees, pomelos, starfruit.

Fruit is generally defined as the part of a plant that contains the pit or seed(s) surrounded in soft flesh. When we think of fruit, it's usually the sweet ones that come to mind, so that's the kind I'm talking about here. Fruit offers us natural sugar for immediate energy, and lots of fiber. They are sources of all the micronutri-

Raw, whole-foods ingredients are much cheaper than processed food. Buying in bulk also reduces your grocery bill, making organics more affordable. It's tempting to cut costs by only purchasing a few ingredients at a time, but variety is key because repetition can be boring, and every bean, grain, or vegetable has different micronutrients.

SECRET FRUIT

We often think of avocado, cucumber, squash (both winter and summer varieties), and tomato as vegetables, but they're technically fruit!

ents that support our health. The pectin grabs toxins, like lead and mercury, and ushers them out of the body. The pigment in apples, berries, and other fruits contains flavanoids which have been found to help prevent heart disease. Natural fructose is great for stabilizing blood sugar levels. The manganese and thiamin (vitamin B1) content is great for energy production and antioxidant defense. Pineapple, especially, has potential anti-inflammatory and digestive benefits; believe it or not, anti-tumor compounds have been found in pineapple stems. Eating fruit is better for your eyes than eating carrots; it protects against macular degeneration, and can also help prevent kidney stones. Eating grapefruit can lower your cholesterol and boost your liver enzymes that clear out carcinogens.

GRAINS

Non-glutinous (or very low gluten): amaranth, buckwheat (and kasha), corn/cornmeal, millet, oats, quinoa, rice; also teff.

Glutinous: barley, kamut, spelt; also bulgur, rye, wheat. (Couscous is not a grain; it's a type of pasta and can be made from wheat or spelt.)

With all the craziness in recent years over low/no-carb diets, I worry that grains (and I'm talking whole grains here) aren't getting the recognition they deserve. Grains are grasses that have their fruit and seed combined in a single entity. (Buckwheat, amaranth, and quinoa are considered grains because we use them in much the same way, but they are not actually grasses.)

When it comes to grains, I find that organic brands are not much more expensive than their conventionally-grown counterparts.

Whole grains (those that still have all their parts intact – bran, germ, and endosperm)

WHEAT

The world's most popular carbohydrate crop, wheat is grown in almost every country (and in the US, in almost every state). And though it is said to be helpful for a range of stress and mental health systems, as well as nurturing the heart and being good for the musculature, it's one of the most common food allergens – but because it's now so commonly used, a lot of us have become intolerant to it (signs of wheat intolerance may include anxiety, eczema, and other skin rashes and digestive issues such as gas, bloating, and loose stools). Many folks around the world eat white-flour (unbleached, all-purpose flour) products, which should really be considered a non-food – white flour may make some of the best baked goods, but refined of its bran and germ, it's lost most of its nutrients (even if it's been "enriched").

Try omitting wheat (this includes bulgur and couscous) from your diet for two weeks and see how you feel. During this time, baked goods and pastas can be derived from other grain sources, like rice or kamut, and be sure to check product labels (including your bottle of soy sauce). After this period, gradually add wheat products back into your diet and see if you feel a difference – you may find you were relieved of certain health ailments.

provide complex carbohydrates that help to balance our blood sugar. Eating grains and legumes together provides you with all the major nutrient groups: fat, protein, carbohydrates, fiber, vitamins, and minerals.

Flours & pastas

I advocate eating whole grains over flour products like baked goods and pasta because whole, unrefined foods have a greater energy value and don't slow down our digestive system as much. I do, however, enjoy baking, and pasta can be fun to cook, so they do make an appearance in my diet a few times a week. While wheat flour is the most widely available, try using different whole-grain flours or pastas – spelt, kamut, rye, and barley flours contain gluten; buckwheat, hemp, corn, chickpea, millet, oat, potato, pumpkin seed, quinoa, rice, soy, and tapioca flours don't. Check package labels to ensure there are no eggs in the ingredients.

LEGUMES

Adzuki (aduki) beans, lentils, split peas, and white beans are said to be easiest to digest.

Black beans, chickpeas (garbanzo beans), kidney beans, and soybeans are the most popular legumes in Western diets, and they're also super-nutritious. Soybeans (including tofu) tend to be difficult to digest unless they've been fermented into tempeh or miso. Soy products can be convenient and work well in many kinds of dishes; and Tetra Pak soymilk or silken tofu typically has a shelf life of one year (until opened, of course).

Legumes (beans and lentils) grow in pods on vines. They nourish our kidneys and ad-

renal glands; their isoflavones protect against heart disease and cancer. Since they are slowly digested they're great for diabetics. Legumes have lots of micronutrients, and provide essential amino acids from which to build new proteins – they contain about 17–25% protein (variable), with the exception of soybeans, which are about 38% (variable). Eat beans and lentils in sprouted form or cooked (at home or from a can) – they're more nutritious when you cook 'em from dried form.

NUTS & SEEDS

Nuts: almonds, cashews, peanuts (actually a legume, since they grow in pods underground, but they have many nut traits), pecans, pine nuts, walnuts; also pistachios, but use in moderation (said to be one of the moldier varieties).

Seeds: flax, poppy, pumpkin, sesame, sunflower.

If you buy nut butter in a plastic container, be sure to transfer it to a glass jar when you get home. Plastic is volatile in the presence of oil, meaning the plastic's chemicals will mix in with the nut butter's oil.

Raw nuts and seeds are good sources of EFAs (essential fatty acids) and protein; almonds and sesame seeds are especially good sources of calcium. Organic seeds are fairly economical; choose organic peanuts over conventional ones which are grown with lots of chemicals. To keep nuts and seeds from going rancid (because of their high fat content), they're best stored in airtight containers in the fridge or freezer; seeds are tasty when toasted in a pan on your stovetop.

* Coconut oil can also be used for baking. It is solid at room temperature (like butter), and contains about 62% medium-chain fatty acids, including the healthy fats like lauric acid, caprylic acid, and capric acid, which metabolize more easily than other saturated or unsaturated fatty acids. This is why coconut oil has the reputation of being a fat that we burn easily. But only use coconut oil occasionally, because of its higher saturated fat content.

OILS

Oils bring out the flavors in food, but they are also important for other reasons. The EFAs in "healthy," cold-pressed oils nourish our cell membranes, are important for supporting brain and immune system functions, and maintain their flavor, aroma, and nutritional value. Olive, peanut, and sunflower oils are among the healthy, cold-pressed varieties, and olive oil is best in terms of matching health benefits and cost, but its flavor is too strong for most baking and it burns at 350°F (180°C), so use another vegetable oil like sunflower, canola (if it's non-GM), or safflower for baking.*

CONDIMENTS, SPREADS & SEASONINGS

Sea salt and tamari or shoyu (naturally brewed soy sauces) are good for flavoring. Also, sun-dried sea salt contains essential and trace minerals, and is necessary to maintain the fluid and acid-alkaline balance in the body. We only need ½ tsp a day, but most people consume 7 times that amount. Herbs, spices, and sea veggies are also excellent seasonings and salt-replacements.

Herbs: basil, coriander, dill, marjoram, mint, oregano, parsley, rosemary, thyme.

Spices: allspice, anise, black pepper, cardamom, cayenne pepper, cinnamon, chili powder, cloves, cumin, fennel seeds, nutmeg, paprika, turmeric; fresh ginger root (can be stored in the freezer for easy grating).

Nutritional yeast (imparts a "cheesy," or savory, seasoning for soups, salads, and popcorn.

Be sure to buy organic herbs and spices as many conventional ones have been irradiated.

For essential sweeteners and baking ingredients, see page chapter ten.

WATER

Our bodies, just like the earth, are made up of about 70% water, and we need to replenish this fluid regularly (2–4 L/day) to keep everything functioning as it should. Water supports our metabolic processes and transports nutrients and minerals to where we need them. It aids in the removal of toxins and waste, both on a cellular level and in the eliminatory process.

According to many health advocates, North American tap water still contains non-health supporting bacteria, chlorine, and fluoride; therefore it's beneficial to have a water filtration system. While it's often true that the more expensive filters remove more contaminants, it doesn't mean that we need to invest in a system that costs more than a month's rent. I use a solid block activated carbon filter, but you should do your own research and make your own decision on which filtration system is best for you, according to your lifestyle, financial situation, geography, and water source (i.e. municipal system or ground source). If you're using a Brita pitcher or similar system, it's best to keep it in the fridge so that bacteria have less of a chance to breed amongst the filter's carbon granules. (But it's a less than ideal system, as you don't want to be drinking cold water.)

Check out *WaterFilterComparisons.net* for more information.

STORAGE

Buy dry goods in bulk whenever you can to reduce packaging and the dent in your wallet. Ideally, bring your own containers to the food co-op or health food stores to stock up; otherwise, be sure to decant your supplies once you arrive home (i.e. transfer from plastic bags into sealable jars, keeping supplies fresh and pest-free). Reuse any glass jars on hand (I use baby food jars); be creative and remember to rotate the contents of your jars so that the older stuff doesn't sit at the bottom.

CHAPTER 6

WHERE TO SHOP

Navigating Food Co-ops,
Farmers' Markets &
Your Local Grocery Store

Many of the ingredients called for in this book can be found at the nearest supermarket, especially if you live in an urban area. As organic food has become more popular, there are often a few aisles devoted to "natural" products in major chain stores.

Sure, there's a lot to be said for easy shopping: quickly getting everything you need so that you have more time for cooking (and the rest of your life), but it may be worth checking out smaller, independent food co-ops or health food stores to support – they often have the whole-foods ingredients you're looking for, and a better relationship with local distributors.

Apart from your local grocers or health food stores, here are a few additional food venues to help you keep your pantry and fridge well-stocked with fresh and healthy food.

FOOD CO-OPS

Food co-ops are owned by the workers and/or the customers who shop there. They can be set up like a small retail grocery store or a buying club, and are generally committed to educating their members about healthy eating, environmental sensitivity, and supporting local farmers.

If you live in the United States, you're lucky to have the Coop Directory Service (coop directory.org) or Local Harvest.org (local harvest.org/food-coops) to help you find a natural foods co-op near you. There's also the Co-operative Grocer's Food Co-op Directory (cooperativegrocer.coop/coops) that may provide some local listings.

I love Karma Co-op in Toronto's Annex neighborhood (karmacoop.org). Even now that I'm living in Montreal, I maintain an out-of-town membership because I appreciate Karma's focus on food issues and education. Most of the products in the store have color-coded labels – green for organic, brown for conventional (and if products are "low-spray," or grown on a farm transitioning to organic that's stated too) – and are marked with the province or country of origin. There's a chalkboard in the produce section touting the number of local items available that day, and there's always a friendly community vibe going on in the store. Oh, and I can't forget to mention that with the relatively modest mark-up, their products are reasonably priced.

Karma is a member-owned co-op and asks its members to work a couple of hours a month (these folks are "working members"). If members choose not to clock any hours, they pay a monthly or per-shop fee on top of the price tag cost. I know of other co-ops, like the impressively huge Park Slope Co-op in Brooklyn, New York (foodcoop.com) that only accepts working members. Other co-ops, like the Big Carrot in Toronto (thebigcarrot.ca), are worker-owned, and therefore committed to the philosophy of their organization, and anyone can shop there.

FARMERS' MARKETS

I love co-ops, but get a romantic feeling about farmers' markets – there's something about the combination of enthusiastic shoppers with the unbleached cloth bags, the lush fresh produce, and the friendly farmers that make them great places for first dates. There are some farmers' markets that are

READING (AND ACTUALLY UNDERSTANDING) LABELS

There is a lot of food jargon used in marketing these days – you might see "made with Whole Grains" on a box of Lucky Charms cereal and think, *Something about that is not right....* So let's try and clear up any confusion about the following terms:

Conventional: a term most often used by people who want to differentiate between organic and non-organic food. "Conventional" food refers to the "regular" produce or food that is not labeled organic and which is produced under current federal agricultural standards that still allow "conventional" food-producing practices, like the use of synthetic pesticides, herbicides, insecticides, irradiation, and factory farming.

GM/GE foods: Genetically modified organisms (GMOs) and genetically engineered (GE) food are hot topics now; there's a battle between big business and consumer groups about whether genetically altered foods should be labeled as such. The benefits of genetically altering seeds and living organisms (i.e. your food) have not yet been proven to outweigh the still unknown risks. As well, with the advent of GM/GE crops (like tomatoes that can survive weeks of shipping and storage), many local, native varieties of produce, legumes, and grains are no longer available because they could not compete in the marketplace. Canadian and US laws do not require the labeling of GM/GE foods. Conventionally-grown foods that are currently said to be genetically engineered include canola, corn, potatoes, soy, and tomatoes – so it's a good idea to get these foods in organic form, thereby supporting your health and agricultural diversity.

Local: Some people define local food as that which is produced no more than 160 km (100 mi) from the place where you buy it. Some people define local by country, province/state, or bioregion. I define local as a relative term: I enjoy fresh strawberries from a nearby farm in the summer (and stock them in my freezer to enjoy them in the winter), thereby avoiding those grown 4,000 km (2,485 mi) away. Food begins to decrease in nutritional value from the moment it's harvested, so food that is closest to where you live will likely have more to offer you than food that's logged more kilometers than you did on your last vacation.

Natural: When I think of "natural," I think of the way a food exists in nature – or pretty close to it. Is an organically-grown apple natural? Yup. Is a jar of applesauce natural? Sure, if it doesn't contain preservatives, simulated flavors, or sweeteners. Is an apple "drink" with just "25% real juice" natural? Nope. Read the ingredient lists, keeping in mind that "natural" is not a regulated term, so any producer or marketer can use it.

Organic: The USDA's Alternative Farming Systems Information Center website states: "Organic agriculture is an ecological production management system that promotes and enhances biodiversity, biological cycles and soil biological activity," and "the principal guidelines for organic production are to use materials and practices that enhance the ecological balance of natural systems and that integrate the parts of the farming system into an ecological whole" (*nal.usda.gov/afsic/pubs/ofp/ofp.shtml*). There are a number of third-party organic certification bodies, including the US Department of Agriculture, Quality Assurance International, and the Organic Crop Improvement Association, which set standards for what it means to farm or purchase "organic"; all bodies agree that foods grown with the use of pesticides, synthetic fertilizers, GM-seeds, antibiotics, growth hormones, and irradiation cannot be considered "organic." If the label says "organic," look for the logo of the certifying body.

Refined/Processed foods: As soon as a whole food begins to be processed, it starts to lose its nutrients and our bodies don't assimilate it as well. Refined foods can seem easier to eat – I'm sure you could eat more slices of a white Italian loaf in a meal, than an equal volume of sprouted or steamed wheat berries – but it would be to the detriment of your health. Also, processed foods can also go "off" faster, hence the common addition of preservatives.

Whole foods: There are two ways to look at "whole foods." There's the whole food itself (like grains of brown rice), and then there's stuff made with them (like cookies made with brown rice flour) – simply, I define whole foods as the opposite of overly processed, refined foods.

open daily, and others that are open one day a week, some are indoors, some outdoors, depending on the size, location, and time of year, and most are open from April to November, if not year-round.

To find the farmers' markets in your area, Google "farmers' markets" and your city, region, province, or state. In the US, there has been a large growth in farmers' markets since the Farmer-to-Consumer Direct Marketing Act was passed in 1976 – there are now over 3,500 farmers' markets in America; as mentioned above, Local Harvest is a good resource to find a market in your area.

And if you live in Canada, check out the listings for Alberta – *albertamarkets.com*, British Columbia – *bcfarmersmarket.org*, Nova Scotia – *nsfarmersmarkets.ca*, or Ontario – *farmersmarketsontario.com*, or search the 'net for other farmers' markets in your neck of the woods.

One of the farmers' markets I frequent in Toronto is located in Dufferin Grove Community Park. It is open once a week, year-round; in winter, they operate out of an ice-rink house. The market also hosts tasting fairs and other fun events. They have a super website (*dufferinpark.ca/market*) that provides a map of all the farms that sell at the market; describes each farm, what it produces, and provides its contact information;

and lists lectures on sustainable agriculture and news articles relating to their goal, "to create direct links between the producers and consumers of local organic food." Vendors must sign an agreement that stipulates no GMOs are allowed in any cooked food, no more than 30% of their produce can be grown off-farm, and growers have priority over non-growers if two farmers are selling the same product.

CSAs

Community Supported Agriculture is often simply known as "food box" programs, in which a group of consumers pay a local farmer (or group of local farmers) for a portion of the harvest and become, in a sense, a partner in the farm. Every week, the farmer will bring boxes of freshly harvested goods to the CSA members at an agreed pick-up point. The most popular programs run from the spring to the fall; there are also farms that offer winter baskets on a bi-weekly basis.

I'll tell you flat out: food grown by someone you've met tastes better. And while there's a fun community vibe at farmers' markets, there's something else going on with CSAs – it's a commitment on the part of the consumers as well as the farmers to show up, week after week. It's nice to have something you can count on.

When buying organic, you might have to adjust your aesthetic standards. Just like real people come in all shapes and sizes, carrots aren't always straight and apples aren't always shiny and scab-free, which is not necessarily an indication that something's wrong with them. You shouldn't tolerate bruised, mushy, or molding produce, or sprouting onions or garlic, but less-than-perfect coloring or shape is just part of the fun of organics.

FOODS I BUY

Do I make everything from scratch? Are you kidding? I certainly try to have a life out of the kitchen (and away from the computer)! Check out my up-to-date list of products and brands that I use at home for you to find at your local grocer or health food store; if they don't carry it, kindly request that they do! getitripe.com

CSA is a relatively new idea in North America. The idea started in both Switzerland and Japan in the 1960s and came to North America in the 80s. Many small farmers have found that becoming a CSA has enabled them to keep their farm economically viable in a time when small farmers are at risk of bankruptcy.

Today, most CSAs are located near urban centers with city dwellers joining nearby farmers to share in the risks and benefits of growing high quality foods in a way that doesn't hurt the environment. Most CSA farmers use organic or bio-dynamic farming methods; some provide a range of produce, including baked goods and firewood. Others, who only grow a single crop, join other farmers in their area to provide the range of vegetables and other products that the members will need year-round. Members of CSAs often make a commitment to visit the farm for a tour, perhaps even helping out at harvest time. Each CSA is different, so it's best to do your research before joining one.

Vote with your dollars!

Who says you have to buy whatever your local grocery or health food store offers you? They want your business, so tell 'em what you want. Be friendly, polite, and sensitive to their business, and you may be surprised by what a letter or phone call can do!

The following is a letter I've drafted to give to local restaurants/cafés/grocery stores/natural foods stores/food co-ops/hair salons/spas or wherever else you regularly spend your dough. You can customize the letter, depending on your particular needs, wants, and interests.

To the fine folks at _____ *(name of establishment – better yet, the name of the most appropriate contact person),*

I think your _____ *(type of establishment)* **is great! I really enjoy**:

☐ the food you serve (better yet, be specific – is it the flavor, presentation, portion-size, etc.?)
☐ the attentive/helpful/friendly staff
☐ the fast service
☐ the fun/creative décor
☐ the comfortable atmosphere
☐ how close you are to my house/work/school
☐ or anything from the list below that they already do

I do, however believe that I would be more inclined to frequent your super establishment if you offered more:

☐ vegan (meat-/egg-/dairy-free) options (feel free to provide specific examples)
☐ wheat-/gluten-free options
☐ naturally-sweetened treats (using fruit, maple syrup, brown rice syrup, stevia, etc. over refined sugar)
☐ non-dairy milk (and/or stevia powder instead of aspartame) for tea or coffee
☐ meals prepared with locally and organically grown foods
☐ fairly traded coffee and teas, and foods made with fairly traded chocolate, sugar, and spices
☐ complimentary filtered water (instead of tap water)
☐ foods heated without the use of a microwave
☐ cloth napkins or unbleached paper napkins, and unbleached paper products in the washrooms
☐ more ecologically-sensitive take-out containers

If you can suggest local resources to help get them going (like Green Shift [*greenshift.ca*] for biodegradable take-out containers), now might be the time to do so.

Thanks so much for taking the time to consider my request(s). I would certainly appreciate hearing back from you regarding this matter.

Warmly, _____ (your name here)

CHAPTER

7

YOUR TOOLS

Essential Kitchen Equipment

Now you've grocery shopped your little heart out, but what good are all those ingredients if you have nothing to prepare them with?

When choosing kitchen tools, avoid using materials that may release toxins into the food you're preparing. **Glass** and **enamel** are the safest options and are considered non-reactive, as are **bamboo**, **wood**, **earthenware**, and **ceramic cookware**. (Some ceramic glazes, however, contain lead; most ceramics are food-safe, but it's worth checking if you're using something that is old or manufactured abroad.) Cookware made of **silicone**, a human-made blend of sand and oxygen (as opposed to a plastic), is also considered inert.

There are some materials (like aluminum and plastic) that are more reactive, and there are some foods (like fats and acidic foods) that are more reactive. Food is more likely to exchange ions with the surrounding cookware when it's hot rather than cold – the trick is to keep the most reactive foods and materials away from one another to keep your food as contaminant-free as possible. In short, don't store hot peanut sauce in a plastic container and don't make spaghetti sauce in an aluminum saucepan.

Remember: the more flexible plastic is, the more reactive it is. So plastic wrap, for example, is more reactive than a hard plastic measuring cup. If you use a microwave, which I don't recommend, *never* use plastic – even if it says it's microwave safe – because the plastic ions combine with the food you're heating. (Microwaves are also said to decrease the "life-force," or energetic value of food, not to mention the fact that they haven't been around for anyone's entire lifespan, so we can't really say what the long-term effects might be.)

If you, like most of us, own plastic or aluminum cookware, don't let it keep you from cooking; just upgrade your equipment when you can, starting with the items you use most.

KNIVES

What is a kitchen without good knives? In the long run, it's worth it to invest in good-quality knives. Cutting onions with a flimsy steak knife is not going to cut it – literally. The essentials are a **paring knife**, at least one good chopping knife (also known as a **chef's knife**), a long, serrated-edged **bread knife**, and a **smaller serrated knife** for tomatoes. Look for products with a handle that feels good in

SHARPEN THOSE KNIVES

Have your knives sharpened regularly, as forcing a dull knife on food can be far more dangerous than using a sharp knife. For best results, sharpen them before each use (home sharpening applies only to non-serrated knives.) My chef pal Dan explains: you want your knife to be sharp and have a straight edge. Using a whetstone or sharpening stone occasionally (about once a week) will keep your knife sharp and using a handheld steel sharpener more often (perhaps daily) will help keep the edge straight. You might also use a cheap, medium grit sharpening stone; I prefer the ceramic ones, but they can be pricey. Most stones are rectangular with a rough side for grinding and a fine side for finishing. Lay the stone on a towel so it doesn't slip and stroke the knife a few times along the entire length of the blade at about 15 degrees. Repeat on the other side. Splash the stone with water to keep it lubricated and cool, and keep going till it's sharp. The steel sharpener should be a very fine grit. Run it along the knife blade a few times at a 15-degree angle. Always give the same treatment to both sides to avoid the edge rolling over.

Xenoestrogens, human-made compounds found within many pesticides, fuels, plastics, detergents, and prescription drugs, are able to imitate estrogen in our bodies and can contribute to an excess of estrogen. Too much estrogen can be a factor in a number of hormone-related health problems, including irregular menstrual cycles, endometriosis, mental health issues (such as depression), and cancers of the breast, cervix, uterus, or prostate. Avoid cooking with plastic by using glass, wood, ceramic, stainless steel, and silicon tools instead.

your hand and has its blade running right through the handle. Prices and brands vary, so go to a few kitchen stores and ask the sales person to show you the selection.

Also, it's handy to have a pair of **kitchen scissors** for snipping fresh herbs or other food items.

CUTTING BOARDS

A large unfinished **wooden cutting board** is essential for preparing food; if you're purchasing a new one, be sure to treat it with a light coating of olive oil or mineral oil before using (sometimes you can purchase ones that have been pre-treated, but make sure you know what it's pre-treated with; if the label doesn't say, you're better off with an untreated board).

Keep a second cutting board on hand to be used exclusively for fruit and other non-pungent items – there's nothing worse than slicing up a mango only to have it taste vaguely of onion. To cleanse an oniony (or garlicky) smelling board, scrub it with a baking-soda-and-water paste before washing in hot soapy water (repeat if necessary) and dry immediately. When washing a wooden board, avoid letting it sit in water as it may crack.

PEELERS, GRATERS, SPIRALIZERS, ZESTERS, MANDOLINES, PRESSES, GRINDERS & REEMERS

I like to use a fruit and vegetable **peeler** with a good handle. There's a lot of nutritional value (fiber, vitamins, minerals) in the skin of fruit or veg, so I keep peeling to a minimum, for a desired texture (like smooth mashed potatoes) or if the produce isn't organic.

Box **graters** are convenient for preparing many kinds of vegetables. In addition, I highly recommend using a **spiralizer** – a mini-appliance that creates long, fine strands of veg, such as beets, zucchini, and daikon – for elegant additions to any cooked dish or salad.

If you like thinly slicing produce or chopping it into matchsticks, I recommend a **mandoline**, which is a super-sharp slicing tool (watch those fingers!) with various attachments for different cuts. You may be able to find a less expensive brand, such as Benrinner, in Chinatown or kitchen shops.

For zesting or fine grating, a **rasp** is an excellent tool. I recommend the Microplane brand because I find their products are best for these tasks; and, with my Microplane, I never bother using a **garlic press**, though I hear Zyliss makes a good one.

I own a nice wooden Peugeot **pepper mill**, which has always served me well.

And my hand-held **citrus reemer** gets daily action when I make my Good Morning Elixir (page 105).

MEASURING CUPS & SPOONS

Some of the best chefs rarely measure their ingredients, but I'm an advocate of precision in the kitchen. I keep a couple sets of stainless steel (i.e. non-flimsy) **measuring spoons** on hand. One of the sets has wider mouths, while the other has narrower mouths for extracting spices from small jars, for example.

When it comes to measuring cups, not everyone is aware that there are **dry measures** and **wet measures**. A dry measuring cup allows you to take a heaping scoop of dry in-

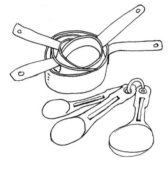

gredient (such as flour) and then scrape along the top with the back of a knife to get a level, accurate measure – no shaking off excess ingredients required, which would compress the ingredient and give it an inaccurate reading. Again, stainless steel is preferred, and choose cups with flat bottoms (so they'll stand on their own) and avoid ones with heavy handles that might cause the cup to tip over.

For liquid measuring cups, I prefer using a 2-cup Pyrex, and occasionally use a 1-cup or 4-cup measure – don't forget to read the measurement at eye level.

MIXING BOWLS

My mum has an old set of English-made, mustard-colored T. G. Green Gripstand ceramic bowls, which I love to use. I also have a decent set of glass bowls that suit me fine. I use wooden bowls for serving salad, though some folks also enjoy using them for baking. Stainless steel can be useful for a clumsy cook; and, of course, avoid plastic bowls (also because they get used-looking so fast).

POTS & PANS

One of my most valued possessions is my **heavy-bottomed soup pot** – it's a 5½-qt (5¼-L), round Dutch oven made of enamel-coated cast iron from the French company Le Creuset (this is quite an investment; I got mine for a gift, but if you're lucky you'll find one on sale or at a discount store). The runner-up to a heavy-bottomed soup pot is a stainless steel soup pot made with a thick, reinforced bottom.

It is also ideal to have a selection of saucepans in varying sizes for steaming vegetables, making sauces, cooking grains and legumes, and boiling pasta (having at least a 1-, 2-, and 3-qt/L saucepan is handy). They should have lids that fit, and it's good to have a pot that comes with one or more stacking **steamer baskets**.*

*CAROLINE'S TRICK FOR STEAMING GRAINS & VEG IN ONE GO

Put a pot of grains with water on the stove to cook. About 15 minutes before they're done (if you're cooking quinoa, that's almost right away, and if you're cooking millet or rice, it's about half way through the cooking time), place the steamer basket full of veggies in between the pot and the lid. The veg will be gently steamed by the grain-cooking water, and any minerals released from the veg will drip down into the grains. Ta-da! More nutrients for your precious bod.

While cast-iron is only moderately reactive, it is not appropriate for cooking soups or acidic foods like tomato sauce. Cast-iron cookware has been touted as having the health benefit of enriching foods with iron, though many health professionals agree that our bodies do not absorb this form of iron easily.

SKILLETS (FRYING PANS)

Cast-iron* skillets are great for cooking Maple Tempeh Strips (page 122), or for protecting yourself from burglars. And they should last a long time if you treat them well – when you first buy it, rinse it with water, dry thoroughly (cast iron pans should always be dried immediately after washing), then cure (season) it by brushing a very light coat of oil over the face of the pan, placing it on medium heat for a few minutes, and then removing it from heat and wiping off excess oil before putting it away. To clean pan,

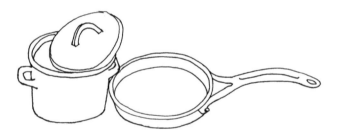

scrub with water and place on a hot stove element until it dries (then immediately remove it from heat and allow it to cool before storing away). If you've cooked something with a strong flavor, wash the pan with soap, but be sure to rinse it well, and re-cure immediately (see above). I've read that Lodge is the best brand, and they're pretty affordable.

Stainless steel frying pans are another option for frying ware and are more stable for acidic foods and liquid-based dishes. If you burn something, avoid scouring a stainless steel pan, as metallic ions more readily leach into food once the surface is scratched. Instead, allow pan to soak with baking soda or detergent overnight.

Teflon-coated pans are handy in a "non-stick" sort of way, but they really aren't safe! Not only do they get scratched up over time, allowing the deteriorating Teflon synthetic coating to come off into your food, but if over-heated, the plastic polymers release carcinogenic fumes. And if that's not enough to keep you away from the stuff, there's an environmental consideration: *Mother Jones* identified Teflon chemicals as "the most persistent synthetic chemicals known to man [sic]" (May/June 2007) – there seems to be no way of removing these toxins from the environment. If you're a non-stick cookware junkie, however, I hear that there are safer pans made with titanium, but they're not cheap.

For cooking large dishes like stir-fries, get a wok. You might find a good but cheap cast-iron wok in Chinatown, or one made of carbon steel in a kitchen store. Follow curing and washing instructions for cast-iron woks (see above), and again, no Teflon coating!

COLANDERS, STRAINERS & FUNNELS

I have a **large stainless-steel colander** for draining pasta and washing salad greens,

giving the greens a good shake over the sink to remove excess water (alternatively, I hear OXO makes a great salad spinner) and a **fine mesh strainer** (which can also be used as a steamer basket to place in a pot) that is essential for rinsing dry grains or legumes.

For funnels, I recommend a **wide-mouth funnel** for pouring bulk ingredients into glass jars for pantry storage; they're also useful for portioning leftovers (especially soups and stews) in jars before for fridge storage. In addition, a **smaller, thinner-nosed funnel** may be helpful for transferring spices and other ingredients into smaller glass containers.

UTENSILS

Silicon spatulas are handy for virtually every recipe. I prefer silicon spatulas for scraping out mixing bowls and the food processor, and they're a step up from rubber brands because they're heatproof to 428°F (220°C). I keep one exclusively for non-onion and -garlic use so it doesn't flavor my baked goods or puddings. You'll also want an **offset spatula** for flipping pancakes and transferring warm cookies to a cooling rack, and a long and narrow **icing spatula** for frosting cakes. I use a **wooden spoon** for stirring stews,  a **slotted spoon** for testing pasta for doneness, and a soup **ladle** for serving. A pair of **tongs** has many uses – such as picking out hot vegetables from the steamer basket. When baking, a **whisk** is good for fluffing up flour when you're too lazy to sift. Assuming you don't spend your entire life in the kitchen, and take advantage of something pre-made from time to time, you'll also need a **can opener**.

ELECTRIC APPLIANCES

If my landlord decided out of the blue to offer me a free month's rent, I might take that money and invest it in a Vita-mix **blender**. They'll pulverize anything, and can grind your whole grains into flour. But right now, I get by with a higher-end **food processor**, which can do more than a typical blender, like process dough for pie crusts, and grate and slice veggies.

I also have a **hand-held blender**, which is invaluable for puréeing soups and making smoothies. **Coffee grinders** can be helpful for the making a fresh pot of coffee, but I use mine for grinding flax seeds, and occasionally for spices.

To clean your grinder well, try running a few tablespoons of dry rice around in it. The grains will whisk away strong scents and flavors of coffee beans or spices.

A **toaster oven** is more practical than an upright slotted toaster, as it can also reheat muffins and bake or grill small items.

A **juicer** might turn out to be either one of your most valued appliances or a dust collector. Let's hope you use it if you have one, because juicing is a great way to get an impressive dose of easily assimilated whole foods-sourced nutrients into your diet. Cheaper, centrifugal-force juicers cost about $100, but they may heat up the produce (thus, killing off some nutrients) and don't extract as much juice as they should (feel how wet the processed pulp is when it comes out the other end); some are also limited to the kinds of produce they can process and, if you're juicing a lot, the motor may burn out pretty quickly. But regardless, the centrifugal juicer may be a good juicer to start with if you haven't juiced before – it's better to spend $100 rather than $400 to find out if you enjoy juicing. Higher quality juicers are in the $300–$400 range or a twin-gear juicer that can cost $700 (The Hippo [from Greenpower] is a more economical brand) – they'll be better bets for juicing greens and grasses and won't heat the produce because of their slower speed. Some will even process nuts into nut butter!

BAKEWARE

Heat-proof bakeware is essential for your oven. I recommend either glass or metal equipment, the occasional ceramic item, and avoiding aluminum whenever possible (although cast-aluminum is better than thin aluminum) because it is reactive. While silicone bakeware is considered safe, I've never had much success baking with it.

Baking sheets or cookie trays should be shiny and light-colored for best heat distribution. (While some recipes may request that the sheet be lightly coated with oil, I prefer to line them with unbleached parchment paper which you can save for future uses – like multiple batches of cookies – and which makes it easy to transfer baked goods to a cooling rack.

When it comes to **cake pans**, get 2 or 3 standard 9-in (23-cm) pans to start. I look for "professional" ones with straight sides that will last longer. I also like baking with **Bundt pans** for their retro look and because cake batters seem to cook through with more ease than in a standard cake pan. Most Bundt pans these days are non-stick, I'm sorry to say (mine isn't, but it's "vintage" from  my parents' basement). Be sure to oil it well and dust with flour (or cocoa) before adding batter, and allow baked cakes to cool completely for easiest removal – a broken Bundt cake can be heartbreaking.

Loaf pans can be glass or metal – I highly recommend lining them with unbleached parchment paper for ease of removal (and to

Your kitchen environment should be a really enjoyable place to work. Ideally, it should have good light and happy plants, including fresh herbs that you can grow on your windowsill (and which also contribute to better air quality). Also, consider how your space is set up (placement of furniture, appliances, and tools) so you can move about and cook with the greatest amount of ease. Music is also crucial for an afternoon of culinary debauchery in my house, so I have a stereo that sits on top of my cookbook shelf.

*The kitchen also needs to be a clean space, and should be kept clean with health- and environmentally-sensitive products. Keep **hand soap** by the sink and scrub your hands well before handling food (keep your fingernails short and remove your rings, too!). Also, use separate **scrubbers** for vegetables and dishes, and separate **sponges** for countertops and floors.*

protect food from the pan if it has non-stick coating).

If you like muffins, have some jumbo or mini **muffin trays** along with a standard tray of 12, and be sure to use unbleached liners.

While you may have a beloved ceramic heirloom **pie plate**, Pyrex glass pie plates are best for baking pies. They're inexpensive and the pies brown better and faster than those baked in a ceramic or metal plate, and it's easy to watch the underside of the pie crust brown.

I keep **casserole dishes** in varying sizes in the drawer under my oven for fruit crumbles, lasagnas, shepherd's pies, and squash au gratin (the 2–3-qt/L ones get the most oven action). Again, I go for Pyrex or other oven-proof glass dishes.

My most valuable piece of baking equipment is my **oven thermometer**. Inexpensive models, which should do you just fine, are available from kitchen or hardware stores for a few dollars.

OVEN MITTS & DISHTOWELS

There's nothing worse than pulling a dish out of the oven with **oven mitts** that are as thin as pillow cases. Some people say the best oven mitts are made by Parvin or Kool-Tek. **Dishtowels** are, of course, useful for drying dishes. Just be sure to wash them regularly. Also, I keep terrycloth **hand towels** next to the sink to use exclusively for drying my hands.

STORAGE CONTAINERS

Long gone are the days when I re-used old yogurt containers to store food in my fridge or pack my lunch. Plastics like that are made for single use, and the more they're used and exposed to heat (like hot water when washing), the more they break down and the greater the risk of xenoestrogen exposure (see page 78). Tupperware-like products are convenient, but should not store acidic foods, or store any foods for a long time. Pyrex and Anchor make sturdy **glass storage ware** (and serving dishes) with plastic lids in various sizes that are great for putting leftovers, even if the food is still hot.

CHAPTER
8

GETTING STARTED

Reading Recipes,
Measuring & Prepping Methods

There are intricacies to executing a recipe that can make or break a meal. If you haven't logged a whole lot of cooking hours in your lifetime, or if meal preparation is more of a mish-mash, throw-it-together affair that produces not so satisfying results, it's best to go over the basics.

READING RECIPES

Before you start, read the recipe from start to finish so there are no surprises. I've tried to provide recipes that are user-friendly, for folks who are already acquainted with preparing whole foods in a decently-stocked kitchen. It's a real drag, though, when you don't pre-read the recipe and are three-quarters of the way through making the dish before realizing that you don't have an essential ingredient or tool. And considering this, it's helpful to set out all the ingredients and equipment called for in the recipe before you start.

Be sure to prepare the ingredient as directed. Particularly, understand the placement of those action words! For example, "1 cup mushrooms, sliced" is different from "1 cup sliced mushrooms": the former directs you to measure 1 cup of whole mushrooms then slice them, and the latter directs you to slice enough mushrooms until you have 1 cup's worth. And here's another example, "1 cup millet, cooked" vs. "1 cup cooked millet": the former would yield four times more cooked millet than the latter.

Be sure you understand the directions. It's also important you have some idea of what all the ingredients are: for example, I once attended a potluck where I overheard, "I didn't

3 teaspoons (tsp) = 1 tablespoon (tbsp)
4 tbsp = ¼ cup
5⅓ tbsp = ⅓ cup
16 tbsp = 1 cup

1 cup = 8 fluid ounces (fl oz) = ½ pint (pt)
2 cups = 1 pt
4 cups = 1 gallon (gal) = 1 quart (qt) or
     1 liter (L) (roughly)

5 milliliters (mL) = 1 tsp
125 mL = ½ cup
250 mL = 1 cup
946 mL = 4 cups
1.89 L = 8 cups

28 grams (g) = 1 ounce (oz)
100 g = 3½ oz
454 g = 1 pound (lb)
16 oz = 1 lb

know what tamari was, so I just put in turmeric – they sound pretty similar!"

Unless otherwise stated, assume: "filtered water" is the cleanest water you can get (see page 69) and produce is washed (see page 86) and any dried ends or scrappy-looking bits are removed before using.

MEASURING

I'm an advocate for precise measuring of ingredients because it will always be the best way to yield exactly what the recipe calls for. Experimenting is fun, and often essential if you don't always have all the ingredients or tools, but I recommend following the recipe as closely as possible, at least when you first make it, in order to taste, see, and smell how the dish is supposed to be, then once you know the ins and outs of the dish, you will be able to experiment with it without ruining it.

For an accurate measurement, the ingredient should be level with the rim of the measuring spoon – I usually level it off with my clean finger or a knife. The only time the volume shouldn't be leveled off is if the recipe calls for a "rounded" teaspoon or a "heaping" tablespoon, etc.

WASHING FRUITS & VEGETABLES

Produce – organically-grown or not – should always be washed well before use. You can wash them before storing them in the fridge or on the counter, but keep in mind that this will break down their protective skins, so they'll need to be consumed sooner.

Root vegetables – use a scrub brush that is used only for this purpose.

Leafy greens – soak them in water mixed with a splash of vinegar to help remove pesticides and bacteria; this includes "pre-washed" salad mixes.

Commercial fruit & vegetable washes (preferably eco-sensitive brands like Nature Clean Fruit and Veggie Wash) can be sprayed on produce and then rinsed off; also, soaking produce in salted water encourages any bugs and slugs to fall off.

PRODUCE OF CONVENIENCE: PRE-WASHED SALAD MIX & PREPARED PRODUCE

If pre-washed salad greens make your life easier, then I say go for it – at least at the start. But pre-sliced veggies and fruit are another story – I recommend staying clear of them because of their decreased vitamin content (and the uncertainty about cleanliness when they were prepped). This goes for baby-cut carrots, too (which are reject bits of big carrots).

To peel or not to peel

Peeling is often an important part of preparing produce. Onions, avocados, citrus, and bananas must be peeled. Some recipes call for peeled potatoes, tomatoes, apples, or peaches, but with these fruits and vegetables, you will retain more nutrients if you don't peel them. On the other hand, pesticides are often concentrated in the peel of conventionally grown vegetables, so peeling them is beneficial for reducing pesticides in your food. I always peel apples for pie and potatoes that will be mashed to achieve a smoother texture in the final dish. Here are a few peeling tips:

Avocado – slice avocado in half lengthwise, around the pit, twist open, then remove pit. Slice fruit while still in its skin, then scoop out slices with a spoon.

Onions – slice a bit off the top of the onion. The papery or tough layers of skin will then be easy to peel away. If you only want to use half the onion, keep the skin on the unused portion and make sure to cover the face of the unused onion, otherwise it can taint the taste of the other food in your fridge.

Ginger – especially if your ginger was conventionally grown, it can be peeled with the edge of a spoon. This is the best technique for saving as much of the fleshy root as possible, as peeling with a knife creates more waste.

CUTTING VEGETABLES

Slicing: cutting a vegetable in one direction to make a particular shape. For example, a carrot can be sliced across to produce rounds or at an angle to produce ovals.

Chopping: cutting in at least 2 directions to produce bite-sized or smaller pieces.

Herbs are best chopped by washing and thoroughly drying them first, then remove and discard thicker stems, roll into a cigar-like shape, and cut across to create the size of leaf you desire.

Dicing: produces smaller pieces than chopping, usually about ⅛–¼ in (3–6 mm) in size.

Mincing: finely dicing that produces the smallest pieces. Strong-flavored vegetables like garlic or ginger are usually minced. It's best to use a large chef's knife and a cutting board or a food processor to make these fine cuts.

Julienne: produces matchstick-sized pieces.

Zesting: a technique that uses a zester or fine grater to remove the outer (colored) layer of citrus fruits called the peel or rind (a zester is also good for finely grating ginger). The resulting zest adds intense citrus flavor to dishes. Always zest lightly, avoiding the underlying white layer called the pith.

CHAPTER

9

PREPARING VEGETABLES, GRAINS AND LEGUMES

Cooking & Sprouting Methods

Over time, much of your daily food preparation will become a no-brainer. But if you're just starting out or if you're relearning your way around the kitchen without your microwave, you can use all the tips you can get.

Let's start with common cooking terms:

Boil: when a liquid boils, bubbles burst all over its surface. Key to remember: *if you're not sure if it's boiling, then it's not boiling*, or if you can stop the bubbles by stirring, it's not at a full rolling boil.

Parboil: to cook briefly (but not completely) in boiling water. Sometimes vegetables like carrots can be parboiled before adding them to a stir-fry to quicken the cooking process.

Roast: to cook in a pan, uncovered, in the oven. This technique gives veggies brown, crispy edges and soft insides, and often a sweeter taste.

Sauté: to sauté, heat a small amount of oil in a skillet, then add ingredients and stir gently while they cook.

Steam:* to steam, place ingredients in a steamer basket or rack in a pot of simmering or boiling water (with just enough water so that it does not touch the basket or rack) and cover with a lid.

STEAMING VEGETABLES

> **You will need:**
> - Vegetable(s) of your choice**
> - Sharp knife & cutting board
> - Stainless steel pot with fitted lid
> - Steamer basket
> - Timer
> - Tongs (or a fork)

Wash your veg well – if using carrots or sweet potatoes, scrub them with a vegetable brush, or peel them if they are not organic.

Fill pot with 1–2-in (2½–5-cm) cold water. Place steamer basket (or rack) in pot – water level should just be under bottom of basket. Place pot on stove over high heat and cover with lid to bring to a boil.

Cut vegetables as desired with a sharp knife (e.g., cut leafy greens lengthwise along stem before chopping widthwise, or slice sweet potatoes in thin rounds; green beans or snow peas just need their tips to be chopped off).

Once water is boiling, place prepared vegetables in steamer basket and cover with lid. Set timer for the appropriate time (see below). Most veg, except for sweet potatoes and squash, are best cooked *al dente*; green vegetables should be bright green when done – they are overcooked if they turn grey or yellow.

Steaming times
- Spinach, Swiss chard leaves: 30 sec
- Bok choy, snow peas: 1–1½ minutes
- Kale, collards, carrots, Swiss chard stalks: 2 min

* I do not recommend steaming (or cooking or reheating) foods in the microwave (just get rid of that microwave!). Along with its yet-to-be-proven long-term health effects, a Spanish study revealed that heating foods in the microwave dramatically decreased vitamin levels.

** There are many kinds of vegetables that can be steamed: including, bok choy, broccoli, Brussels sprouts, carrots, cauliflower, collards, green beans, kale, squash, sweet potatoes, and Swiss chard. Steaming allows you to retain more vitamin and mineral content than if you were to boil the vegetables; and they are more digestible and fibrous the closer they are to their raw state; this is why they are best steamed al dente.

- Broccoli, cauliflower, beets, green beans: 2½ min
- Brussels sprouts: 3–4 min
- Squash, sweet potatoes, corn on the cob: 8–10 min

Once steamed, remove pot from heat and uncover to stop steaming process. Remove veggies with tongs or a fork, and serve, topped with homemade dressing, flax/hemp seed oil and tamari, or with soup.

ROASTING SQUASH

> **You will need:**
> - Squash of your choice*
> - Sharp chef's knife & cutting board
> - Baking sheet
> - Olive oil, sea salt & maple syrup (optional)
> - Timer
> - Tongs (or a fork)

Roasting squash is quite simple to do and makes a great foundation for a cool-weather meal.

Preheat oven to 375°F (190°C).

Wash outside of squash well.

Slice in half lengthwise – this may require some effort, but if you rock the knife back and forth as you cut down, you should be able to do it.

Scrape out seeds and pulp and discard or set aside. (You can separate seeds from pulp, toss them in salt, and roast them on a baking sheet alongside squash until golden. They're tasty and nutritious!)

Pour about 1 tbsp oil onto each squash half and rub it over flesh and skin. Place squash halves flesh-side down on a baking sheet (lined with parchment paper if desired). Roast for about 40 minutes, until the flesh is *almost* soft.

Remove from oven, flip squash flesh-side up, sprinkle flesh with sea salt and drizzle with maple syrup (if desired), and roast for another 10 minutes (to enhance the sweetness and the crisp edges). If you're planning to use this squash in another recipe, omit this step and simply bake flesh-down for another 10 minutes or until soft.

Serve hot, alongside greens and a grain or legume dish.

COOKING GRAINS

(See chart on next page.)

> **You will need:**
> - Grain(s) of your choice filtered water, sea salt
> - Fine mesh strainer
> - Stainless steel pot with fitted lid
> - Timer

* There are many varieties of winter squash to choose from for roasting: including acorn, ambercup, buttercup, butternut, carnival, delicata, Hubbard, kabocha, pumpkin, and spaghetti. I might recommend roasting about ½ lb (230 g) raw squash per serving. Most varieties of squash have vibrantly colored orange flesh, which is rich in beta-carotene and will beautifully brighten up any dinner plate. (If you want to roast other root vegetables – see recipe for Maple Roasted Roots on page 185 – omit maple syrup if desired.)

COOKING GRAINS

Grain	Water: grain	Cooking time	Approximate yield (based on 1 cup dry grain)	Nutritional values & additional notes
amaranth	2:1	20–30 min	2 cups	very high in fiber, protein & calcium; easy to digest
barley* (hulled)	2–3:1	1–1½ hr	3½–4 cups	selenium, phosphorus & copper; warming properties
barley* (pearl)	2–3:1	30–50 min	3½ cups	fiber, selenium, phosphorus & copper; supports bowel health; warming properties
buckwheat	2:1	10–15 min	2 cups	lowers risk of high cholesterol & high blood pressure
bulgur*	2:1	20 min	3 cups	avoid with wheat allergies
cornmeal	3:1	30 min	3 cups	B vitamins, which support lung health, memory & energy when under stress
kamut*	3:1	1–2 hr	2½ cups	a type of wheat but higher in proteins, minerals, vitamins & unsaturated fatty acids than common wheat
millet	2:1	20–30 min	3½–4 cups	most alkalinizing grain
oats* (whole)	2¼:1	30 min–1 hr	2–2½ cups	nourishes nervous system
oats* (rolled)	2:1	5–10 min	4 cups	nourishes nervous system
quinoa	2:1	15–30 min	3–3½ cups	highest protein of any grain; more calcium than cow's milk; vitamins B & E & iron
rice, brown	2:1	25–35 min	3 cups	manganese, selenium, magnesium & B vitamins
rice, wild	2–4:1	45 min	4 cups	manganese, selenium, magnesium & B vitamins
rye berries*	3:1	2½ hr	2½ cups	manganese & dietary fiber help prevent gallstones
spelt*	3:1	2 hr	2¼ cups	riboflavin (vitamin B2) aids in relieving migraine symptoms & niacin (B3) protects against atherosclerosis
wheat berries*	3:1	1–2 hr	2½ cups	shown to have unique benefits in preventing breast and colon cancer; high in manganese; avoid if intolerant to wheat

Contains gluten – except for oats, which have been recently deemed non-glutinous, although they're often processed in a mill with other grains that are glutinous, so they're not always safe for those with gluten allergies.

FOR A NUTTIER FLAVOR

Another method of cooking grains that imparts a nuttier flavor, is to pan roast them first for 3–5 minutes (stirring or flipping grains in pan until they are light brown but not burnt). Then transfer to simmering salted water or vegetable stock and cook. Remove from heat and let them sit for 10 minutes in a sieve or colander to drain. Fluff with a fork and serve. Cooking time for this method will be shorter.

Not sure how much to soak? 1 cup dried legumes before soaking generally equals about 2½ cups cooked.

Storage of uncooked grains

Grains should be stored in clean, airtight containers in a cool, dry place. With wheat, spelt, and kamut's hard outer layers, they can be stored for many years under the right conditions. Rice will store for about two years. Millet may go rancid if stored too long.

Measure grains (about ¼–½ cup dry grains per serving), pour into a fine mesh strainer, and rinse under cold running water.

Place rinsed grains in a saucepan and combine with appropriate amount of filtered water. Add a pinch of sea salt (except when cooking amaranth, kamut, spelt, or wheat berries).

Place on stove and turn heat to high. Bring to a boil, then reduce heat to low, cover, and allow to cook (do not uncover and/or stir grains while cooking; stirring breaks the grains' cells and the result is a starchy, sticky mess) until done. Fluff with a fork and serve.

Many grains cook at a 2:1 ratio, water to grain; it does vary, but when in doubt, this is the safest measurement to follow.

COOKING LEGUMES (beans, lentils & peas)

(See chart on next page.)

> **You will need:**
> - Legume(s) of your choice, filtered water, kombu, sea salt
> - Fine mesh strainer
> - Stainless steel pot with fitted lid (or a pressure cooker)
> - Timer

Much like Amélie Poulain from the film *Amélie*, I also love plunging my hand into a container of dried beans....

I'm not all that amazed anymore when I meet vegans and vegetarians, or even omnivores, who don't know how to cook dried legumes. While we're all hopefully aware that legumes are an essential part of our diet, they have a reputation for taking a long time to cook, but cooking beans yourself is less expensive and less draining on the world's resources, and more nutritious over canned varieties. Cooking legumes from their dried form is pretty simple once you've done it a few times. Try it and see.

Soak

To start, it's important to soak beans before cooking because it will help them cook faster and more evenly. I usually put dried legumes in a glass or ceramic bowl, pour a generous amount of filtered water over them (about 4:1, water to legumes), cover, and allow to soak for 6–24 hours (depending on the type of

If you have soaked legumes but aren't able to cook them within 24 hours, be sure to drain and cover them with fresh water and store them in the fridge. Cook within 2–3 days.

COOKING LEGUMES

Legume	Soaking time	Water*: legume	Cooking time	Nutritional values & additional notes
adzuki (aduki) beans	2–4 hr	3:1	1–1½ hr	easy to digest; tones kidneys according to traditional Chinese medicine
black beans	6–12 hr	4:1	1½ hr	most antioxidants of any legume
black-eyed peas	4–12 hr	3:1	1 hr	protein, minerals, B vitamins, isoflavones
cannellini (white kidney) beans	6–12 hr	3:1	1–1½ hr	molybdenum, folate & tryptophan
chickpeas (garbanzo beans)	6–12 hr	4:1	2 hr	more iron than any other legume; protein & molybdenum
kidney beans	6–12 hr	3:1	1½–2 hr	molybdenum, folate, tryptophan & protein
lima beans	6–12 hr	2:1	1½ hr	molybdenum & tryptophan
lentils	0 min–1 hour	3:1	45–60 min	molybdenum, folate & tryptophan; easy to digest (less gassy than other legumes); second highest amount of protein of any legume
navy beans	4–12 hr	3:1	1–1½ hr	controls blood sugar; tryptophan, folate & manganese
pinto beans	6–12 hr	3:1	1½ hr	molybdenum, folate & tryptophan
split peas	0 min–1 hour	3:1	45–60 min	easy to digest
soybeans	6–12 hr	4:1	3–5 hr	highest amount of protein of any legume (can be difficult to digest though); molybdenum, tryptophan & manganese

* With the exception of lentils and split peas, cook legumes in liberal amounts of water and then drain off excess at the end.

If you cook legumes often, or would like to, purchasing a pressure cooker may be a wise investment. A pressure cooker is a pot with a super seal on the lid to pressurize the heat and allow the legumes to cook at a faster rate. Be sure to carefully read the directions for your pressure cooker before using.

legume). If you're in a rush, quick-soak them in just-boiled water for only 1–2 hours. Be sure not to put any salt in this soaking water. Some lentils do not need to be pre-soaked.

Drain & rinse

After soaking, when the lentils or beans have plumped up a bit, transfer to a sieve or colander and strain off soaking water (you can use this water for your plants, unless you used the quick-soak method), then rinse thoroughly under cold running water. Rinsing legumes is important to, as my friend Dan frankly explains, get rid of the farts.

Cook

Place soaked and rinsed beans in a heavy-bottomed pot. Add enough filtered water to cover about 2 inches above the legumes. Then you can add a 2–4-in (5–10-cm) piece of kombu* if desired.

Place pot on high heat and bring to a boil. Once boiling, reduce heat to simmer, and cover until beans are soft but not falling apart. Skim off any foam that may rise to the surface while cooking.

Don't take beans off heat until they are fully cooked (not *al dente*), unless they will be

cooked in something like a soup or stew later. When beans are undercooked, they put extra stress on your digestive system and are more likely to give you gas.

All legumes when combined with the essential amino acids in grains become excellent, low-fat sources of protein; they also provide cholesterol-lowering fiber.

Enjoy in salads, soups, stews, dips, grain dishes, or anything you like.

Legume tips

• Freezing cooked beans changes the texture, so they won't be good for bean salads, but they would be fine for use in soups or blending into dips, such as hummus.

• Shelf life: the only way to tell if your dried beans or lentils are fresh is to soak them – if they become wrinkled, they're old; if they become plump, they're fresh!

---

* *Kombu is a type of sea vegetable (seaweed) that comes in long green strips and is available from your local natural foods store or Asian market. Cooking legumes with mineral-rich kombu increases the nutritional value of the dish and helps make the legumes more digestible. Ensure you remove and discard kombu after cooking. Kombu will not lend a "seaweedy" taste to the legumes.*

SPROUTING

(See chart on next page.)

> **You will need:**
> - 1–4 tbsp viable seeds, nuts, grains, or legumes (use organic; if your seeds have been irradiated, they cannot be sprouted), filtered water
> - commercial sprouter,* or a wide mouth, ½ – 1-L glass jar, food-grade screen, mesh, or a piece of cheesecloth (to cover mouth of jar), and a rubber band (to hold screen in place)

Why sprout?

• Sprouts are super good for you. They're much more nutritious than the seed, nut, bean or grain they come from, or the plant they would become.

• Sprouts are the storehouses of the energy that is needed to produce the next generation of their plant. They're packed with everything they need to make the transformation from seed to plant.

• Sprouts have all the essential amino acids, plus vitamins, minerals, chlorophyll, and enzymes.

• The nutrients in the sprout are much more bioavailable (able to be absorbed by the body) than they are in the seed or plant.

• All sorts of enzymes that facilitate its growth, and are also good for us, are produced in the sprouting process. Those extra enzymes help with the digestion of anything you eat with sprouts.

• Sprouting takes only a few days and very little effort.

• You can do it right in your own kitchen without any expensive equipment. Food doesn't get any more local than this.

• Since sprouts can be grown any time of year in any climate you have no excuse not to start sprouting!

Aim to eat ½ cup of sprouts each day. Enjoy them in salads, sandwiches, smoothies, stir-fries or other entrées, or on top of soups.

Soak

Place seeds, nuts, grains, or legumes in jar (no more than ⅓ full), cover with mesh screen or cheesecloth, and secure with rubber band. Add water to rinse seeds, etc., then drain immediately. Cover rinsed seeds, etc., with cool or room-temperature filtered water (about 3 in/7½ cm above seeds, etc.). Soak for recommended time (see package of seeds or the chart on page 96).

Drain & rinse

Drain off and discard water after soaking, as it contains enzyme inhibitors. Then rinse and drain sprouts (no soaking) at least twice a day. (In hot weather, do this three times a day to prevent mold growth.) Ensure they're really drained well each time by propping jar upside down on dish-drying rack to drain on an angle in a bowl.

Eat & enjoy

Sprouting takes 2–5 days and sprouts are ready when they are as long as the grain or legumes themselves; small seeds are ready when hulls begin to break away from their two

* If using a commercial sprouter, follow its directions; otherwise follow directions below for using glass jar method.

tiny leaves. Once sprouted, place in a container with a folded piece of paper towel on the bottom to absorb any excess water and then store in fridge. Eat within 4 days.

SPROUTING

Seed	Amount of seeds, grains, or legumes (to yield about 4 cups sprouts)	Soaking time	Sprouting time
adzuki (aduki) beans	1 cup	12 hr	3–5 days
alfalfa	2 tbsp	6 hr	5–6 days
chickpeas (garbanzo beans)	1 cup	12 hr	3–5 days
fenugreek	½ cup	8 hr	3 days
lentils	½ cup	8 hr	3 days
mustard seeds	¼ cup	6 hr	5–6 days
mung beans	½ cup	8 hr	2–4 days
radish	¼ cup	6 hr	5–6 days
rye	1 cup	12 hr	3 days
red clover	2 tbsp	6 hr	5–6 days
sunflower seeds	2 cups	12 hr	2 days
soybeans	1 cup	12 hr	3–5 days
wheat berries	1 cup	12 hr	3 days

long grain brown rice

mille[t]

red quinoa

wild rice

brown jasmine rice

amaranth

short grain brown rice

yellow quinoa

sweet brown rice

cornmeal

kamut

pearl barley

hulled barley

buckwheat

kasha

wheat

oats

rye

spelt

(Left to right:) Blueberry Buckwheat Muffins (page 127), Spiced Squash Muffins (page 131), Cinnamon Swirl Biscuits (page 133), and Banana Chocolate Chip Muffins (page 126)

Cranberry Ginger Granola (page 116)
with Get Up & Go Smoothie (page 108)

CHAPTER
10

MAKING GREAT
BAKED GOODS

Healthy baked goods have had a pretty bad rap. They've often been considered to be dense, dry, crumbly, bland, or tough. When you're enjoying a cookie or slice of cake, you don't necessarily want the first thought to be, "Oooh, healthy." You want, "Mmmm, delicious! Decadent! To die for!"

Over the years of playing around in the kitchen *sans* eggs and dairy products, I have come to pride myself on being a relatively skilled vegan baker. This chapter will provide you with some general guidelines for impressive baked goods; more specific details will be found in chapters thirteen, nineteen, and twenty.

FLOURS

Not all flours are created equal.

Wheat flour, while it is commonly used in conventional baking, is not used in these baking recipes. Instead, most call for **spelt flour**.

WHY WHEAT-FREE?

Along with dairy, wheat is one of the most allergenic foods. Our constant exposure to wheat in our diets is a likely culprit. And unless your diet's already pretty varied and whole foods-based, I'd be willing to bet that you have wheat every day in some form – bread, pasta, cereals, baked goods, and soy sauce – and are due for a change.

Spelt has as much protein as high-protein wheat flour and tends to be less of an allergen than wheat flour. Spelt gluten is sensitive, so you should avoid overworking it; it requires about ¾ of the liquid that whole wheat requires in baking.

Alternate grain flours

Here is a list of alternative, non-wheat flours that can be used – usually in smaller quantities – in baking (see page 25 for additional nutritional information).

Amaranth flour offers calcium as well as calcium co-factors (minerals that help calcium to be absorbed), and is high in protein. Amaranth adds a spicy, sweet, and nutty flavor to pancakes, waffles, or muffins, and is usually added in small quantities to leavened products; flat breads can have more amaranth. (No gluten.)

Brown rice flour has a mild, nutty taste. It is good in pie crusts or pizza crusts and can be used to make cookies, pancakes, and waffles. Provides B vitamins and vitamin E. (No gluten.)

Buckwheat flour offers more protein than many other grains, and is typically added to pancakes, waffles, and pasta. (Very low gluten.)

Cornmeal offers a hearty texture to muffins, breads, and of course, polenta. It contains its bran and germ. Blue cornmeal has a higher protein content than yellow cornmeal. (No gluten.)

Millet flour gives baked goods a delicate taste and works well with other gluten free flours. For yeast breads, up to 30% millet flour may be used, but because millet is gluten free, it needs to be combined with glutinous flours to enable the bread to rise. It provides protein, calcium, iron, magnesium, potassium, and phosphorus. (No gluten.)

Oat flour also contains its bran and germ, and is often combined with flours that contain gluten to aid rising. It offers a sweet cakelike crumb that makes it really nice in baked goods. (Low gluten.)

Oat bran is a good source of (soluble) fiber, and makes a good substitute for wheat bran. (Low gluten.)

Quinoa flour has a delicate, nutty taste. It can be used as the sole flour when making crepes, pancakes, cookies, or muffins, and should be mixed 50-50 with a gluten flour when baking bread. It is a complete protein and contains calcium, iron, phosphorus, vitamin E, and lysine. (No gluten.)

Rye flour also has low gluten content so breads made with it can be dense but moist. To make rye breads less dense, add some spelt flour or whole wheat flour (if tolerated). (Low gluten.)

Soy flour is a good source of protein. It has no gluten, so again, you will need additional flours with gluten to help it rise. (No gluten.)

Tapioca flour can be used as a thickener. It is a nice addition to gluten-free breads giving them a better texture. (No gluten.)

Teff flour has a malty flavor and is rich in calcium, protein, and iron. It can be used to thicken soups and sauces. Combine it on a 1:5 ratio with spelt or wheat so that bread rises. (No gluten)

RAISING AGENTS

Baking soda, or sodium bicarbonate, is a chemical raising agent that looks like white powder. This is how it works: when you add liquid and acid to the powder, carbon dioxide gas is produced. These carbon dioxide bubbles in your batter cause it to rise. Cream of tartar, or lemon or yogurt generally provide the acid. Make sure the one you buy doesn't have aluminum as one of the ingredients.

Baking powder consists of baking soda and at least one acid that will, with the addition of liquid, create carbon dioxide and cause rising. Double-acting baking powder has an acid that reacts at room temperature and one that reacts at the higher temperatures of cooking so that your baked goods get that extra lift.

BAKING TIPS

1 | **Read the recipe** from start to finish, before you do anything. Set out all ingredients to ensure you've got everything you need.

2 | **Preheat oven** to correct temperature (it's best to use an oven thermometer).

3 | **Prepare baking sheets, trays, or pans** to be used – cut and/or fold parchment paper as needed to fit in pan, and/or lightly coat bottom and sides with any good oil (coconut, sunflower, or olive) and dust with flour, cocoa powder (for chocolatey recipes), or cornstarch. For loaf and cake pans, lightly oil pan, lay down parchment, and lightly oil it too (just to be safe). Just line cookie sheets with parchment, no oiling required.

4 | **Measure ingredients precisely**. Use a

OTHER WHEAT-BASED PRODUCTS COMMONLY USED IN BAKING

Enriched flour

Graham flour

Gluten flour

Semolina

Ubut flour (unbleached untreated flour)

Unbleached flour

Wheat bran

Wheat germ

White flour

Whole durum wheat

Whole pastry flour

IS YOUR BAKING POWDER FRESH?

Baking powder should be replaced every year. When you bring a new container of baking powder home, label it with the date. After 6 months, test it to see if it still works: add 2 tsp baking powder to 1 cup hot water – if it fizzes and bubbles, it's still usable.

If there's a baked good that you like to make often, or if you're going to bake something in a few days but have some time now, make a mix: take a container with a sealable lid and fill it with the measured dry ingredients required for the recipe. Label it with any further instructions, recipe title, or simply list quantities of wet ingredients needed to complete the recipe.

Lining baking pans or trays with parchment is also a good idea if you're baking with pans that are looking a little worse for wear or are made from a more reactive material (like aluminum or Teflon – see page 80).

liquid measuring cup for wet ingredients (e.g., oil, non-dairy milk, or maple syrup), and dry measuring cups for dry ingredients (e.g., flour, sugar, or cocoa powder). Measure ingredients at eye level and use your clean finger or a knife to level off dry ingredients.

5 | **Sift or whisk** together dry ingredients before adding wet ingredients, and always sift baking powder, baking soda, and cocoa powder to remove clumps. When measuring ingredients to be sifted, don't pack them into the cup or spoon.

6 | **Cream sugar with fat** (in this book, often coconut oil) then gradually add to mixed dry ingredients. The light, fluffy sugar-and-fat mixture contains air, which will make your baking lighter as it cooks.

7 | **Avoid overmixing**. When you mix too much, gluten develops in batter and your cakes and muffins won't rise as well. When combining wet and dry ingredients, gently fold with a silicone spatula or wooden spoon – your baked goods will be lighter and have nicer crumb texture.

8 | **Use cold ingredients for biscuits or pie crusts**, work cold fat into cold flour, then add cold liquids and mix quickly before rolling

or patting out dough. Cold ingredients keep the fat from melting into flour before baking. When dough is baking, the melting fat leaves air pockets that make biscuits or pie crusts light and flaky.

9 | Once wet and dry ingredients are combined, **put batter in oven as quickly as possible**. (This goes for cakes, muffins, and biscuits in particular!)

10 | **No peeking in the oven**.

Avoid opening oven before baking is complete (especially with cakes, loaves, and muffins). If you do open it, close it gently – allowing it to slam could cause your cake to fall.

11 | **Test for doneness** with a skewer, toothpick, or knife. Slide it into the center of the baked good – if it comes out clean, it's done. If there's still sticky batter, bake it for another 5–10 minutes. Other signs of doneness: cakes and muffins that have domed tops, golden color on top of vanilla cakes or on bottoms of light-colored cookies, and cracks in tops of loaves or loaves pull away from sides of pan. Sometimes, brownies and cookies can be removed from oven before they look completely done so that they are chewy when they cool.

12 | **Allow baked goods to cool completely** in their pans for 10 minutes before transferring to a cooling rack before storing or serving. If cookies are overcooked, however, transfer them to a rack right away. Allow cakes to cool completely before frosting and pies to cool and set for half an hour before serving.

13 | **Store in airtight containers** at room

temperature for 2–7 days (depending on the item), but cookies will be good from a week up to a month. Baked goods should only be stored at room temperature for a couple of days before refrigerating or freezing, if desired.

EGG REPLACERS (EQUIVALENT TO 1 EGG)

- ½ medium or large banana: for desserts, or sweet things like pancakes or smoothies
- 3 tbsp–¼ cup applesauce: for sweeter recipes
- ¼ cup soft/silken tofu: use a food processor to make it very smooth before using
- 1 tbsp psyllium seed husks + 2 tbsp water: for breads & baking
- 1½ tsp powdered "egg replacer" + 2 tbsp water: available in most health food stores

Flax eggs, version 1: great for pancakes, breads and other baking.

- ⅓ cup whole flax seeds
- 1 cup filtered water

Blend seeds to an even meal in a blender or small food processor. Slowly add water and continue blending until mixture resembles a thick milkshake. Store in an airtight container in your fridge for up to 6 days.

Makes 6 "eggs"; 3 tbsp = 1 egg.

Flax eggs, version 2: great for fancier baked goods, or when you want egg-replacer to be as neutral-tasting and textured as possible.

- ½ cup flax seeds
- 3 cups filtered water

Combine flax seeds and water into a saucepan on high heat. Bring to a boil, then reduce heat to simmer for about 20 minutes, stirring often (I mean it) to prevent seeds from sticking, until mixture becomes "gloppy" (will thicken more as it cools). Strain out the flax seeds and discard or add to homemade granola bar batter.

Makes about 1 dozen "eggs"; ¼ cup = 1 egg. Store in a jar in fridge for up to 2 weeks, or in an airtight container in freezer for a few months.

The average Canadian consumes 30–40 kg (66–88 lb) refined sugar each year, but we seldom think about what is in it, where it comes from, or why it is so cheap.

The most common sugar is granulated, refined white sugar. It is made from sugar cane or sugar beets. The juice of these plants is boiled until the concentration of sugar is so great that it begins to crystallize out. The liquid that remains is used to make molasses, and the crystals of granulated white sugar that remain contain simple carbohydrates, with no micronutrients. Variants of white sugar include icing or powdered sugar, which is made from finely ground, granulated sugar crystals, with cornstarch added to prevent clumping; and light and dark brown sugars that are colored and moistened with molasses. Turbinado sugar is made by steaming unrefined raw sugar from sugar cane. It looks like pale brown sugar and can be used to replace brown sugar.

Baking can be finicky, but I encourage you to try sugar substitutions.

SUGAR SUBSTITUTIONS

Here are some general recommendations to replace 1 cup of refined, white sugar:

Agave nectar (¾ cup). Reduce liquid in recipe by ¼ cup for every cup of agave used.

Barley malt (1¼ cups). Reduce liquid in recipe by ¼ cup. If a recipe calls for honey, molasses, or rice syrup, barley malt can be substituted measure for measure (but substituting barley malt for molasses may not work, as molasses has a very strong taste). Barley grains are treated with enzymes that digest the grains' complex carbohydrates into a more simple sugar producing sweet, maltose-rich syrup.

Brown Rice Syrup: *see* barley malt.

Maple sugar (1 cup). If a recipe calls for honey, molasses, or rice syrup, but you want to use maple sugar, it can be substituted measure for measure.

Maple syrup (1 cup). Reduce liquid by ¼ cup for every cup of maple syrup used.

Molasses (½ cup). Reduce liquid in recipe by ¼ cup. Molasses contains significant amounts of a variety of healthy minerals (iron, calcium, copper, manganese, potassium, and magnesium). It is made from the liquid left after the first crystallization

of sugar from sugar cane juice. This liquid is boiled again to produce light molasses, but further boiling make the liquid darker, and more bitter as more and more sugar is extracted – the second boiling produces dark molasses, and the third, blackstrap.

Rapadura & Sucanat (1 cup). Rapadura is made of sucrose crystals that have been coated in mineral-rich cooked cane juice. Sucanat is made the same way, and has a molasses-type taste, which can be too strong for some recipes. Jaggery, gur, piloncillo, and panela are other names for rapadura or Sucanat.

Stevia (⅛ tsp whole leaf powder = 1 tsp sugar; ³/₈ tsp = 1 tbsp sugar; 2 tbsp = 1 cup sugar; amounts differ if using liquid or white powder form, see product's label). Stevia, an extract from the stevia plant, is much sweeter than sugar and therefore less needs to be used; it also has very few calories. Many Western health authorities have yet to acknowledge stevia as a safe sugar substitute, stating that there are not enough studies on the plant; however, stevia has been used in South America for centuries and there have been many studies that report that stevia is a safe and useful sugar replacement, especially for people with diabetes or hypertension (some folks feel that this lack of support may have something to do with pressure from the artificial sweetener companies). Stevia is available at health food stores and some grocery stores.

BE FAIR!

Remember when I mentioned that between the 17th and 20th centuries, Europeans colonized many areas of the planet and took over control of agriculture practices which benefited themselves and left the indigenous peoples working for a little more than survival wages? The 20th century saw the signing of global trade agreements that further eroded the power of "the people" (i.e. non-corporations) to control what they could charge for their goods and labor. Here are some interesting facts from Fair Trade Toronto (fairtradetoronto.com), a volunteer group that works to increase the awareness about, and availability of, fair trade products.

• Six corporations control approximately 70% of world agricultural trade, while agriculture supports the livelihoods of 70–80% of people living in low-income countries.

• Since 1975, GDP per capita in industrialized countries has increased by 50%; it has fallen by 15% in the world's least developed countries.

• Over the past 20 years, the least developed countries (representing 20% of the world's population), have suffered a 50% decline in their share of world trade.

• Since 1960, the gap between the rich and poor has increased by 250%. Reacting to these global inequities, concerned consumers began to organize and promote new standards for producing goods for trade. Goods that met the standards were certified "fair trade" items by the countries between which they were being traded.

Below is a list of the goals of fair trade also from Fair Trade Toronto:

• Improve the livelihoods and well being of producers by improving market access, strengthening producer organizations, paying a better price and providing continuity in the trading relationship.

• Promote development opportunities for disadvantaged producers, especially women and indigenous people, and to protect children from exploitation in the production process.

• Raise awareness among consumers of the negative effects on producers of international trade so that they exercise their purchasing power positively.

• Set an example of partnership in trade through dialogue, transparency, and respect.

• Campaign for changes in the rules and practice of conventional international trade.

• Protect human rights by promoting social justice, sound environmental practices, and economic security.

Fairly traded goods are widely available in sugar, cocoa, and chocolate products, coffee, tea, spices, quinoa, and bananas. Encourage your local grocery store to stock these products.

THINGS TO CONSIDER WHEN BUYING SUGAR

Most sugar comes from sugar cane, which is usually harvested by poorly paid workers in less than comfortable conditions. As vegans, we are concerned with animal rights and therefore should also be concerned about the rights of the people who produce our food. If you use refined sugar, consider buying organic, fair trade sugar to support organic farming and fair working conditions for workers (and the communities in which they live). Organic and fair trade sugar is available at most large grocery stores as well as health food stores.

CHAPTER 11

DRINK UP

Good Morning Elixir • "Apple Pie" Fiber Drink • Almond Milk • Coconut Milk
Get Up & Go Smoothie • Green Smoothie • Decadent Date Smoothie
Immune Boost Juice • Easy Tea • Turmeric Ginger Tea • Hot Iron

GOOD MORNING ELIXIR

I am not typically a routine-oriented person, but I do drink my lemon water every morning. In traditional Chinese medicine, sour tastes are linked to the liver, which makes this drink a great daily detox for our bodies; it also stimulates hydrochloric acid production in our bellies (for good digestion) and is a more refreshing way to start the day than drinking coffee.

If you are new to cleansing, work your way up to using ½ a lemon. On your first morning, you may want to use just one lemon slice, on the second and third days, a ¼ lemon, and by the fourth day, the entire ½ lemon. I make a large amount in a 1-qt/L glass Mason jar, but feel free to use a smaller quantity of water for a large mug's worth.

up to ½ organic lemon (see note in intro), washed well before slicing

1½–3 cups room temperature filtered or spring water

½–1 cup just-boiled filtered water

Using a reamer, release all the lemon juice into a large mug (or glass jar), then drop the lemon in too (if your lemon isn't organic, skip this step).

Fill mug about ⅔ full with the room temperature water, then top up with just-boiled water.

After drinking, follow with another glass of water, or at least a swish of plain water in your mouth to remove the acidic lemon juice from your teeth.

Picture your liver smiling.

MAKES 1 SERVING.   GF, SF, NF, R

Juicing Citrus

To get the greatest amount of juice out of a citrus fruit, follow these simple steps:

• Using your palm, roll fruit around on kitchen counter or tabletop.

• Wash it well (this is especially important if you are using the rind).

• Slice open widthwise over your mug or glass to catch any juicy goodness.

• With a reamer (I prefer the hand-held reamers to tabletop ones, unless there is a lot of juicing to do) extract as much juice and pulp as possible. If you don't have a reamer, a fork will do – just twist it to loosen the pulp.

➤ "Apple Pie Fiber" Drink ➤

1¼ cups filtered water

⅓ cup organic unclarified apple juice (contains apple pectin)

1 tbsp flax seeds, freshly ground (fiber source & bowel lubricant)

2 tsp psyllium seed husks, if tolerated* (fiber bulking agent)

1 tsp wheat bran, if tolerated (fiber that removes toxic methylmercury)

1 tsp chicory root extract powder (contains inulin, a prebiotic)

½ tsp slippery elm powder (soothes intestinal lining & is anticarcinogenic)

½ tsp cinnamon (discourages unhealthy bowel flora & normalizes blood sugar levels)

½ tsp non-dairy probiotic formula powder containing *Lactobacilli acidophilus* and *Bifidobacterium longum*

Many of us don't get enough fiber in our diets, which means we often aren't eliminating enough waste from our bodies. And when we're not eliminating that waste, it gets reabsorbed. It's a rotten cycle, literally. Here's a great drink (slightly adapted from naturopathic doctor Sat Dharam Kaur's recipe) to get you going. The apple juice and cinnamon make it tasty too.

All ingredients should be available at health food stores, but if you can't find them all, just mix up what you've got. You can drink this daily, between meals, or up to four times a day under a supervised cleansing regime.

Combine all ingredients in a 2-cup glass jar and screw on lid.

Shake vigorously, then drink immediately, chewing each mouthful a few times before swallowing.

Follow by refilling jar with extra water and drinking that too.

MAKES 1 SERVING. GF (if omitting bran), SF, NF

* Some folks find psyllium seed husks make them bloated. If you're not sure if they do, try making the drink with psyllium one day and without another day and see how you feel.

ALMOND MILK

It's nice to be able to make raw, non-dairy milk right in your own kitchen, and not rely on soymilk Tetra Paks to enjoy your cereal in the morning!

Drain water from soaked almonds.

Place soaked almonds in a food processor or blender, along with filtered water, salt, and nectar, syrup, or stevia, and give it a whirl for about 2 minutes, until almonds are completely pulverized.

Strain almond milk* into a sealable glass jar (if a smoother consistency is desired, use a fine mesh strainer or a nut milk bag).

Stores in fridge for up to 4 days. Blend again or shake well before serving.

MAKES 3–4 CUPS.   GF, SF, NF, R

½ cup raw almonds, soaked in filtered water overnight (or for 4–8 hours)

3–4 cups filtered water (to thicken milk as desired)

⅛ tsp sea salt (optional)

up to 1 tbsp agave nectar or brown rice syrup or ¼ tsp green stevia powder (to sweeten as desired; optional)

* Save leftover almond pulp as a baking ingredient or to sprinkle on cereal. Be creative!

Spilt milk
If you find your food processor or blender leaks out the top while processing, try covering the top with a piece of plastic wrap, letting some hang over the sides. Fit the lid over the plastic wrap, and blend as usual.

⟿ COCONUT MILK ⟿

1 fresh coconut

1¾ cups just-boiled filtered water

This is no task for a culinary slacker, but if you're up for busting open a coconut, it's smooth sailing after that. (Anna Lappé and Bryant Terry's book Grub *first inspired me to try making this stuff from scratch.)*

Pound holes through the eyes of the coconut using a clean nail and hammer. Drain coconut water and discard (or drink it if you like – it's very sweet!). To crack coconut open, you will require some muscle. Place coconut on a tea towel on a cutting board and crack it hard with the hammer until it breaks open (though sometimes I go to my front stoop, where I whack the shell down onto the concrete).

Pry the flesh away from the inside of shell using a knife, slicing into flesh and prying it away. Peel off brown skin from flesh if desired.

Add coconut flesh to a food processor or blender and give it a good whirl, pouring in just-boiled water slowly, until pulp is very fine.

Allow to sit for about 10 minutes before straining through a few layers of cheese-cloth or a fine mesh strainer (or ideally, a nut milk bag) into a sealable glass jar or container.

Stores in fridge for up to 3 days, or in freezer for 1–2 months.

**MAKES AT LEAST 1½ CUPS (equivalent to one 14-oz / 398-ml can of coconut milk).
GF, SF, NF**

⟿ GET UP ᴀɴᴅ GO SMOOTHIE ⟿

1 cup organic non-dairy milk

1 ripe banana

3 tbsp hemp protein powder (or another high-quality non-dairy protein powder)

1 tbsp flax seeds, freshly ground

1 tbsp carob powder

½ tsp cinnamon

1 tsp brown rice or maple syrup, or agave nectar, or ¼–½ tsp green stevia powder (optional)

⅓–½ cup filtered water (to thin smoothie as desired)

This tasty meal-in-a-glass is high in fiber and includes blood-sugar balancing cinnamon and protein to get you through the morning. You may choose to use a frozen banana for a cooler, thicker smoothie, but this drink is better assimilated by your body at room temperature.

Whirl all ingredients together in a food processor or blender, adding the water slowly to desired consistency.

Drink immediately.

MAKES 1 SERVING.   GF, SF, NF

⇌ GREEN SMOOTHIE ⇌

Is it possible you don't get enough greens in your daily diet? Here's a great way to get some before you head off to work in the morning. "But spinach in a smoothie?" you say. Relax, the sweetness from the fruit balances it out. Just try it and see.

Add the banana, fruit, spinach, juice, and spirulina into a blender or food processor.

Whirl ingredients for about 30 seconds, until all fruit has been processed. Slowly add water and re-blend to desired consistency.

Pour into a glass and enjoy.

MAKES 1 LARGE SERVING AS A MEAL (2¼ CUPS), OR TWO SMALLER SERVINGS. GF, SF, NF, R

1 ripe banana

1 cup fresh or frozen organic fruit (e.g., berries, mango, kiwi, peach, pear, cherries), chopped if needed

1 cup packed organic baby spinach

½ cup fruit juice* (pear, mango, or berry nectar is nice)

1 tsp spirulina (and/or 1 tbsp greens powder blend [optional])

¼–½ cup filtered water

* For a creemier smoothie, substitute non-dairy milk for the juice.

While blending, you may add 1 tbsp freshly ground flax seeds or anything else you may like in your smoothie.

⇌ DECADENT DATE SMOOTHIE ⇌

This makes an extra special breakfast treat or a delicious milkshake-like dessert.

Place the dates in a small dish and pour just-boiled water over them. *Let them sit for a few minutes until they soften.

Add softened dates and their water, along with the banana, milk, almond butter, and cinnamon into a food processor or blender and give it a whirl until smooth. If needed, thin with additional milk (or filtered water).

Pour into a fancy glass, sprinkle with the almonds if desired, and serve cold.

MAKES 1 SERVING (ABOUT 1¾ CUPS).
GF, SF, NF, R (if using raw milk or nut butter)

5–6 dates, pitted & chopped

2 tbsp just-boiled water (enough to cover dates)

1 medium-large banana, frozen

¾ cup non-dairy milk

2 tbsp almond butter (or other nut or seed butter)

½ tsp cinnamon

raw almonds, finely crushed (for garnish)

* Reconstituting dried fruit by soaking overnight or quick soaking in just-boiled water helps make it more digestible and usable in smoothies (especially dates or gogi berries). Pre-soaked raisins are good for baking as they are less likely to burn.

IMMUNE BOOST JUICE

3 large or 4 medium carrots

1 small or ½ medium beet

1 medium apple

1 thumb-sized piece fresh ginger root

Optionals (choose 2)

½ lemon, peeled

1 small or medium cucumber

2 stalks celery

4 stalks kale

This is a tasty fresh juice that I've always found easy to make in a centrifugal juicer (more on juicers on page 81). Carrots offer vitamins A, B3, and E, the beet helps to build your blood, and the ginger is warming and aids circulation and digestion. For an extra nutrient-packed drink: pour juice into a jar, add 1 tsp spirulina powder, cover with lid, and shake it up!

Scrub all produce well, and trim off ends of carrots and beet – no need to peel anything. Your juicer may have a wide enough mouth for whole apples, but I recommend quartering them and removing the seeds (as they contain small amounts of cyanide – this is especially important if you plan to use the pulp in Juice Pulp Muffins, page 130). Process all ingredients in juicer according to machine's directions.

Drink immediately (centrifugal juicers produce juice that oxidizes quickly), sipping slowly for maximum nutrient absorption.

MAKES 1 SERVING (ABOUT 1¾ CUP). GF, SF, NF, R

EASY TEA

1 part lemon balm

1 part nettle leaves

1 part oatstraw

1 part peppermint leaves

just-boiled filtered water

To emphasize good digestion, add:

1 part fennel seeds

To make this calming, add:

1 part chamomile flowers

My dear friend Melina Claire, who's a herbalist, created this simple and tasty tea blend for me. I enjoy it after dinner as it helps to ease digestion and allows me to wind down for the evening. Use organic and locally-grown herbs whenever possible.

Combine all the herbs together in a large bowl.

Measure 1 tsp herb blend for each cup of water or 1 heaping tbsp for 4 cups of water.

Place herb blend in a tea strainer or cloth tea bag and place in a teapot. (Transfer remaining dried herbs into a glass jar with a secure-fitting lid and use over the next few months.)

Pour the water through strainer or over bag into teapot, cover with a lid and tea cozy or a dishtowel, and allow to steep for 10–20 minutes.

Pour into mugs, sip slowly, and enjoy.

MAKES 1–4 CUPS. GF, SF, NF

⟿ TURMERIC GINGER TEA ⟾

My friend Cheendana shared this recipe from a herbalist friend, saying, "You won't believe how delicious this is!" Enjoy this warming drink in the evening, as it can help with digestion. Traditional Chinese medicine says that the liver is most active between 1 and 3 a.m., so it's beneficial to consume things that are liver-supporting, such as turmeric, before bed.

Be warned: turmeric stains in a major way. If you have a glass saucepan, now's the time to use it. Same goes for a glass mug. They'll wash clean with greater ease. Oh, and be careful of your counters and your clothes, too!

1 tsp fresh grated turmeric root (or ½ tsp turmeric powder)*

1 tsp grated fresh ginger root (or ½ tsp ground ginger)

2–3 twists of black pepper* from a pepper mill (optional)

1½ cups filtered water

juice of ½ lemon

2 tsp maple syrup, or to taste

Combine the turmeric, ginger, pepper, and water in a saucepan (preferably glass, see note above) on medium-high heat to simmer for 5–10 minutes; be careful not to boil.

Pour into a mug, add the lemon juice and syrup, and stir.

MAKES ABOUT 1½ CUPS. GF, SF, NF

* Curcumin, which lends turmeric its bright yellow color, has been identified as a strong but safe anti-inflammatory agent, great for those with inflammatory bowel disease. Also, its antioxidant properties make it impressively anticarcinogenic and useful for rheumatoid arthritis sufferers. Turmeric supports liver detoxification too, and seems to be most effective when consumed with black pepper.

⟿ HOT IRON ⟾

When I lived on Stowel Lake Farm on Salt Spring Island, I noticed that a few of the farmers drank molasses in hot water first thing in the morning instead of coffee. Molasses offers a decent amount of iron. And so do nettle leaves. Iron is a mineral we need for good energy levels and healthy immune systems, and vitamin C from the lemons is needed to absorb the iron … so drink up!

1 heaping tbsp nettle leaves (or 2 tea bags of nettle leaves)

4 cups just-boiled filtered water

juice of ½ lemon

1 tbsp organic blackstrap molasses

Place the loose nettle leaves or tea bags in a teapot or 1-qt/L glass Mason jar. Pour in the just-boiled water, and cover with a lid and tea cozy or a dishtowel, and allow to steep for 15–30 minutes before straining out leaves or removing tea bags.

Stir in the lemon juice and molasses, and enjoy.

MAKES 2–3 SERVINGS, OR ENOUGH FOR 1 PERSON TO DRINK OVER A FEW HOURS. GF, SF, NF

CHAPTER

12

BREAKFASTS

━ FRESH FRUIT SALADS ━

My friends Heather and Karla had a good laugh when I told them I was writing fruit salad recipes. "Who needs a recipe for fruit salad?!" Heather almost howled. I've had some pretty un-wonderful fruit salads in my life, so I figure some people might. And with that, I humbly offer you some simple guidelines for preparing tasty and refreshing bowls of mixed fresh fruit. Enjoy them for breakfast, as a snack, or on a picnic. As far as good digestion is concerned, eating fruit after a meal ain't the best idea, so if you're having it as dessert, wait for at least 30 minutes after your meal.

Prepared fruit doesn't last too long (and its vitamin content decreases as soon as you slice into it), so only prepare the amount that you will eat in the next day or two.

A fruit salad doesn't need to include everything but the kitchen sink – too many flavors in one bowl can be overwhelming. A good salad features 3–5 fruits – you can even make something as simple as an all-melon salad, using orange-, yellow-, pink-, and green-fleshed varieties.

It's good to balance softer fruits like berries, mangoes, and kiwis with a base of fleshy or substantial fruits, like chunks of melon or peeled and thinly sliced apple. I've never been a huge fan of bananas in fruit salad, as they can get slimy and discolored, so if you're going to use them, slice them in just before serving. And avoid using canned fruit. It's been depleted of many of the vitamins it once had, so why bother?

Allow for 1 cup of prepared fruit per serving.   **GF, SF, NF, R**

In summer, we have lots of locally-grown fruit options (see page 62 for essential organics):

Apples & pears (later in the season)	Grapes	Stone fruits: peaches, nectarines, plums, apricots, cherries
Berries	Melon*	

Tropical fruits can also make a nice accent:

Kiwi	Orange	Pomelo
Lychee	Papaya	Starfruit
Mango	Pineapple	

These additions can make a fruit salad memorable:

Fresh chopped mint, basil, or sage leaves	Fresh lemon and lime juices, which help to keep fruit from turning brown	A dash of pure vanilla extract
Grated fresh ginger root or ground cardamom		Coconut milk (for tropical-themed salads)

---

* Cantaloupe rinds can sometimes be infected with strains of salmonella. While washing fruit before cutting it open is always a good idea, in this case, it does not make much of a difference. Food safety experts recommend the following:

• Choose melons that are clean, and free of bruises or blemishes. Steer clear of precut melons.

• Cut cantaloupes with a sharp knife: a dull knife can cause contamination by pushing the rind into the flesh.

• Slice away the rind before eating or storing, and refrigerate any leftover flesh within an hour or two of cutting.

• Wash your cutting board well with hot soapy water after cutting melons.

Sweeteners can intensify flavors, but use sparingly:**

Agave nectar

Grain malt or syrup (e.g., barley or brown rice)

Maple syrup

** If sweetener is too thick, mix it with lemon juice (or excess juice from the ingredients) then pour it into the bowl.

ALL~PURPOSE APPLESAUCE

8 medium apples,* peeled, cored & chopped

1 cup filtered water

2 tsp fresh lemon juice

1 tsp cinnamon (optional)

Tart and juicy apples, like Cortland, Fuji, Golden Delicious, Granny Smith, Jonagold, McIntosh, or Northern Spy, are preferable for this recipe.

Applesauce is a staple in my kitchen, often taking the place of eggs in baked goods, and sometimes as a simple snack slightly warmed in a saucepan. If you have an inclination to can (a great skill to have), use this recipe at apple harvest time, doubling, tripling, or quadrupling it, depending on how many apples you have. See the Index for all the recipes in this book that use applesauce.

Place the apples and water in a pot on medium heat. Cover and simmer for 30 minutes, stirring occasionally.

Remove from heat, add the lemon juice and cinnamon, and mash. Allow to cool slightly before serving or using, and cool completely before storing in the fridge.

MAKES ABOUT 4 CUPS. GF, SF, NF

Pink Sauce

I often choose not to peel the apples before cooking. The skins will break down to a certain degree, but there will likely be some curly bits remaining. If using apples with any red in the skins, the resulting sauce will have a pretty pink tinge.

GOOD MORNING MUESLI

4 cups cereal flakes (I like Nature's Path Organic Heritage Flakes or Millet Rice Flakes)

2 cups rolled oats

1 cup puffed grains (I like Nature's Path Organic Kamut Puffs)

½ cup organic raisins

½ cup dried fruit, chopped if needed (e.g., dried apple, unsulphured apricots, dried cranberries, coconut flakes, dates, or additional raisins)

½ cup raw almonds or other nuts, chopped

½ cup seeds (sunflower, pumpkin, flax &/or sesame seeds)

1 tsp cinnamon

Muesli is a breakfast cereal with a base of uncooked rolled oats and dried fruit. Here's my version. If you live in a cereal-hungry household, you may want to make a double batch. Serve with non-dairy milk or yogurt.

Combine all ingredients in a large bowl and toss well.

Stores in an airtight container for up to 1 month.

MAKES 9 CUPS, ABOUT 8–12 SERVINGS. SF, NF

ROCO'S GRANOLA

I vividly remember two things about my first visit to Halifax, Nova Scotia: the record-breaking lack of sun that persisted for more than two weeks, and Rebecca's homemade granola with soymilk served in rustic ceramic bowls handmade by Adrienne. The dried fruit is mixed in at the end to avoid drying it out any further and making it too tough.

Preheat oven to 325°F (165°C). Lightly oil a 2½- or 3-qt/L casserole dish.

Combine the oats, bran, germ (if using), coconut, grain syrup or malt, molasses or maple syrup, almonds, oil, sunflower and sesame seeds, and cinnamon in a large bowl.

Transfer to the casserole dish, evenly distributing granola, and bake for 25 minutes, removing from oven to stir a couple of times for even baking.

Remove from oven, mix in the raisins and apples, and allow to cool.

Stores in an airtight container for 1 month or more.

MAKES ABOUT 6 CUPS, OR 6–12 SERVINGS.   SF, NF

3 cups rolled oats

½ cup oat or spelt bran (or wheat bran, if tolerated)

½ cup wheat germ (or additional non-wheat bran)

½ cup shredded unsweetened coconut

½ cup brown rice syrup or barley malt*

2 tbsp organic blackstrap molasses or maple syrup

¼ cup chopped or crushed almonds

¼ cup olive, sunflower, or softened non-hydrogenated coconut oil (plus extra to coat dish)

2 tbsp sunflower seeds

2 tbsp sesame seeds (unhulled preferred)

½ tsp cinnamon

½ cup organic raisins

½ cup dried apples, chopped

* Maple syrup can be substituted for the grain syrup or malt, although it may not create the same crunchy granola clusters.

CRANBERRY GINGER GRANOLA

3 cups rolled oats

1 cup oat or spelt bran

½ cup shredded unsweetened coconut

½ cup chopped raw cashews

¼ cup raw pumpkin seeds (chopped if desired)

¼ cup softened non-hydrogenated coconut oil or sunflower oil (plus extra to coat dish)

⅔ cup brown rice syrup or barley malt *

1 tbsp grated fresh ginger root

¾ cup dried cranberries**

* A ½ cup maple syrup or agave nectar can be substituted for the grain syrup or malt, although it may not create the same crunchy granola clusters.

** Use fruit-sweetened cranberries when you can.

The fresh ginger in this cereal gives it a great little zing. Serve with non-dairy milk or yogurt.

Preheat oven to 325°F (165°C). Lightly oil a casserole dish.

Combine the oats, bran, coconut, cashews, pumpkin seeds, oil, and syrup or malt in a large bowl. Squeeze the grated ginger over the bowl, then add the pulp too (for a better distribution of gingery flavor).

Transfer to the casserole dish, evenly distributing granola, and bake for 25 minutes, removing from oven to stir a couple of times for even baking.

Remove from oven, mix in cranberries, and allow to cool.

Stores in an airtight container for a month or more.

MAKES ABOUT 6 CUPS, OR 6–12 SERVINGS.   SF, NF

CHEWY FRUIT and NUT GRANOLA BARS

I've come up with this version of the classic breakfast-on-the-go/anytime-of-day snack using a gloppy, high-fiber flax and amaranth mixture to bind them together. I like the look of the cute little amaranth in there (it's a grain I don't use too often), and the flavor's pretty lovely. They make for great road-trip food.

Preheat oven to 350°F (180°C).

Spread the oats on an unoiled baking sheet and toast them for 20 minutes, stirring once halfway through baking time to prevent browning. Remove from oven and set aside. Reduce oven temperature to 325°F (165°C).

Combine the water, flax seeds, and amaranth in a small pot on the stove on high heat (you can do this while the oats are toasting). Bring to a boil, stir, and then reduce heat to a simmer for 8 minutes, or until noticeably thickened. Remove from heat and set aside.

Whisk together the bran, flour, coconut, cranberries, cinnamon, and salt in a large bowl. Add toasted oats to bowl, along with the syrup, oil, zest, and flax-seed mixture and stir well to combine.

Lightly oil an 11x7x2-in (28x18x4-cm) baking pan. Transfer mixture into pan, pressing down evenly. Score into 16 bars (one lengthwise cut, 7 widthwise cuts).

Bake for 30 minutes. Allow to cool before cutting.

Stores in an airtight container on your countertop for about 4 days or in fridge for up to a week (although they might get soggy in the fridge).

MAKES 16 BARS. **SF, NF**

3 cups rolled oats (not quick oats – may substitute with kamut or rye flakes, but oats nourish your nervous system)

1 cup filtered water

¼ cup flax seeds, partially ground (a couple quick pulses in the coffee grinder)

2 tbsp amaranth

½ cup oat bran (or wheat bran, if tolerated)

½ cup whole grain flour (e.g., spelt, kamut, or wheat)

½ cup shredded unsweetened coconut

½ cup dried cranberries

1 tsp cinnamon

¼ tsp sea salt

⅔ cup maple syrup

½ cup sunflower or olive oil (plus extra to coat pan)

zest of 1 organic orange

Flavor to your fancy

To experiment with the flavoring, you can substitute the same amount of dates for cranberries and lemon zest for orange, or instead of the cranberries and coconut, try raisins and walnuts, or ginger and cashews (oooh, what about candied ginger?!).

∙— COZY OATMEAL —∙

1/3 cup rolled oats (not quick oats)

3/4 cup filtered water or pure fruit juice

7 (or so) whole raw almonds, coarsely chopped, or 1–2 tbsp raw sunflower seeds

1 tbsp organic raisins or chopped pitted dates

1/4 tsp cinnamon

1 pinch of sea salt

1/2 apple or pear, cored & chopped (optional)

1 tbsp flax seeds, freshly ground

maple syrup to taste (optional)

organic non-dairy milk to taste (optional)

Oats are good for your nervous and immune systems, and are wonderfully warming in the colder months. While my Scottish ancestors might have considered it sacrilegious to add so many things to a pot of porridge, I got the idea from the zine Vegan Mary and it's been one of my favorite breakfasts for years.

Combine the oats, water or juice, almonds or seeds, raisins or dates, cinnamon, salt, and apple or pear in a small pot on medium heat.

Cook for about 8 minutes, stirring occasionally, until oats have softened as desired.

Transfer to a cereal bowl, sprinkle with the flax seeds, and drizzle with syrup and milk.

MAKES 1 SERVING. **SF, NF**

∙— THE MORNING KAMUT —∙

1/3 cup whole grain kamut

3/4 cup filtered water

1/4 cup pear or apple juice

1/2 tsp cinnamon

1/8 tsp sea salt

1-2 tbsp flax seeds, freshly ground

barley malt, or brown rice or maple syrup, to taste (optional)

organic non-dairy milk to taste

Who knew kamut kernels had such a fun texture?! If you have time, presoak them in the water (but using just-boiled water is best) in a small saucepan the night before – it'll cut down on the cooking time in the morning (only by 5–10 minutes, but some days that can make a big difference!).

Bring the kamut and water to a boil in a small saucepan (or if presoaked, just turn on the heat!), stirring to ensure it doesn't stick to the bottom of the pot.

Once boiling, reduce heat to low (or medium-low depending on your stove), and stir in the juice, cinnamon, and salt. Cover and cook for about 50 minutes, stirring occasionally – careful not to let it stick – until kamut is *al dente* or chewy, but not crunchy.

Transfer to a cereal bowl, sprinkle with flax seeds, and drizzle with malt or syrup and milk.

MAKES 1 SERVING. **SF, NF**

BANANA PANCAKES

Would you laugh at me if I said that Jack Johnson's song "Banana Pancakes" has cast a more romantic light on this weekend breakfast staple for me than ever before? This recipe's been with me since I first became vegan. If you want to make waffles instead, just bump up the oil to 1 tbsp and milk to 1½ cups.

Serve with your favorite pancake toppings – maple syrup, chopped nuts or seeds, nut butter or non-hydrogenated margarine, cinnamon....

Whisk together the flour, baking powder, cinnamon, and salt in a medium bowl.

Add the banana, milk, sweetener, and oil and stir just until flour is absorbed.

Lightly oil a skillet and place on medium to medium-high heat. Portion ¼ cup batter per pancake onto the skillet and fry for about 4 minutes, until golden, then flip and fry for 2 minutes, until golden. Continue until all batter is used.

MAKES 2–3 SERVINGS.   SF (if using SF milk), NF

1 cup spelt flour

2 tsp baking powder

¼ tsp cinnamon (optional)

¼ tsp sea salt

1 ripe banana, mashed (about ⅓ cup)

1 cup organic non-dairy milk (or more to thin batter as desired)

1 tbsp maple or brown rice syrup or barley malt, or ½ tsp green stevia powder

1 tsp non-hydrogenated coconut oil or sunflower oil (plus extra for frying)

Pancake pointers

The first pancake is almost always a flop. Perhaps from too much oil in the pan making the pancakes too oily, or too little oil, making them stick to the pan. But don't get discouraged – just make the necessary adjustments and proceed with the rest of the batter.

The oiled pan should be fairly hot when you pour on the batter. Test by sprinkling a few drops of water onto it. If it sizzles, your pan is ready. For cooking pancakes, it's a fine balance to get just the right temperature – too much heat can burn the outsides while the insides stay raw, not enough heat can make them very dry.

Flip each pancake only once – flipping them back and forth dries them out.

Don't press down on your pancakes with the spatula (I'm talking to you, fidgety cooks!). Let them do their thing in the pan; otherwise, they will be thin and tough.

For crêpes, thin out the batter, adding water or non-dairy milk, 2 tbsp–¼ cup at a time, to batter until desired consistency is achieved.

To keep pancakes warm and moist while cooking rest of batter, put a plate covered with a clean tea towel in the oven at a low temperature (say, 175–200°F/80–95°C). Stack cooked pancakes on the plate, under the tea towel.

Fry up all the batter into pancakes – even if you don't eat them all, you can freeze the leftovers to be warmed up in the toaster oven at a later date.

And you know what's especially nice? Warm maple syrup. Heat a bit up in a small saucepan 5 minutes before you sit down to eat.

⟩ Li'l Blue Corn Cakes ⟨

⅔ cup non-GM blue cornmeal (may substitute with yellow cornmeal)

1 cup just-boiled water

⅔ cup millet flour (or other whole grain flour)

2 tbsp flax seeds, ground

1 tbsp baking powder

1 tsp cinnamon

½ tsp sea salt

1 cup organic non-dairy milk

⅓ cup applesauce (see page 114)

1 tbsp maple or brown rice syrup, or ½ tsp green stevia powder

1 tbsp olive or sunflower oil

additional sunflower or non-hydrogenated coconut oil (for frying)

I first made these a few summers back when I was regularly visiting my friend Karla's farm. The blue cornmeal in her pantry just drew me in to make pancakes every time. Oh, and did you notice? With millet flour, they're gluten-free!

Serve hot, with molasses or maple syrup and any other delicious pancake toppings.

Mix the cornmeal and just-boiled water in a bowl and set aside.

Combine the flour, flax seeds, baking powder, cinnamon, and salt in a large, separate bowl. Add the milk, applesauce, sweetener, oil, and cornmeal mixture, and stir until a relatively uniform batter is achieved and there are no big clumps.

Lightly oil a skillet and place on medium heat (or medium-high, depending on your stove). Once oil is hot, portion batter (2–3 tbsp each) onto pan and cook for about 4 minutes, until golden, then flip and cook for 3 minutes, until golden. Continue until all batter is used; you will need to re-oil pan between batches.

MAKES 4–6 SERVINGS, OR 20–26 SMALL PANCAKES.   GF, SF, NF

◆ BLUEBERRY BREAKFAST POLENTA ◆

This is a simple breakfast treat. Serve drizzled with maple syrup or barley malt if desired – it's even tastier served with Cashew Creem (page 219).

Mix the cornmeal, cinnamon, salt, and juice in a small bowl.

Bring the water to a boil in a 3-qt/L saucepan. Once boiling, slowly stir in cornmeal mixture.

Cook uncovered on medium-low heat for 20–30 minutes, stirring frequently to prevent scorching, until thick and smooth. It's done when you can jam a spoon into it and it'll stand on its own.

Remove from heat. Stir in the oil using a silicone spatula, then gently fold in the blueberries. Scrape polenta into a lightly oiled or parchment-lined baking dish or pie plate, and smooth out evenly. Allow to set for about 30 minutes.
(It'll firm up on its own; you'll see.)

Cut the polenta however you like – I slice it evenly into quarters and then cut each quarter into 4 triangles.

Store any remaining polenta in an airtight container in the fridge for up to 4–5 days and warm it up in a skillet or toaster oven before serving.

MAKES ABOUT 5 SERVINGS.   GF, SF, NF

1 cup non-GM cornmeal

½ tsp cinnamon (optional)

½ tsp sea salt

1½ cups fruit juice (apple, pear, or other non-citrus fruit)

1½ cups filtered water

1 tsp non-hydrogenated coconut oil, or sunflower or olive oil (plus extra to oil dish)

1 cup blueberries (fresh or frozen, but not thawed)

SWEET POTATO ROUNDS WITH CINNAMON DRIZZLE

2 fist-sized or 1 large orange-fleshed sweet potato, scrubbed & sliced into 1/8-in (1/2-cm) rounds

2 tbsp organic nut butter (e.g., almond, cashew, or natural peanut butter)

2 tbsp flax seed oil (I like Omega Nutrition's Orange Flax Oil Blend)

2 tsp organic blackstrap molasses or maple syrup

2 tsp cinnamon

1/8 tsp sea salt

Who says sweet potatoes can't be a breakfast food? They're substantial and grounding – two qualities I look for in a morning meal.

This "drizzle" is a very flavorful alternative to margarine. It's also got an amazing nutritional profile: there's protein in the nut butter; the EFAs (essential fatty acids) in the flax seed oil promote good brain function, among other things; there's iron and calcium in the molasses; and the cinnamon discourages unhealthy bowel flora and normalizes blood sugar and insulin levels. You can also try the drizzle on waffles or toast.

Steam the sweet potato rounds for 8–10 minutes, until soft (see steaming directions on page 89, if needed).

Combine the remaining ingredients in a small bowl and mix well.

Dish out the steamed sweet potatoes into 2 cereal-sized bowls and garnish with the drizzle.

MAKES 2 SERVINGS.   **GF, SF, NF**

MAPLE TEMPEH STRIPS

9 oz (250 g) organic, non-GM tempeh, sliced lengthwise into 1/4-in (2/3-cm) strips (about 18 strips)

2 tbsp tamari soy sauce

2 tbsp maple syrup

1 tbsp filtered water

1/2 tsp apple cider vinegar

1 large clove garlic, grated or pressed

1/4–1/2 tsp chipotle pepper powder (if unavailable, use 1/4 tsp cayenne pepper) (or to taste)

2 tbsp non-hydrogenated coconut oil, or olive or sunflower oil (for frying)

1/3 cup filtered water

A tasty replacement for bacon. It's worth seeking out chipotle pepper powder for this recipe as it offers a nice smokey kick. Serve alongside pancakes (pages 119–120), in a sandwich, or on top of salad (see chapter fifteen).

Place the tempeh strips in a shallow dish.

Combine the tamari, syrup, water, vinegar, garlic, and chipotle in a small bowl and stir. Pour over tempeh and marinate for at least 15 minutes (or overnight).

Heat 1 tbsp oil in a large skillet on medium-high. Once pan is hot, lay half of strips in pan to fit in 1 layer. Cook for 3–4 minutes, until they begin to brown, but be careful not to let them burn. Flip and carefully drizzle on half the water. Cook for another 2–3 minutes, then remove and set aside.

Add remaining 1 tbsp oil and repeat.

MAKES 4–5 SERVINGS.   **GF**

TOFU SCRAM

A tasty alternative to scrambled eggs! Serve with whole grain toast and fresh salad.

Place the tofu in a shallow dish.

Combine the tamari and ginger in a small bowl and mix well. Pour over tofu and marinate for 10–20 minutes.

Heat the oil in a skillet on medium-high. Once skillet is hot, add tofu and marinade and sprinkle with nutritional yeast and turmeric.

Stir with a silicone spatula for about 6 minutes, until heated through.

MAKES ABOUT 4 SERVINGS.   **GF, NF**

1 lb (454 g) medium or firm tofu, roughly chopped or crumbled

3 tbsp tamari soy sauce

1 tbsp grated fresh ginger root

1 tbsp non-hydrogenated coconut oil or olive oil

1–2 tbsp nutritional yeast (optional)

1 tsp turmeric

CRISPY~FRIED TOFU

This is a simple and very tasty way to prepare tofu, loved by vegans and omnivores alike. You might also call it tofu bacon, but the meat reference is unnecessary. Serve alongside a fresh salad and whole-grain toast, in a sandwich, or with a bowl of steamed greens and grains.

Pour the tamari into a saucer (or small plate), and shake nutritional yeast into another. Place a few tofu slices at a time in tamari for 10–60 seconds, then carefully flip to other side for another 10–60 seconds (the quickest marinating you'll ever do!). Hold each slice above saucer to let excess tamari drip off, then coat each side with nutritional yeast and set aside. Repeat until all tofu is used.

Heat 1 tbsp oil in a large skillet on medium. Once skillet is hot, lay enough strips in pan to fit in 1 layer. Fry for about 4 minutes, until golden, then flip to other side and fry for another 3 minutes, until golden.

Repeat until all tofu is fried, using 1 tbsp oil to coat pan for each batch.

MAKES ABOUT 4 SERVINGS.   **GF, NF**

3 tbsp tamari soy sauce

1/3–1/2 cup nutritional yeast

1 lb (454 g) firm tofu, thinly sliced (ideally, no more than 1/6-in [1/2-cm] thick)

1/4 cup olive oil (for frying)

These are best eaten straight outta the pan (well, wait about a minute or two so you don't burn yourself). If you let them sit for too long (say, 15 minutes), they're not nearly as scrumptious.

CHAPTER 13

MUFFINS, BISCUITS AND QUICK BREADS

TIPS FOR MAKING MUFFINS

It's fun to think that within just half an hour from the time you're pulling ingredients off your shelf you could be slicing open and buttahrin'-up a fresh, steaming, warm muffin. *Mmmm . . .*

• If you've got empty cups in a muffin tray, pour a little bit of water into each of them so you don't mess with the humidity in the oven.

• Avoid over-mixing! When you mix the batter too much, gluten develops in the batter and your muffins won't rise as well. When you put your wet and dry ingredients together, gently combine them with a silicone spatula. Your baked goods will be lighter and have nicer crumb texture.

• Muffins should be removed from the baking tray five minutes after they come out of the oven. You want to allow them a few minutes to set (and be cool enough to handle for a few seconds), but you don't want the steam coming off them to condense, making the muffin soggy. A dinner knife (or, better yet, a grapefruit knife) can help get them out. Allow to cool completely before storing.

➤ APPLE CINNAMON MUFFINS ➤

I make this recipe all the time because I usually have all the ingredients on hand, and it's simple to make.

Preheat oven to 375°F (190°C). Prepare a 12-cup muffin tray with paper liners or a light coating of oil.

Whisk together the flour, baking soda, cinnamon, and salt in a large bowl. Add the apple, applesauce, raisins, milk, syrup, oil, vinegar, and seeds or nuts. Stir just until all flour is absorbed.

Portion the batter into muffin cups and bake for 20–22 minutes, until the tops are domed and a toothpick inserted in center comes out clean.

Stores in an airtight container for up to 3 days, or in fridge for up to a week.

MAKES 12 MUFFINS. SF, NF

2 cups spelt flour

1 tsp baking soda

¾ tsp cinnamon

½ tsp sea salt

1 medium apple, peeled & diced

1 cup applesauce (see page 114)

¾ cup organic raisins

⅓ cup organic non-dairy milk

⅓ cup maple syrup

3 tbsp sunflower or olive oil (plus extra if using to coat pan)

1 tbsp apple cider vinegar

½ cup flax or poppy seeds, or chopped walnuts or almonds

> **Plump 'em up!**
> *If your oven tends to burn raisins in baked goods, try presoaking them in the liquid that is called for in the recipe. (For example, in this recipe, presoak them in the applesauce, milk, syrup, oil, and vinegar.) For extra plump raisins, reconstitute them in water overnight (discarding the soaking water before use).*

Banana Chocolate Chip Muffins

1¾ cups spelt flour

1½ tsp baking powder

½ tsp baking soda

½ tsp cinnamon

½ tsp sea salt

1½ cups mashed ripe bananas*
(about 4 medium or 3 large
bananas)

⅔ cup maple syrup

⅓ cup softened non-hydrogenated coconut oil, or sunflower
or olive oil (plus extra if using to
coat pan)

⅔ cup non-dairy chocolate chips
(organic & fair trade if possible)

½ cup walnuts or pecans,
chopped (optional)

*Choosing ripe bananas over
slightly greener ones makes for
a significantly better muffin; as
the peel develops brown flecks,
the fruit inside becomes sweeter
and less starchy.*

This is one of those treats that stands out vividly from my memories of childhood. As soon as my mum would bake them, they'd be gone in a flash. As bananas make such a great replacement for eggs in baking, I can't imagine why anyone would use a banana muffin or bread recipe that called for eggs.

Preheat oven to 375°F (190°C). Prepare a 12-cup muffin tray with paper liners or a light coating of oil.

Whisk together the flour, baking powder and soda, cinnamon, and salt in a large bowl. Add the banana, syrup, and oil. Stir just until all flour is absorbed. Fold in the chocolate chips and nuts.

Portion the batter into muffin cups and bake for about 25 minutes, until the tops are domed and a toothpick inserted in center comes out clean.

Stores in an airtight container for up to 3 days, or in fridge for up to a week.

MAKES 12 MUFFINS.   SF, NF

Chocolatey goodness
I can't get enough of the slightly melted chocolate chips in these muffins, but if you're not a fan of chocolate, substitute the same quantity of organic raisins or chopped pitted dates.

— BLUEBERRY BUCKWHEAT MUFFINS —

I used to insist that there could be either vegan baked goods or gluten-free baked goods, but it was next to impossible to bake something that was both vegan and gluten-free and not wind up with a big disappointment. But after playing around in the kitchen a bit, I proved myself wrong! These babies are impressive – and free of refined sugar to boot.

Rinse the buckwheat, then combine it in a bowl with the room temperature filtered water and soak overnight (or combine with the just-boiled water and soak for 1 hour).

Preheat oven to 375°F (190°C). Prepare a muffin tray with paper liners or a light coating of oil (you'll need to prep 16 cups instead of the standard 12).

Pour soaked buckwheat (along with any unabsorbed water) into a food processor or blender, add the syrup, milk, flax seeds, oil, lemon juice, zest, anise, and salt, and give it a whirl for about 1 minute, until the buckwheat kernels are broken down. Add the baking powder and soda, and whirl again for another 10 seconds to combine.

Pour the batter into a large bowl and fold in the blueberries with a silicone spatula.

Portion batter into muffin cups, filling them to the top, and bake for 25 minutes, until the tops are domed and a toothpick inserted in the center comes out clean.

Stores in an airtight container for up to 2 days, or in fridge for up to a week.

MAKES 16 MUFFINS. **GF, SF, NF**

1¾ cups whole buckwheat (raw, not toasted)

2 cups filtered water (room temperature or just-boiled)

½ cup maple syrup

⅓ cup organic non-dairy milk

⅓ cup flax seeds (golden preferred)

¼ cup softened non-hydrogenated coconut oil or sunflower oil (plus extra if using to coat pan)

2 tbsp fresh lemon juice

zest of 1 organic lemon (about 2 tsp, lightly packed) (if organic is unavailable, omit)

1 tsp anise seeds, ground (optional)

½ tsp sea salt

1 tbsp baking powder

½ tsp baking soda

2 cups fresh or frozen (not thawed) blueberries

Soaked but not forgotten
If you soak the buckwheat but don't get around to making the muffins the next morning, all is not lost. It will keep in the fridge for a day or two – just allow it to warm to room temperature for about half an hour before proceeding with recipe.

Ghost muffins
When a muffin tray is on its way into the oven but not all the cups are filled, pour about ½ in (1 cm) water into each empty cup to promote the same level of humidity in the oven.

— RAISIN BRAN MUFFINS —

¾ cup just-boiled water

⅓–½ cup maple syrup

¼ cup organic blackstrap molasses

1 cup organic raisins

1½ cups oat or spelt bran (or wheat bran, if tolerated)

1½ cups spelt flour (or whole wheat pastry flour, if tolerated)

⅓ cup flax seeds

1 tsp baking powder

1 tsp baking soda

1 tsp cinnamon

½ tsp sea salt

⅓ cup olive or sunflower oil (plus extra if using to coat pan)

¼ cup applesauce (see page 114)

1 tbsp apple cider vinegar

zest of 1 organic orange (optional) (if organic is unavailable, omit)

There are indeed lots of ways to get much-needed fiber in your diet, but this is a pretty popular one.

Preheat oven to 350°F (180°C). Prepare a 12-cup muffin tray with paper liners or a light coating of oil.

Combine the just-boiled water, syrup, molasses, and raisins in a medium bowl and set aside.

Whisk together the bran, flour, flax seeds, baking powder and soda, cinnamon, and salt in a large bowl. Add the oil, applesauce, vinegar, zest, and raisin mixture. Stir just until all flour is absorbed.

Portion the batter evenly into muffin cups and bake for 20–22 minutes, until the tops are domed and a toothpick inserted in center comes out clean.

Stores in an airtight container for up to 3 days, or in fridge for up to a week.

MAKES 12 MUFFINS.   SF, NF

ZUCCHINI DATE MUFFINS

One thing I learned out in the fields is that squash have a knack for hiding – zucchinis in particular. I would visit the squash patch regularly, peer through the leaves, and not notice anything worth harvesting for days, until – ta-da! – all of a sudden, gigantic zucchinis would appear. The dates make these lightly spiced muffins sweet without the addition of refined sugar – how about that!

Place the dates in a glass or ceramic bowl, pour in the just-boiled water, cover with a pot lid or a plate, and allow to soak.

Preheat oven to 375°F (190°C). Prepare a 12-cup muffin tray with paper liners or a light coating of oil.

Whisk together the flour, baking powder and soda, cinnamon, nutmeg, ginger, and salt in a large bowl. Stir in the zucchini and flax seeds and mix until zucchini is well coated in flour.

Uncover the soaked dates and mash (no need to drain water) with a fork until relatively smooth (no big chunks). Add date mash and oil to dry ingredients. Stir just until all flour is absorbed. Add the vinegar and stir just until evenly distributed.

Portion the batter into muffin cups and bake for about 22 minutes, until the tops are domed and a toothpick inserted in center comes out clean.

Stores in an airtight container for up to 2 days, or in fridge for up to a week.

MAKES 12 MUFFINS.   SF, NF

1½ cups chopped pitted dates

¾ cup just-boiled water

2 cups spelt flour

2 tsp baking powder

2 tsp baking soda

2 tsp cinnamon

1 tsp nutmeg

1 tsp grated fresh ginger root
(or ½ tsp ground ginger)

½ tsp sea salt

2 cups grated zucchini

½ cup flax or sunflower seeds,
or chopped walnuts

½ cup sunflower oil

1 tbsp apple cider vinegar (plus
extra if using to coat pan)

Date-ing pointers
To make date-chopping a less sticky affair, lightly oil your chef's knife before using. The date pieces will just slide right off the blade.

JUICER PULP MUFFINS

2 cups spelt flour

1 tsp baking soda

½ tsp sea salt

1 tsp ground ginger

1⅓ cup lightly packed juicer pulp from Immune Boost Juice (page 110)*

¾ cup fruit juice or organic non-dairy milk

⅓ cup maple syrup

¼ cup softened non-hydrogenated coconut oil or sunflower oil (plus extra if using to coat pan)

1 tbsp fresh lemon juice or apple cider vinegar

*You may use pulp from other veggie and fruit juice combinations, just choose your flavors wisely!

I felt bad about all the leftover juicer pulp from making my Immune Boost Juice going to waste, so I've come up with this rather satisfying recipe for my tastebuds and conscience. These muffins are gingery and moist, so be sure to refrigerate or freeze them if they're going to be around for more than a day or two.

Preheat oven to 350°F (180°C). Prepare a 12-cup muffin tray with paper liners or a light coating of oil.

Whisk together the flour, baking soda, salt, and ginger in a large bowl. Add the pulp, juice or milk, syrup, and oil. Stir just until all flour is absorbed. (If beets and carrots are in pulp, the batter may look like salmon mousse. Don't worry, the color will change when baked.) Add the lemon juice or vinegar and mix quickly, just until evenly distributed through batter.

Portion the batter evenly into muffin cups and bake for 22–24 minutes, until tops are domed and a toothpick inserted in center comes out clean.

Stores in an airtight container for up to 2 days, or in fridge for up to a week.

MAKES 12 MUFFINS.   SF, NF

SPICED SQUASH MUFFINS

These are a treat for me in the cooler months. I use butternut squash, but another winter variety would be fine too. They're especially nice served with pumpkin seed butter (Omega Nutrition makes a particularly good one).

Preheat oven to 375°F (190°C). Prepare a 12-cup muffin tray with paper liners or a light coating of oil.

Whisk together the flour, bran, cinnamon, nutmeg, cloves, baking soda, and salt in a large bowl. Stir in the squash to coat with flour. Add the seeds, ginger, syrup, milk, oil, and vinegar, and stir just until all flour is absorbed.

Portion the batter evenly into muffin cups and bake for 20–22 minutes, until tops are domed and a toothpick inserted in center comes out clean.

Stores in an airtight container for up to 3 days, or in fridge for up to a week.

MAKES 12 MUFFINS. SF, NF

1¾ cups spelt flour

½ cup oat bran

2 tsp cinnamon

1 tsp nutmeg

½ tsp ground cloves

1 tsp baking soda

½ tsp sea salt

1½ cups (lightly packed) peeled & grated winter squash

⅓ cup pumpkin or sunflower seeds

2 tsp grated fresh ginger root

⅔ cup maple syrup

½ cup organic non-dairy milk

⅓ cup sunflower oil (plus extra if using to coat pan)

1 tbsp apple cider vinegar

➤ Buttahmilk Biscuits ➤

3½ cups spelt flour

2 tbsp baking powder

1 tsp baking soda

2 tsp sea salt

½ cup non-hydrogenated coconut oil or non-dairy, non-GM margarine, cold

1½ cups "sour milk" (1 tbsp apple cider vinegar or lemon juice + organic non-dairy milk to make 1½ cups)

1 tbsp sweetener (maple or brown rice syrup, or agave nectar)

organic non-dairy milk or oil for brushing biscuit tops

My high school friend Adrienne first introduced me to buttermilk biscuits. She uses a heart-shaped cutter to form them, so they look really sweet. Biscuits make a great accompaniment to any soup or fresh green salad. Enjoy them while they're still warm!

Preheat oven to 425°F (220°C).

Whisk together the flour, baking powder and soda, and salt in a large bowl. Cut in the coconut oil or margarine until mixture is crumbly (pea-sized) and there are no large chunks of oil (they should be pea-sized).

Stir in the "sour milk" and sweetener. Lightly mix and knead just until all flour is absorbed.

Roll out onto a countertop or board to about ¾-in (2-cm) thick and cut into biscuits using a biscuit cutter or upside-down glass or mug.

Brush the tops with milk or oil and bake on an unoiled baking sheet for 13 minutes, until lightly browned.

Stores in an airtight container for up to 3 days, or in fridge for up to a week.

MAKES ABOUT 12 BISCUITS.   SF, NF

Cold ingredients + hot oven = best biscuits
In order to get the best textured biscuits, make sure the fat (in this case, coconut oil or margarine) doesn't melt into the flour before the biscuits enter the oven. Ensure it is refrigerated so that it's solid like butter and all other ingredients are cold. Cut the fat into the flour with a pastry cutter or two knives; avoid using your warm fingers. When biscuits are cooking, the fat will melt, leaving air pockets that make the biscuits light and fluffy.

And why is the oven temperature so high? Biscuits cook best in a hot oven (make sure yours is preheated to the correct temperature); the steam facilitates rising.

~ CINNAMON SWIRL BISCUITS ~

Mmmm! Here's an impressive brunch or tea-time treat. If you're serving more than three people, you may wanna make a double batch. Serve fresh out of the oven.

Preheat oven to 425°F (220°C). Line a baking sheet with parchment paper (or lightly oil) and set aside.

Pour the just-boiled water over the cornmeal in a small bowl and set aside to soak for about 15 minutes.

Whisk together flour, baking powder and soda, and salt in a large bowl. Cut in the coconut oil or margarine (with a pastry cutter or 2 knives) until pieces are sort of pea-sized.

Stir in the syrup, soaked cornmeal, and "sour milk" just until all flour is absorbed.

Turn out the dough onto a clean, floured surface and shape into a 9x7-in (23x18-cm) rectangle. (If your dough is very sticky, feel free to sprinkle on an extra 1–2 tbsp flour.)

Combine the swirl ingredients in a small bowl, then brush it evenly over top of dough.

Roll it up lengthwise (do this carefully and evenly to make a really nice "swirl") and gently slice into 10–12 pieces. Place them swirl-side up on the baking sheet, reshaping each biscuit as needed. Dollop any swirl mixture that dripped off back on top.

Bake for 12 minutes.

Stores in an airtight container for up to 3 days, or in fridge for up to a week.

MAKES 10–12 BISCUITS.   **SF, NF**

¼ cup just-boiled water

⅓ cup non-GM cornmeal

1½ cups light spelt flour

2 tsp baking powder

1 tsp baking soda

½ tsp sea salt

⅓ cup non-hydrogenated coconut oil or non-dairy, non-GM margarine, cold (plus extra to coat pan)

2–3 tbsp maple syrup

½ cup "sour milk" (1 tbsp apple cider vinegar or lemon juice + organic non-dairy milk to make ½ cup)

Swirl

2 tbsp non-hydrogenated coconut oil, room temperature (or slightly melted)

2 tbsp Sucanat or organic sugar (fair trade if possible)

1 tsp cinnamon

⅛ tsp sea salt

~ MOLASSES CORNBREAD ~

1½ cups spelt flour

1 cup non-GM cornmeal

2 tsp baking powder

½ tsp baking soda

½ tsp sea salt

½ tsp cinnamon (optional)

1½ cups "sour milk" (1 tbsp apple cider vinegar or lemon juice + organic non-dairy milk to make 1½ cups)

⅓ cup olive or sunflower oil (plus extra if using to coat pan)

¼ cup applesauce (see page 114)

¼ cup maple syrup

3 tbsp organic blackstrap molasses

Molasses adds a rich taste (along with minerals like iron and calcium) to this bread, making it a nice deep brown color. It's great served warm with Cannellini Kale Soup (page 168) or the Southern Bowl (page 182).

Preheat oven to 350°F (180°C). Lightly oil and flour an 11x7-in (28x18-cm) baking pan and set aside.

Whisk together the flour, cornmeal, baking powder and soda, salt, and cinnamon in a large bowl. Add the "sour milk," oil, applesauce, syrup, and molasses. Gently mix together just until all flour is absorbed. (The batter will seem pretty thin, but the cornmeal will absorb liquid as it bakes.) Pour into the prepared pan.

Bake for 45–50 minutes, until bread pulls away from the sides of pan and there are a few small cracks on surface.

Remove from oven and allow to cool for at least 10 minutes before slicing into squares or rectangles.

Stores in an airtight container for up to 3 days, or in fridge for up to a week.

MAKES 12 SERVINGS.   SF, NF

GINGERBREAD

This is a lovely treat during autumn and wintertime. I like to wrap it up with a bow and give it as gifts during the holidays.

Preheat oven to 350°F (180°C). Lightly coat 2 (8½x 4½-in/22x11½-cm) loaf pans or 4 mini-loaf pans with oil and a dusting of cocoa or carob powder, then line them with parchment paper for greatest ease of removal at the end.

Whisk together the flour, baking soda, cinnamon, cocoa or carob powder, ground ginger, allspice, cloves, nutmeg, and salt in a large bowl. Add the oil, milk, molasses, syrup, applesauce, and ginger root, and stir just until all flour is absorbed. Quickly stir in vinegar just until it's evenly distributed.

Portion the batter evenly into pans and bake for about 36 minutes (for mini loaves) or 45 minutes (for regular loaves), until the tops are domed and a tooth-pick inserted in center comes out clean.

Stores in an airtight container for up to 2 days, or in fridge for up to a week.

MAKES 2 REGULAR LOAVES OR 4 MINI-LOAVES.   **SF, NF**

Easy molasses
If you measure the oil before the molasses, the molasses will easily slip out of the measuring cup.

2½ cups spelt flour

2 tsp baking soda

1 tsp cinnamon

1 tsp cocoa (fair trade if possible) or carob powder (plus extra for dusting)

1 tsp ground ginger

½ tsp allspice

½ tsp ground cloves

½ tsp nutmeg

½ tsp sea salt

½ cup softened non-hydrogenated coconut oil or sunflower oil (plus extra to coat pan)

½ cup organic non-dairy milk

½ cup organic blackstrap molasses

½ cup maple syrup

⅓ cup applesauce (see page 114)

2 tbsp grated fresh ginger root

1 tbsp apple cider vinegar

ALMOST FOCACCIA BREAD

3 cups spelt flour (plus extra for dusting)

1 tbsp baking powder

1 tsp baking soda

1 tsp sea salt

2 tbsp fresh rosemary leaves (or 1 tbsp dried) (plus extra for sprinkling)

1 tbsp fresh basil leaves (or 1 tsp dried)

1 tsp fresh thyme leaves (or ½ tsp dried)

1 tsp fresh sage leaves (or ½ tsp dried)

1 tsp fresh marjoram leaves (or ½ tsp dried)

1½ cups "sour milk" (1 tbsp apple cider vinegar or lemon juice + organic non-dairy milk to make 1½ cups)

½ cup applesauce (see page 114)

½ cup olive oil (plus extra to coat pan)

* I avoid using yeast in baked goods because chemical yeast is a common allergen for people.

This is a herbed quick-bread* version of focaccia. It goes great with soups like Portobello Soup (page 176), Cashew Creem Tomato Soup (page 169), Creemy Corn Soup (page 170), or Green Pea Soup (page 172).

Preheat oven to 375°F (190°C). Prepare 2 (8½x 4½-in/22x11½-cm) loaf pans or 4 mini-loaf pans with a light coating of oil and a dusting of flour, then line them with parchment paper for greatest ease of removal at the end.

Whisk together the flour, baking powder and soda, salt, rosemary, basil, thyme, sage, and marjoram in a large bowl. Add the "sour milk," applesauce, and oil. Stir just until all flour is absorbed.

Portion the batter evenly into pans, sprinkle with additional rosemary, and bake for about 35 minutes (for mini loaves) or 45 minutes (for regular loaves), until the tops are domed and a toothpick inserted in center comes out clean.

Stores in an airtight container for up to 2 days, or in fridge for up to a week.

MAKES 2 MEDIUM LOAVES OR 4 MINI-LOAVES.   SF, NF

CHAPTER

14

DIPS AND SPREADS

Hummus Three Ways • Red Lentil Hummus • White Bean Dip

Cilantro Black Bean Dip • Baba Ganouj

Great Guacamole (and sprouting an avocado plant) • Fresh Summer Salsa

Caroline's Raw Veggie Paté

HUMMUS THREE WAYS

2 cups cooked chickpeas (garbanzo beans) (or 1 [19-oz/540-mL] can, drained & rinsed)

2 medium cloves roasted or raw garlic (roasted imparts a mellower flavor)

2 tbsp tahini

2 tbsp fresh lemon juice

2 tbsp flax seed oil or olive oil (optional)

1 tsp sea salt

freshly ground black pepper to taste

¼ cup filtered water (to thin hummus as desired)

A great spread for sandwiches, burgers, or falafels, or as a dip for veggies and tortilla chips. If you want to make more to bring to a party or potluck, simply double or triple ingredients as needed.

 Classic Hummus

Toss all ingredients into a food processor or blender and give it a whirl, slowly adding water as needed and stopping to scrape down sides with a silicone spatula, processing until smooth. Add additional water if necessary (but don't let it get too runny!).

Serve, or store in an airtight container in fridge for at least a few days.

MAKES 2 CUPS. GF, SF, NF

 Green Herbed Hummus
Follow the directions for Classic Hummus (above), adding ½ cup chopped fresh parsley and using only 2 tbsp filtered water.

MAKES 2 CUPS. GF, SF, NF

 Hummus with Caramelized Onions

1 tbsp olive oil (for frying)

1 small-medium onion, diced

1 batch Classic Hummus (above) (using only 1 tbsp flax seed oil or olive oil called for in recipe)

Heat the oil in a small skillet on medium. Add the onions and cook for 20–30 minutes, adjusting heat as needed so they don't get crispy and stirring continually, until soft, sweet, and caramel in color. Remove from heat and allow to cool.

Scrape Classic Hummus into a serving bowl using a silicone spatula and fold in caramelized onions.

MAKES ABOUT 2¼ CUPS. GF, SF, NF

RED LENTIL HUMMUS

Lentils tend to be easier to digest than chickpeas (a.k.a. garbanzo beans), and they cook up a lot faster. This variation from your standard hummus makes a great spread for sandwiches, burgers, or falafels, or as a raw veggie dip.

Combine the lentils with water in a 3-qt/L saucepan and bring to a boil.

Reduce heat to simmer and skim off any foam from surface.

Stir in the tomatoes (if using), cumin, turmeric, and salt, cover and cook for 20 minutes, stirring occasionally, until tender.

Remove from heat, uncover, and allow to cool for 10–20 minutes.

Combine the lentil mixture with red peppers (if using), oil, tahini, garlic, and cayenne in a food processor or blender and process, stopping to scrape down sides with a silicone spatula, until smooth. Adjust seasonings to taste. Chill in fridge for 1 hour before serving.

Stores in an airtight container in fridge for up to 5 days.

MAKES 3½ CUPS. **GF, SF**

1 cup dried red lentils, rinsed

2¾ cups filtered water

⅓ cup sun-dried tomatoes (dry form, not in oil) or roasted red peppers

1½ tsp cumin

1 tsp turmeric

½ tsp sea salt

¼ cup flax seed oil or olive oil

¼ cup tahini

4–5 medium cloves garlic, chopped

⅛ tsp cayenne pepper (or to taste)

WHITE BEAN DIP

White beans are a great source of calcium. Serve with raw veggies, on rice cakes, or as a sandwich spread.

Toss all ingredients into a food processor or blender and give it a whirl, slowly adding water as needed and stopping to scrape down sides with a silicone spatula, processing until smooth. Adjust seasonings if necessary.

Stores in an airtight container in fridge for up to 4 days.

MAKES 1½ CUPS. **GF, SF, NF**

1½ cups cooked cannellini or navy beans (or 1 [14-oz/398-mL] can, drained & rinsed)

1 large or 2 medium cloves garlic

3 tbsp flax seed oil or olive oil

½ tsp sea salt (or to taste)

freshly ground black pepper to taste

⅓ cup chopped fresh parsley

1 tsp fresh minced dill weed (or ½ tsp dried) (optional)

up to 3 tbsp filtered water (to thin dip as desired)

CILANTRO BLACK BEAN DIP

2 cups cooked black beans
(or 1 [19-oz/540-mL] can,
drained & rinsed)

²⁄₃ cup packed chopped
cilantro (leaves & stems)

2 medium cloves garlic

2 tbsp fresh lime juice

1 tbsp tomato paste*

1 tbsp flax seed oil or olive
oil (optional)

1 tsp sea salt

½ tsp chipotle pepper powder**
or cayenne pepper (or to taste)

½ tsp ground coriander

½ tsp cumin

¼ cup filtered water (to thin
dip as desired)

*If you avoid tomatoes, the
tomato paste can be omitted;
but you may want to compensate the flavor by bumping up
the coriander seed to 1 tsp.*

**You may substitute chipotle
pepper powder with ½–1 whole
chipotle pepper from a can,
minced.*

Black beans are a great source of fiber and iron, and have more antioxidants than any other legume! Cilantro is good for digestion and is said to have anti-anxiety properties. This dip-with-a-kick is good served with non-GM tortilla chips and raw veggies, or as a sandwich or burger spread.

Toss all ingredients in a food processor or blender and give it a whirl, stopping to scrape down sides with a silicone spatula, processing until smooth and adding additional water if necessary (but don't let it get too runny!). Adjust seasonings to taste.

Stores in an airtight container in fridge for up to 4 days.

MAKES 1¾ CUPS. GF, SF

BABA GANOUJ

I don't love all baba ganouj – especially the kinds that contain mayonnaise – but I love this one. Serve with wedges of toasted flat bread, raw veggies, or as a sandwich or burger spread.

Preheat oven to 500°F (260°C). Line a baking sheet with aluminum foil.

Poke skin of the eggplants all over with a fork and place them on baking sheet.

Roast for 50–60 minutes, turning every 15 minutes, until they're soft throughout when you press them (with tongs of course, not your precious fingers).

Remove from oven and allow eggplants to cool enough to handle. Slice lengthwise and scoop out the flesh into a fine mesh strainer. Discard the skins. Allow flesh to drain for a few minutes before transferring to a food processor or blender. Add the tahini, parsley, garlic, lemon juice, salt, and pepper and process until almost smooth. Adjust seasonings if necessary, and give it another quick whirl.

Transfer to a sealable container and allow to cool in fridge for about an hour.

Drizzle the oil on top just before serving.

Stores in an airtight container in fridge for up to 2 days (but it's best consumed fresh).

MAKES 2 CUPS. GF, SF

2 lb (910 g) eggplant*

¼ cup tahini

¼ cup minced fresh parsley leaves

1–2 medium cloves garlic, minced

1 tbsp fresh lemon juice

½ tsp sea salt

freshly ground black pepper to taste

1 tbsp olive oil or flax seed oil

* For this recipe, use 2 large globe eggplants – the standard variety that are plumper at the bottom – or 5 medium Italian eggplants – the thinner variety.

3 ripe Hass avocados*

2–3 medium cloves garlic, minced, grated, or crushed

2 tbsp fresh lime or lemon juice

½ tsp cumin

½ tsp chili powder

½ tsp sea salt

½ tsp red chili flakes (or ¼ tsp cayenne pepper or chipotle pepper powder), or to taste

1 medium ripe tomato, diced small (optional)

Once opened, avocados tend to oxidize quickly – the lime juice should help avoid this, but you can also leave the avocado pits in the prepared guacamole to help retain the green color, then remove 'em just before serving.

I sometimes get crazy cravings for avocados. This could have something to do with the fact that it gives me the opportunity to use their silly nickname, "alligator pear," or maybe it's because they're a rich source of "good" fats (the monoun-saturated kind, including oleic acid), vitamins B6, C, and K, as well as fiber, potassium, folate, and copper.

Serve with non-GM tortilla chips and Fresh Summer Salsa (page 144), inside a burrito with Pinto's Refried Beans (page 197), or as a burger topping.

Slice each avocado open lengthwise and remove the pit (be careful when using your knife). Score a grid pattern into the flesh with knife and scoop out cubes of flesh into a medium bowl using a spoon.

Add the garlic, lime or lemon juice, cumin, chili powder, salt, and chili flakes. Mash mixture with a fork until you get desired guacamole consistency.

Stir in the tomato.

Serve immediately, and store any leftovers in an airtight container in fridge (with avocado pits*) and use within 1–2 days.

MAKES 1½ CUPS.　GF, SF, R

SPROUTING AN AVOCADO PLANT

Growing an avocado plant is a nice way to utilize all the parts of an avocado; practice patience, and it makes a great addition to your home.

1 avocado pit

toothpicks

glass jar

water

patience

pot

soil

Rinse avocado pit well to remove any flesh.

Determine which end of the pit is the top. (as shown)

Insert 3–4 toothpicks on a downward angle about 5-mm into the middle of the pit (be careful, this will require a jabbing force, and some toothpicks may break).

Fill the jar with water and immerse at least half of the pit in the water, letting the top be above water; then place by a window.

Top up water every few days and wait. . . . When I say wait, I mean it.

After a few months go by (yup, it's that long), one day you'll notice that the bottom of the pit has cracked open and is revealing a root. At this point, prepare a small pot of soil. Remove the pit from water and gently twist out toothpicks. Plant pit carefully, so you don't injure the root, ⅝ths deep into soil, with top peeking out.

Water it regularly – keep soil moist for first 3 months then every 5 days or so – before you know it, a shoot will emerge from the top … and then a couple of leaves!

These babies grow quickly – mine shot up to about my height within two years.

Re-pot as needed.

Note: I've grown banana trees, mango plants, and avocado plants in my homes in Québec and Ontario, and I sadly have never seen any fruit. These houseplants won't grow fruit unless they're cross-pollinated with other avocado (or banana or mango) plants. And, if you're considering bringing the plant outdoors for the summer, don't just plunk it in the ground anywhere – the leaves can easily scorch in the sun. Introduce the tree to direct sunlight slowly, 1 hour a day at first. Bring it indoors again before it gets chilly in the fall.

— FRESH SUMMER SALSA —

4 small or 3 medium ripe organic/local tomatoes (about 1½ lb/680 g), diced small

½ small red onion, minced (about ½ cup)

⅓ cup minced fresh cilantro (leaves & stems)

1 small jalapeño pepper, stemmed, seeded & minced (about 1 tbsp) or ½–1 tsp chili flakes

2 large or 3 small garlic cloves, grated or pressed

1 tbsp fresh lime juice

½ tsp sea salt

The store-bought stuff has nuthin' on fresh homemade salsa! In the warmer months, locally-grown tomatoes, onions, cilantro, chilies, and garlic should all be available. Serve with non-GM tortilla chips and Great Guacamole (page 142), inside a burrito with Pinto's Refried Beans (page 197), or as a burger topping.

Combine all ingredients in a large bowl and mix well. Cover and chill in the fridge for 1–2 hours to allow flavors to meld before serving.

Store any leftovers in an airtight container in fridge for up to 4 days.

MAKES 3⅔ CUPS.   **GF, SF, R**

— CAROLINE'S RAW VEGGIE PÂTÉ —

1 cup sunflower seeds (or ½ sunflower & ½ pumpkin seeds), soaked for 4–8 hours, then drained

1 medium carrot, chopped

1 stalk celery, chopped

½ cup packed chopped fresh parsley or cilantro (leaves & stems)

1 medium clove garlic, chopped

2 tbsp fresh lemon juice

2 tbsp mellow-flavored miso (e.g., white Shiromiso)

Caroline Dupont is a holistic health hero! She was one of my teachers in nutrition school and I really admire her approach to life. She's particularly inspiring when it comes to including more living (raw) foods in our diets. This pâté is from Caroline's book Enlightened Eating. *She says it's delicious on slices of raw yam – and I agree!*

Toss all ingredients in a food processor or blender and give it a whirl, stopping to scrape down sides with a silicone spatula, processing for 1 minute, until smooth.

Store leftovers in an airtight container in fridge for up to 5 days.

MAKES ABOUT 2⅓ CUPS.   **GF, NF, R**

Blueberry Breakfast Polenta (page 121) with Immune Boost Juice (page 110)

(Top to bottom:) Cilantro Black Bean Dip (page 140), Red Lentil Hummus (page 139), and White Bean Dip (page 139)

Coconut Cauliflower Chana (page 106)

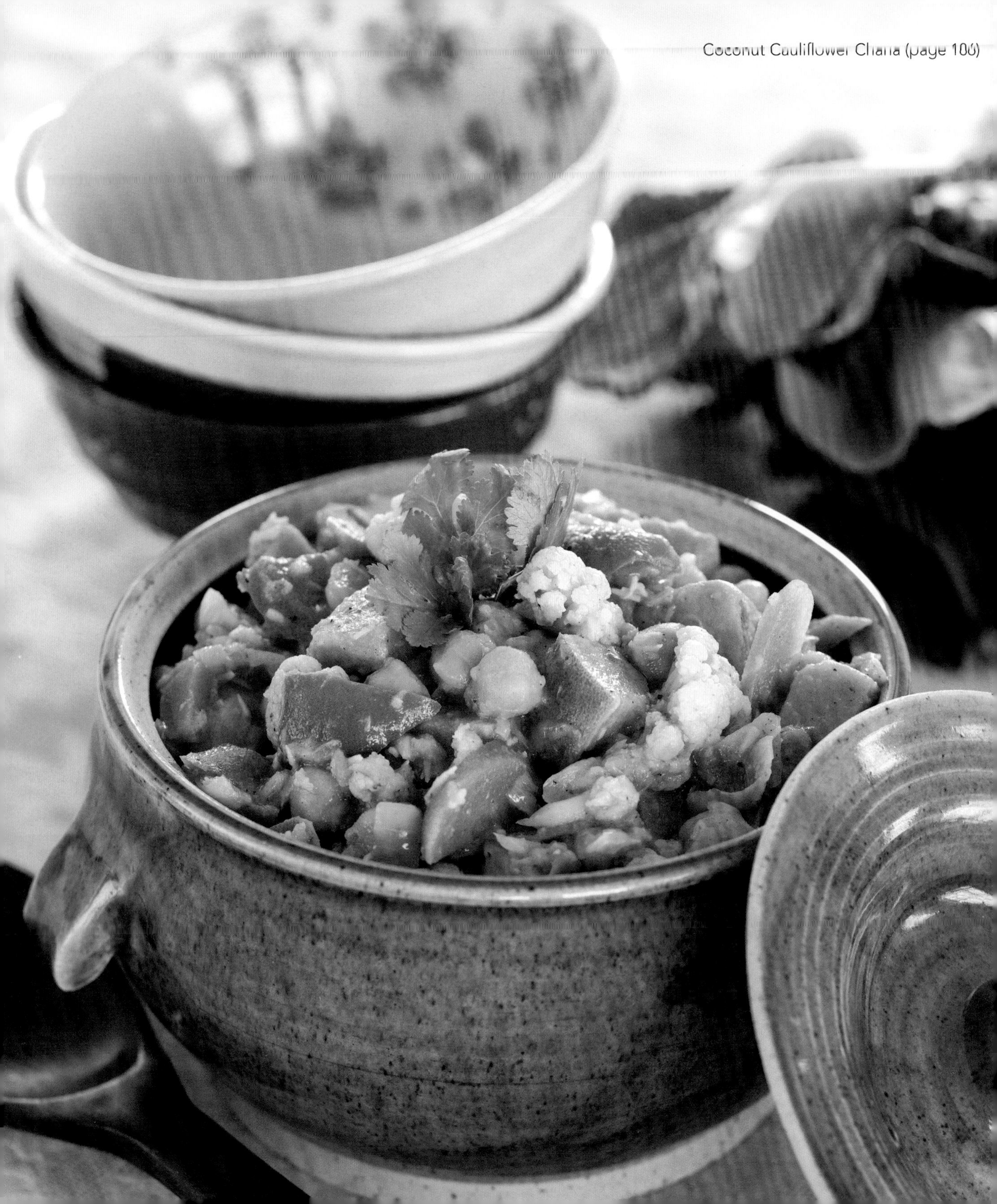

CHAPTER

15

SALADS AND DRESSINGS

BUILD A SALAD

When I was twenty, I worked at an all-boys summer camp in the Haliburton Highlands, Ontario; newly-turned-vegan me and close to 300 omnivorous boys. Yikes. My veganism was the source of much heckling that summer. I have a distinct memory of walking through the crowded dining hall to the kitchen for my "special" dinner one night while the entire room of boys bellowed at me, "You don't make friends with salad! You don't make friends with salad!" (I was up on my pop culture enough to know that the song was part of an episode of The Simpsons *in which Lisa becomes a vegetarian.)*

I used to think that making a salad into a meal was downright unfeminist. I'd protest: How can we really be nourished by a bowl of lettuce leaves with a pale wedge of tomato and the dressing on the side? Women have appetites, and we need not be ashamed to eat a decent meal! But I have since taken a more creative and educated approach; salads are not limited to greens, and they're a great way to get fresh, organic living foods into our diets.

Here are a whole bunch of options for building some amazing meals:

Start with a lovely bed of fresh greens (about 2 cups per serving) – choose organic if you can. Try a mesclun mix – e.g., baby spinach, arugula, mizuna, and mâche – or simply freshly chopped romaine, red lettuce, or spinach. You may start with very lightly steamed (2 minutes max) kale or Swiss chard.

Then throw on any of the following (the energetic properties of food listed on pages 27–32 may help you make the best choices):

• Nutrient-dense chopped fresh herbs: parsley (for vitamins K, C, and A, and iron), cilantro (a great detoxifier), and dandelion greens (stimulates digestion and supports liver function)
• Grated carrots, beets, cabbage, ginger root, and garlic
• Chopped or sliced snowpeas, baby bok choy, cucumbers, bell peppers, scallions, wild leeks, or red onions
• Fruit: an option that's not often considered, but pieces of strawberry, pear, apple, or orange can be really nice
• Sprouts (go organic, or grow your own – see page 95): mung beans, alfalfa, sunflower, quinoa (when sprouted it's a complete protein, did you know?), lentils and other seeds, grains, and legumes

Neat Nutritional Fact
Because beta carotene (a precursor for vitamin A) is water soluble and vitamin A is fat soluble, you need to eat fat at the same time as your brightly colored vegetables in order to absorb their vitamin A properties.

• Beans and lentils (cooked or canned): chickpeas (garbanzo beans), white beans, and green lentils can help make very satisfying salads

• Marinated and grilled tempeh, tofu, eggplant, zucchini, and/or bell peppers

• Sea vegetables like soaked and drained arame seaweed or a shake of dulse flakes

• A sprinkling of raw seeds or chopped nuts: sesame seeds, sunflower seeds, pumpkin seeds (I like to pulse seeds in the coffee grinder a couple times), hemp seeds, walnuts, and almonds

• A sprinkling of nutritional yeast

• And don't forget dressing. A good way to get in your daily dose of essential fatty acids (EFAs) for good immune system function (among other things) – try one of the dressings in this chapter, or just a drizzle of cold-pressed flax or hemp seed oil with a squeeze of fresh lemon.

Try these combinations with your bowl of chosen greens:

jae's All-Out Daily Deluxe

Chopped dandelion greens; spiralized (or grated) beets; chopped cucumber; chopped green onion; mung bean sprouts; cooked chickpeas (garbanzo beans); sunflower seeds; and House Dressing (page 148)

The Beagle

Cooked green lentils; tomato wedges; chopped fennel bulb; fresh basil leaves; and Duma dressing (page 147)

Sweet Caroline

Cubed mango; cubed avocado; red pepper, chopped into triangles; chopped fresh cilantro leaves; sunflower sprouts; unpasturized sauerkraut (optional); and Simplest Salad Dressing (page 148)

HOUSE DRESSING

1 tbsp miso paste

1 tbsp nut butter (almond, cashew, or natural organic peanut)

1 tbsp maple syrup

1 tbsp tamari soy sauce

3 medium cloves garlic, grated or pressed

freshly ground pepper to taste

¾ cup flax seed &/or olive oil

⅓ cup apple cider vinegar

This flavor combination is perfect, if I do say so myself. I predict this dressing will become a staple in your kitchen – it has in mine.

Mix the miso, nut butter, syrup, tamari, garlic, and pepper in a small bowl.

Transfer the mixture into a glass jar and add the oil and vinegar. Screw on a lid and shake well to combine. Give another good shake before pouring over salad.

Stores in fridge for up to a week.

MAKES 1⅓ CUPS. **GF, NF**

Miso Paste
* *A salty, fermented paste that originates from China, folks in the East have been enjoying miso's savory taste, as well as the probiotics (good bacteria) and B vitamins it contains, for millennia. The plastic packages of miso found on the grocer's shelf have been heat-treated to preserve them, killing all those beneficial cultures, so it's best to buy the stuff stored in the refrigerated section, which can still be considered a living food.*

SIMPLEST SALAD DRESSING

½ cup flax seed or olive oil (or a blend of both – and you may add a bit of hemp seed oil)

juice of 1 lemon (about ¼ cup)

1 medium clove garlic, grated or pressed

½ tsp Dijon mustard (optional)

1 tsp agave nectar, or maple or brown rice syrup (optional)

¼ tsp sea salt

freshly ground black pepper to taste

Sometimes all you want on your salad is simple oil and lemon. This dressing features both.

Place all ingredients in a glass jar, screw on lid, and shake well to combine. Give another good shake before pouring over salad.

Stores in fridge for up to a week.

MAKES ABOUT ¾ CUP. **GF, SF, NF, R**

BALSAMIC VINAIGRETTE

Reducing balsamic vinegar gives it a sweeter and more intense flavor. This dressing is especially nice over a fresh green salad with chopped heirloom tomatoes or ripe organic strawberries and almonds or walnuts.

Pour the vinegar into a small saucepan. Bring to a boil on high heat, then reduce to simmer for 5–8 minutes, until liquid is reduced by about half.

Transfer to a small bowl. Drizzle in the oil while whisking with other hand to emulsify mixture. Stir in the garlic, salt, and pepper.

Serve over salad.

Pour any leftovers into a clean glass bottle or jar and store in fridge for up to a week.

MAKES ¾ CUP. GF, SF, NF

½ cup balsamic vinegar

½ cup flax seed, walnut, or extra virgin olive oil (or a blend of all three)

1 clove garlic, grated or pressed

½ tsp sea salt

freshly ground black pepper to taste

DUMA DRESSING

I jotted down a version of this recipe that was posted on the fridge at the Duma House, an intentional community in Oregon that I visited a few years ago. It's great on salads and its savory flavor makes it a great addition to pasta. This dressing is meant to be served cold (so as not to spoil the flax seed oil), so if using as a pasta sauce, let the cooked pasta stand at room temperature to cool down a bit before tossing in the sauce. Deelish!

Toss all ingredients into a food processor or blender and give them a whirl for about 30 seconds, until smooth. Serve.

Pour any leftovers into a clean glass bottle or jar and store in fridge for up to a week.

MAKES ABOUT 2⅔ CUPS. GF, NF, R

½ cup olive oil

¼ cup flax seed oil (or additional olive oil)

¼ cup filtered water

½ cup apple cider vinegar

⅓ cup tamari soy sauce

1 small onion, chopped (about 1 cup)

⅓ cup nutritional yeast

⅓ cup raw sunflower seeds

2 tsp fresh dill weed (or 1 tsp dried)

GREEN TAHINI DRESSING

¾ cup filtered water

⅔ cup tahini (raw preferred)

⅔ cup minced fresh parsley

2 large cloves garlic, chopped

2 tbsp fresh lemon juice

½ tsp sea salt

This creamy dressing seems to go well with everything! It also makes a delicious sauce for falafels.

Toss all ingredients into a food processor or blender and give them a whirl for 2 minutes, until smooth. Serve.

Pour any leftovers into a clean bottle or jar and store in fridge for up to a week (it may need to be thinned with a small amount of water mixed in before serving).

MAKES ABOUT 1½ CUPS. **GF, SF, NF, R**

SESAME MISO DRESSING

2 tbsp miso paste*

2 tbsp toasted sesame oil

2 tbsp flax seed oil or olive oil

2 tbsp rice vinegar

2 tbsp filtered water

1½ tsp grated fresh ginger root

1 medium clove garlic, grated

½ tsp brown rice syrup

a pinch (¹⁄₁₆ tsp) cayenne pepper (optional)

* See note on miso paste on page 148.

Toasted sesame, ginger, and miso – a classic Japanese flavor combination! This recipe can easily be doubled – just remember that 4 tbsp equals ¼ cup. Serve salad with sprouted mung beans and sprinkle with sesame seeds.

Mix the miso and sesame oil in a medium bowl.

Transfer into a glass bottle or jar and add remaining ingredients. Screw on lid and shake well to combine. Give another good shake before pouring over salad.

Stores in fridge for up to a week.

MAKES ½–⅔ CUP. **GF, NF**

— MANGO SALAD —

This fresh, sweet salad comes from my friend, Dan Olsen, who is a chef. He made it when he threw an Asian Birthday Feast for his brother a few years ago – I refused to leave the party without the recipe.

Gently combine all ingredients in a medium bowl.

Cover and refrigerate for 1–2 hours, and toss lightly before serving.

MAKES 4 SERVINGS (ABOUT 4 CUPS).   **GF, SF, R**

2 large firm mangos, peeled & julienned

1 red bell pepper, julienned

juice of 3 smallish limes

2 tbsp fresh basil leaves

2 tbsp fresh cilantro leaves

2 tbsp fresh mint leaves

1 tbsp grated fresh lemongrass

½ tsp sea salt

freshly ground black pepper to taste

— COLORFUL PRESSED SALAD —

This recipe is adapted from The Hip Chick's Guide to Macrobiotics by Jessica Porter – a great, accessible introduction to a healthful Eastern diet. Leave it to the macrobioticas to come up with a smart way to make beautiful raw red cabbage more digestible and flavorful – just press it.

Use a mandoline (not the musical instrument, silly, the super-sharp slicing tool – see page 78) to reduce the prep time; if you don't have one, use the sharpest knife you've got in the kitchen to slice these veggies as thin as you can.

Place the red and Nappa cabbages, carrots, apple, and parsley or dandelion leaves in a flat-bottomed bowl (if unavailable, use a skillet).

Add the salt and toss to combine, squeezing produce with clean hands. Place an inverted plate directly on ingredients and press* for about half an hour to encourage the release of water from the produce.

Transfer to a strainer to discard pressed water and rinse.

Squeeze again and transfer to a serving bowl.

Toss with vinegar, dulse flakes, and walnuts, and serve.

MAKES ABOUT 4 SERVINGS.   **GF, SF, NF, R**

1 cup thinly sliced red cabbage

1½ cups thinly sliced Nappa cabbage (Chinese cabbage)

1½ cups fine julienned carrots

1½ cups thinly sliced Granny Smith apple

1 cup lightly packed minced fresh parsley or dandelion leaves

1 tsp sea salt

½ tsp umeboshi or brown rice vinegar (optional)

1 tsp dulse flakes

⅓ cup chopped toasted walnuts

* "Press" with any heavy object available in your kitchen – something relatively stable that can sit on top of the inverted plate, like a few cans or a fruit bowl full of apples. Place the object on the plate and allow the weight to slowly press water from the produce.

GINGER SESAME PASTA SALAD

1 lb (454 g) brown rice fusilli pasta (or other whole grain pasta)

1 cup snow peas, tips & stems removed

1 small-medium cucumber (or zucchini, quartered lengthwise and sliced, or 1 cup sprouted mung beans)

2 medium carrots, finely julienned

1 medium red bell pepper, finely julienned

3 scallions, minced, or ⅓ cup minced garlic scapes*

⅓ cup chopped fresh cilantro (leaves & stems are fine)

1 recipe Ginger Salad dressing (below)

¼ cup raw sesame seeds

½–1 lb (227–454 g) firm tofu, marinated & fried or baked (optional; see page 161)

Garlic scapes are the long, thin, green shoots of garlic bulbs that are available in the spring.

This makes a great potluck or picnic dish. I also like to take it for lunch when I'm out and about. Aesthetically, I like to use a mix of brown (unhulled) and black sesame seeds for the garnish.

Cook the pasta according to package directions. During last 30 seconds, add the snow peas. Strain and rinse with cold water.

Transfer the pasta and snow peas to a large bowl and stir in the cucumber, carrots, red pepper, scallions or scapes, and cilantro. Add Ginger Salad Dressing and toss gently to coat.

Cover and chill for 2 hours.

Remove from fridge, uncover, and toss salad again. Sprinkle with sesame seeds and top with tofu just before serving.

Store any leftovers in fridge for up to 2 days.

MAKES ABOUT 4 SERVINGS.   GF

GINGER SALAD DRESSING

¼ cup flax seed or olive oil

3 tbsp rice or apple cider vinegar

2 tbsp toasted sesame oil

1 tbsp sweetener (brown rice or maple syrup)

2 tbsp tamari soy sauce

1 tbsp grated fresh ginger root

⅛ tsp cayenne pepper (or to taste)

Combine all ingredients in a jar. Cover with lid and shake well to combine. Give another good shake before serving.

Stores in fridge for up to a week.

QUINOA TABOULEH

Try this – it's simple and nutritious, and especially nice for a packed lunch or a summertime dinner. It also is a great filling for a pita or a wrap. The addition of chickpeas (garbanzo beans) and the substitution of quinoa for couscous adds extra protein to this traditional grain salad.

Combine all ingredients in a large bowl.

Cover and chill in fridge for at least 30 minutes.

Remove from fridge, uncover, toss lightly, and serve.

Store any leftovers in fridge for up to 2 days.

MAKES ABOUT 4 SERVINGS.   GF, SF

1½ cups cooked quinoa, cooled

2 cups cooked chickpeas (garbanzo beans) (or 1 [19-oz/540-mL] can, rinsed)

1 medium cucumber, quartered lengthwise then sliced

2 medium tomatoes, diced

1½ cups chopped fresh parsley leaves

¼–½ cup chopped fresh mint leaves

2–3 cloves garlic, minced

¼ cup flax seed or olive oil

2 tbsp lemon juice

1 tsp sea salt

freshly ground black pepper to taste

CHICKPEA SALAD

This is a simple, satisfying salad that I've been making for as long as I've known how to cook. It is ideal for a packed lunch; the protein from the chickpeas should tide you over till dinner-time. I often like to eat it on top of fresh salad greens, but it stands just fine on its own.

Combine all ingredients in a large bowl.

Cover and chill in fridge for 30 minutes, and toss before serving.

Store any leftovers in fridge for up to 3 days.

MAKES 2–4 SERVINGS.   GF, SF

2 cups cooked chickpeas (garbanzo beans) (or 1 [19-oz/540-mL] can, rinsed)

1 green or yellow bell pepper, diced

1 ripe tomato, diced

½ cucumber, quartered lengthwise then sliced

1 medium carrot, grated (optional)

½ cup diced red onions or thinly sliced scallions

1 large or 2 medium cloves garlic, pressed or minced

2 tbsp flax seed or olive oil

1 tbsp freshly squeezed lemon juice

1 tbsp unhulled (brown) sesame seeds

1 tsp sea salt

freshly ground black pepper to taste

BEET AND GREEN BEAN TOSS

2 cups green beans (organic strongly preferred), stemmed & halved

1 cup spiralized,* grated, or julienned beets

¼ cup salad dressing**

1 tbsp unhulled sesame seeds (brown or a mix of brown & black)

* I have a great tool called a spiralizer that I use to peel root vegetables into long, delicate strands. It's a popular tool among raw foodists for making veggies look like spaghetti noodles and such, and is available at kitchen stores or online. And yes, the beets stay raw in this recipe – I'm amazed at how often people are surprised that I don't steam my beets!

** Of course, homemade dressing is best, and you've got a bunch to choose from in this chapter. For this recipe, I recommend picking something without too much color (and without balsamic vinegar, unless it's white balsamic) so that the bright and beautiful reds and greens can shine through.

This dish looks pretty, is darn simple to make, tastes good, and is good for you. Find locally-grown green beans and beets in the summer and early fall at your local farmers' market.

Serve as a side dish or on top of steamed grains, sweet potatoes, or fresh salad greens for a full meal.

Lightly steam green beans for 3–4 minutes, to *al dente*. Transfer to a medium bowl and toss with beets, dressing, and seeds.

MAKES 2 SERVINGS OVER GRAINS OR ADDITIONAL VEGGIES, OR 4 SERVINGS AS A SIDE DISH.   GF, SF, NF

CHAPTER 16

SAUCES, GRAVIES AND MARINADES

Fresh Tomato Sauce • Fresh Basil Pesto • Fresh Cilantro Pesto
Date Apple Chutney • Perfect Peanut Sauce • Red Star Sauce • Cashew Gravy
Miso Gravy • Basic Tofu Marinade • Tempeh Marinade

FRESH TOMATO SAUCE

1½ lb (681 g) ripe organic tomatoes (about 3 medium-large or 4 small-medium)

¼ cup olive oil

1 medium clove garlic, grated or pressed

¼ cup minced fresh basil

½ tsp balsamic vinegar (optional)

½ tsp red pepper flakes (optional)

½ tsp sea salt

freshly ground black pepper to taste

This raw recipe is reserved for gorgeously ripe summer tomatoes — otherwise, don't bother. Serve over pasta, spaghetti squash, or zucchini "noodles" (spiralized zucchini, see page 78).

Slice the tomatoes in half, remove cores and seeds, and dice ½-in (1-cm) thick.

Toss with the oil, garlic, basil, vinegar, red pepper flakes, salt, and black pepper in a large glass or ceramic bowl.

Store any leftovers in fridge for up to 3 days.

MAKES ABOUT 3 CUPS, ENOUGH FOR 1-LB (454-G) DRIED PASTA.
GF, SF, R

FRESH BASIL PESTO

¼ lb (114 g) fresh basil (2½–3 cups basil leaves)

½ cup pine nuts or other raw nuts or seeds (e.g., walnuts, cashews, almonds, or sunflower seeds)

2 medium cloves garlic

½ tsp sea salt

freshly ground black pepper to taste

⅓ cup olive oil

¼ cup hot filtered water

Pesto is a superb addition to pasta, on pizza, or in a salad dressing (you could add 1 or 2 tsp to Simplest Salad Dressing [page 148], for example). Make a triple or quadruple batch when local, fresh basil is available and then freeze it to enjoy through the colder months.

Wash the basil, remove stems, and add to a food processor or blender along with the pine nuts or other nuts or seeds, garlic, salt, and pepper. Pulse a few times to break up and combine ingredients. Add the oil and water and process until desired consistency (or coarse paste) is achieved.

Store in fridge for up to a week, or in freezer for up to 4 months.

MAKES ABOUT 1 CUP.   GF, SF, NF, R

FRESH CILANTRO PESTO

Not only is cilantro (also sometimes known as fresh coriander) cheaper than the ever-popular pesto-making herb basil, but it's also an amazing detoxifier – it actually pulls heavy metals out of the body. Let's hear it for detoxifying foods! This pesto freezes well, so make a large batch when local cilantro is available.
   Serve over pasta or dolloped onto pizza.

1½ cups packed, chopped fresh cilantro (leaves & stems; about 1 bunch)

½ cup flax seed oil &/or olive oil

3 medium cloves garlic, minced

3 tbsp fresh lemon juice

1 tbsp filtered water (optional)

⅓ cup sunflower seeds

⅓ cup pumpkin seeds

½ tsp sea salt

½ tsp dulse powder (or an additional ¼ tsp sea salt)

freshly ground black pepper to taste

Combine all ingredients in a food processor or blender and process until desired consistency (or coarse paste) is reached.

Serve cold or at room temperature.

Store in fridge for up to a week, or in freezer for up to 4 months.

MAKES ABOUT 1½ CUPS.   **GF, SF, NF, R**

DATE APPLE CHUTNEY

Serve this with any Indian-inspired dish or just to make a bowl of steamed greens and grains more exciting.

1 tbsp non-hydrogenated coconut oil or olive oil

1 medium-large onion, diced

1 cinnamon stick (unbroken)

1 tbsp fresh lemon juice or apple cider vinegar

2 tsp ground coriander, toasted

2 tsp ground cumin

2 medium apples, peeled, cored, & roughly chopped

½ cup filtered water

¾ cup pitted dates (lightly packed)

1 tsp sea salt

Heat the oil in a 3-qt/L saucepan on medium. Add the onions and cinnamon stick and sauté for about 5 minutes, until onions are softened.

Reduce heat slightly and add the lemon juice or vinegar, coriander, and cumin. Cover and cook for 10 more minutes, stirring occasionally to prevent sticking.

Add the apples, water, dates, and salt, stir, and simmer for 45–60 minutes (may need to adjust heat to simmer), stirring occasionally, until apples and dates are broken down (the dates will turn chutney dark brown as they melt). The chutney is done when there is almost no liquid remaining – the mixture should be a sticky, gooey mess (but in a good way).

Remove from heat, discard cinnamon stick, and allow to cool completely before using.

Stores in an airtight container in fridge for up to 3 weeks.

MAKES ABOUT 2½ CUPS.   **GF, SF, NF**

➤ PERFECT PEANUT SAUCE ➤

1 tbsp non-hydrogenated coconut oil or olive oil

1 medium onion, puréed* or minced (about 1½ cups)

5 medium or 3 large cloves garlic, minced

1 tbsp grated fresh ginger root

½ tsp curry powder

1 cup organic natural peanut butter (smooth or chunky)

3 tbsp tamari soy sauce

¼ tsp cayenne pepper (or to taste)

1 cup just-boiled water (to thin sauce as desired)

½ cup coconut milk (or additional water)

Using puréed onion helps to make a smoother sauce.

My stepfather and I have an ongoing contest about who makes a better peanut sauce. Today, I win. Serve hot over stir-fries or Asian-inspired vegetable and/or grain dishes.

Heat the oil in a medium saucepan on medium or medium-high. Add the onions and sauté for about 8 minutes, until translucent. Add the garlic, ginger, and curry powder and sauté for another 2 minutes.

Stir in the remaining ingredients until smooth, slowly adding water until desired consistency. Simmer for another 5 minutes on medium-high heat, stirring frequently.

Store any leftovers in a glass jar in fridge for up to a week, or in freezer for up to 8 weeks.

MAKES ABOUT 3 CUPS.   GF

➤ RED STAR SAUCE ➤

¼ cup nutritional yeast (Red Star brand recommended)

2 tbsp whole grain flour

½ tsp sea salt

1 clove garlic, crushed

¼ tsp mustard powder

freshly ground black pepper to taste (a few generous twists)

1 cup filtered water

½ cup unsweetened organic non-dairy milk

2 tbsp olive oil

This vegan classic is often used as a replacement for cheese sauce. But it's possibly more enjoyable when you don't expect it to be a cheese substitute; enjoying it for what it is. Red Star Nutritional Yeast is a great source of B12 vitamins and also contains protein. Serve over cooked macaroni, baked potatoes, or steamed broccoli.

Combine the nutritional yeast, flour, salt, garlic, mustard, and pepper in a medium bowl.

Mix in the water, milk, and oil until smooth.

Pour mixture into a small skillet on low heat and stir continually (like you're making gravy) for about 5 minutes, until it thickens to a gravy-like consistency, then immediately remove from heat.

Store any leftovers in fridge for up to 5 days.

MAKES 1½ CUPS.   GF (if using GF flour), SF, NF

CASHEW GRAVY

This recipe is adapted from one of the first vegan cookbooks I owned – a Seventh-day Adventist book that my friend Cheendana introduced me to called A Good Cook … Ten Talents *by Frank and Rosalie Hurd. The cookbook is a treasure and cultural experience; keep your eyes peeled for it in used bookstores. Serve the gravy, not the cookbook, over steamed or roasted veggies (page 89 or 185) or baked tofu (page 161).*

Heat the oil in a medium saucepan or skillet on medium heat. Add the garlic and sauté for 2–3 minutes (but don't let it get crispy!).

Add the cashews, celery seeds, water, and tamari, and stir to combine. Increase heat to medium-high and stir in the starch mixture, stirring continually until mixture comes to a boil. Remove from heat, add pepper and serve.

Store any leftovers in an airtight container in fridge for up to a week.

MAKES 2 CUPS. **GF, NF**

2 tbsp olive oil

1 large or 2 medium cloves garlic, crushed or grated

½ cup cashews,* ground (to a powder, not a paste)

½ tsp celery seeds (optional)

1½ cups filtered water

2–3 tbsp tamari soy sauce, to taste

2 tbsp arrowroot powder or cornstarch, dissolved in an additional ½ cup water

freshly ground pepper to taste

* I prefer to buy raw whole cashews, roast them for 5 minutes, then grind 'em.

MISO GRAVY

1 tbsp organic miso paste*

¼ cup filtered water

2 tbsp olive oil

1 medium leek, ** root & green top removed, then minced (about 1 cup)

1 medium clove garlic, grated or minced

1 tsp fresh thyme leaves (or ½ tsp dried)

3 tbsp whole grain flour

¾ cup unsweetened organic non-dairy milk

1 tbsp tamari or shoyu soy sauce

freshly ground black pepper to taste (a few good twists)

Buy miso paste from the grocer's refrigerated section – it is the most nutritious as it contains probiotics (good bacteria) and B vitamins. The plastic packages of miso found on the grocer's shelf have been heat-treated to preserve them, killing all those beneficial cultures, so it's best to buy the stuff stored in the refrigerated section, which can still be considered a living food. This also explains why you don't want to let it come to a boil.

** *Leeks can be sandy between the layers of the stalks when you purchase them, so rinse 'em well. Leeks may be substituted with a small yellow onion.*

I adapted this recipe from Rebecca Wood in my friend Michelle's Sackville, New Brunswick kitchen while dancing around to the Arcade Fire (having just seen them at the Halifax Pop Explosion music festival). It was a November-grey day outside and the gravy was the perfect thing to serve with baked squash, sautéed mushrooms, and steamed greens.

Mix the miso with water in a small bowl until smooth, then set aside.

Heat the oil in a medium skillet on medium heat. Toss in the leek and garlic and sauté for about 5 minutes, until leek is lightly browned. Add the thyme and flour, and stir continually for another 2–3 minutes, until mixture is lightly colored and creamy, not grainy. (Reduce heat if needed to prevent browning.)

Whisk in the milk and tamari and stir continually for about 3 minutes, until mixture thickens. Stir in the miso mixture and cook for another 2 minutes – but don't let it boil! Grind in the pepper. Serve immediately.

Store leftovers in fridge for up to 3 days.

MAKES 1⅓ CUPS.   GF (if using GF flour), NF

Basic Tofu Marinade

Straight-up, plain tofu is a bit of a yawn. Let's give it some flava!

Combine all ingredients in a glass jar, cover, and shake well.

To marinate tofu

Cut the tofu into ½–1-in (1–2½-cm) cubes, or slice into "cutlets" or strips, then carefully place in a glass baking dish in one layer. Pour the marinade over top, distributing evenly.

Marinate for 1–4 hours, gently flipping tofu with a silicone spatula halfway through time.

Serve, or fry or bake before serving (see below).

For 1 lb (454 g) firm tofu

¼ cup tamari soy sauce

2 tbsp apple cider vinegar

2 tbsp filtered water

1 tbsp olive oil

1 medium clove garlic, grated or pressed (optional)

½–1 tsp dried herb or spice of your choice (e.g., rosemary, thyme, coriander, cumin, or turmeric) (optional)

BAKED TOFU CUBES

Serve with almost anything – vegetables, grains, you name it.

Preheat oven to 350°F (180°C). Lightly oil a baking dish. Place the marinated tofu in a dish in 1 layer. Cover with remaining marinade, or not for a milder flavor.

Bake for 20 minutes. Remove from oven, gently flip tofu to other side with a silicone spatula, and bake for another 10 minutes.

Store leftovers in fridge for up to 4 days.

MAKES ABOUT 4 SERVINGS.   GF, NF

TEMPEH MARINADE

For 1 (9-oz/255-g) cake of firm tempeh

¼ cup tamari soy sauce

1 tbsp apple cider vinegar

2 tbsp filtered water

1 tbsp olive oil

1 medium clove garlic, grated or pressed (optional)

½ tsp ground coriander

½ tsp cumin

½ tsp turmeric (optional)

a pinch (¹⁄₁₆ tsp) cayenne pepper (or to taste)

I think tofu's popularity often overshadows tempeh's greatness. This is a tasty way to prepare tempeh before adding it to a stir-fry and serving with Perfect Peanut Sauce (page 158).

Combine all ingredients in a glass jar, cover, and shake well.

To marinate tempeh

Cut the tempeh into ½–1-in (1–2½-cm) cubes, or slice into strips, then carefully place in a glass baking dish in one layer. Pour marinade over top, distributing evenly.

Marinate for 1–4 hours, gently flipping tempeh when halfway through time.

MAKES 3–4 SERVINGS.   GF, NF

CHAPTER

17

Soups

VEGETABLE STOCK

2 tbsp olive oil

1 large or 2 medium onions, chopped

3 cloves garlic, chopped or crushed

10–14 cups chopped vegetables & vegetable scraps*

filtered water (to cover veggies)

16 peppercorns (or 1 per cup of water)

2 bay leaves

Types of veggies to use for stock: carrots, celery, leek greens, parsley stalks, parsnips, mushrooms, zucchini ... (but don't use leafy greens or green bell peppers; they'll make the stock bitter).

Vegetable stock can replace water in soups and a number of other recipes (like stews, sauces, and gravies). Making stock is a great way to use veggies that would otherwise go to the compost, and it adds more minerals and flavor to the recipe you prepare.

As far as I know, there are no hard and fast rules to making a veg stock – just work with what you've got. Any vegetable scraps you use should be clean – sorry-looking scraps are okay, dirty and moldy ones aren't.

Heat the oil in a large soup pot on medium heat. Add the onions and sauté for about 10 minutes, until onions soften. Stir in the garlic and sauté for a couple of minutes. Throw in the remaining ingredients and stir to combine.

Increase heat to bring to a boil. Once boiling, cover and reduce heat to simmer for 30–45 minutes.

Remove pot from heat and strain liquid into a large container or another pot (be careful when handling hot liquid and a heavy pot), extracting as much as possible. Discard veggies (or better yet, compost them). Allow stock to cool completely.

Stores in airtight containers in the fridge for up to 3 days or in freezer for up to 3 months.

MAKES 3¼–4¼ QT (3–4 L).   **GF, SF**

Pulp it up
Once I made a stock using pulp from a batch of home-pressed carrot/ apple/ginger root/beet juice. I scooped out the pulp from the juicer and stored it in sealed containers in the freezer. When I was ready to make stock, I thawed the pulp and used it in lieu of veggies. Needless to say, a stock with apple and ginger pulp only complements certain recipes, so be aware that if you use juicer pulp for making stock, you need to choose your flavors wisely.

Too much salt can ruin a soup
If you use a store-bought stock instead of this one (which has no added salt), reduce salt in your recipe by ½ tsp; you can always add more salt later.

APPLE CARROT SOUP WITH CORIANDER

When my friend Daniel made this soup at the vegan restaurant Aux Vivres in Montreal, I practically begged him to write down a version for me for at-home use. He kindly obliged. I'd never before made a soup with apple that I loved the taste of, but this one's great.

Heat the oil in a soup pot on medium (or medium-high, depending on your stove). Add the onions and sauté for 6 minutes, until softened. Add the garlic and celery and sauté for another 4 minutes.

Add the carrots and stock water and increase heat to bring to a boil. Once boiling, reduce heat to low, cover, and simmer for 12 minutes.

Add the apple, coriander, fennel, cinnamon, salt, and pepper, stir, and cook for another 20 minutes.

Remove from heat, and using a hand blender (be careful of hot liquid), purée until very smooth (otherwise, transfer to a food processor or blender to purée).

Adjust seasonings as desired. Garnish with cilantro before serving.

MAKES 6–8 SERVINGS. GF, SF, NF

2 tbsp olive oil

2–3 medium onions, chopped

3–4 cloves garlic, minced

2 stalks celery, diced

2 lb (910 g) carrots, scrubbed (or peeled if not organic) & chopped

5 cups vegetable stock (see page 164) or filtered water

3–4 fist-sized apples, peeled, cored & chopped

1 tbsp coriander seeds, toasted then ground

1 tbsp fennel seeds, ground

1 tsp cinnamon

2 tsp sea salt (or more to taste)

freshly ground black pepper to taste

minced fresh cilantro leaves (for garnish)

Hand blenders, also known as immersion blenders, are invaluable when it comes to making smooth soups because there's no need to transfer hot liquid to a food processor and back to the soup pot, which can be quite a mess. When I purée soups, I am sure to wear an apron, and hold the blender in one hand and the pot's lid between me and the soup with the other (to act as a shield). Finally, be sure that the blender's electric cord doesn't dangle over the stove's hot elements!

⟶ BEAUTIFUL BORSCHT ⟶

1 tbsp olive oil

2 medium or 1 large onion, chopped

2 medium or 1 large carrot, scrubbed (or peeled if not organic) & sliced

2 stalks celery, diced

6 cups vegetable stock (see page 164) or filtered water

1 large orange-fleshed sweet potato or 2 fist-sized potatoes, cubed (about 2 cups)

1 large or 2 medium beets,* diced (about 2 cups)

1 tsp sea salt (or more to taste)

2 cups shredded red cabbage

1 tbsp apple cider vinegar

1 tbsp agave nectar or maple syrup

3 tbsp fresh dill weed (or 1 tbsp dried)

freshly ground black pepper to taste (be generous)

Use red beets for this recipe, not candy cane beets that have red and white stripes; they are surprisingly bitter and will not make a traditional borscht with its rich inspiring color.

I think I love the color of this soup just as much as its taste! Be sure to wear an apron when you're preparing this, as beet juice can stain. Beets are known to be detoxifying, with powerful cleansing effects on our kidneys and blood. Serve with a nice rustic loaf of bread and a dollop of organic non-dairy yogurt or sour cream.

Heat the oil in a soup pot on medium heat. Add the onion and sauté for about 8 minutes, until softened (add a small amount of water if needed to prevent sticking). Add the carrot and celery, and sauté for another 5 minutes.

Add the stock or water, sweet or regular potatoes, beets, and salt, and stir. Increase heat to bring to a boil. Once boiling, reduce heat, cover, and simmer for 20 minutes.

Add the cabbage, vinegar, nectar or syrup, dill, and pepper, stir, and allow to simmer for another 5 final minutes, and serve.

MAKES ABOUT 8 SERVINGS.   GF, SF, NF (if using sweet potatoes)

— BROCCOLI CREEM SOUP —

This is a really lovely soup with delicate flavor. Broccoli is high in vitamins A, C, and K, folate, and fiber, and like other cruciferous vegetables, is known for its detoxifying and cancer-prohibiting properties.

Heat the oil in a soup pot on medium. Add the onion, bay leaf, and salt, and sauté for 8–10 minutes, until onions are translucent. Add 4 cups broccoli, the zucchini, and stock or water, stir, and cook for another 10 minutes or until broccoli is very tender (it may not seem like there's enough liquid, but don't worry, the soymilk's coming in just a moment).

Remove from heat. Remove bay leaf and purée soup with a hand blender (be careful of hot liquid) while slowly adding soymilk (otherwise transfer to a food processor or blender to purée and add soymilk, then return to pot), adding additional soymilk if a thinner soup is desired.

Whisk in remaining ingredients, adding an extra ½ tsp salt if desired. Heat gently, being careful not to boil (which may cause soymilk to curdle).

Serve hot, garnished with the steamed broccoli florets.

MAKES ABOUT 4 SERVINGS.   GF, NF

1–2 tbsp olive oil

1 medium onion, chopped (about 1½–2 cups)

1 bay leaf

½ tsp sea salt

4 cups chopped broccoli (florets & stalks)*

1 small zucchini, diced (about 1 cup)

1½ cups vegetable stock (see page 164) or filtered water

2 cups organic soymilk** (unsweetened preferred)

½ tsp thyme

¼ tsp allspice

freshly ground black pepper to taste

1 cup broccoli florets, thinly sliced & lightly steamed (for garnish)

* Be sure not to waste those broccoli stalks – I always chop off the dry end, peel off the tougher skin, and then use the tender part inside. It's just as good as broccoli tops!

** Soymilk is best for this soup because it is creemier than other non-dairy milks.

CANNELLINI KALE SOUP

1–2 tbsp olive oil

4 large or 6 medium garlic cloves, minced or grated

6 cups cooked cannellini beans* (white kidney beans)

4–5 cups vegetable stock (see page 164) or filtered water

3 tbsp tomato paste

2 tsp fresh minced sage leaves (or 1 tsp dried)

2 tsp sea salt

fresh ground black pepper to taste

5 cups chopped kale leaves* (from 5–6 large leaves)

¼ cup non-GM cornmeal (finely ground preferred)

2–3 tbsp fresh lemon juice, to taste

If you are in a pinch, white navy beans can stand in for cannellinis and collard greens can replace kale.

I enjoy hearty soups. This recipe is both hearty and creamy (without the use of milk or tofu), and I'm certain you'll enjoy it thoroughly! Serve with Molasses Cornbread (page 134) and a fresh green salad that includes tomatoes; as the soup is based on both beans and greens, it can also make a fine meal-in-a-bowl on its own.

Heat the oil in a soup pot on medium. Add the garlic and sauté for 30–60 seconds, until fragrant but not browning. Add only 3 cups of the beans and 2 cups of the stock or water, and cover.

Purée remaining beans and stock or water, tomato paste, and sage in a food processor or blender until smooth. Transfer mixture into pot and stir in the salt, pepper, and kale. Simmer for about 20 minutes, until kale is tender, stirring occasionally and reducing heat if soup begins to boil.

Mix the cornmeal and lemon juice in a liquid measuring cup and pour in additional filtered water until the mixture reaches the 1-cup mark. Pour this mixture into the soup slowly, and stir well to keep lumps from forming.

Simmer soup for another 10–15 minutes, stirring occasionally; you'll likely need to reduce heat to prevent scorching. Taste and adjust seasonings if necessary. Serve hot.

MAKES ABOUT 6 SERVINGS.   GF, SF

CASHEW CREEM TOMATO SOUP

It's funny the way my cooking has evolved. Once upon a time, I had a strong love for dairy. Then my veganism kicked in and I had to learn how to make things creemy using soy products instead. And now that I'm conscientious about not eating soy every day, I try to make rich dishes with other whole foods. Here, we have cashews to thank. They complement ripe organic and locally-grown tomatoes beautifully. Serve with a side of salad or steamed greens, or alongside a sandwich.

Process the soaked cashews and water in a food processor or blender for about 1 minute, until very smooth, and set aside.

Heat the oil in a soup pot on medium-high heat. Add the onions and sauté for about 8 minutes, until onions soften and begin to turn translucent. Add the 3 cups tomatoes, garlic, basil or dill, syrup, salt, and cayenne, and stir to combine.

Increase heat to bring to a boil. Once boiling, reduce heat, cover, and simmer for 20–30 minutes (the longer the better), stirring occasionally.

Remove from heat. Purée soup with a hand blender (be careful of hot liquid) while slowly adding cashew milk (otherwise transfer to a food processor or blender to purée and add cashew milk then return to pot) for about 30 seconds or until smooth.

Stir in the 2 diced tomatoes for finishing and re-heat for another 5 minutes.

MAKES 5–6 SERVINGS.   GF, SF

1 cup raw cashews, soaked in filtered water for 4–8 hours, then drained & rinsed*

1½ cups filtered water or vegetable stock (see page 164)

1 tbsp olive oil

1 large or 2 medium onions, chopped (about 3 cups)

3 cups diced fresh tomatoes (or 1 [28-oz/796-mL] can diced or crushed tomatoes in juices)

3 large or 5 medium cloves garlic, minced

2 tbsp minced fresh basil leaves (or 1 tbsp dried) or 2 tsp fresh dill weed (or 1 tsp dried)

2 tsp maple syrup (or other natural sweetener)

1 tsp sea salt

⅛ tsp cayenne pepper (or to taste)

2 medium-sized ripe tomatoes, diced (about 2 cups) (for finishing)

* If you've soaked the cashews but can't make the soup right away, drain off the soaking water, rinse, and place them in an airtight container in the fridge, covered with fresh water (will keep for about 2 days.) Drain and rinse before using.

CREEMY CORN SOUP

1 tbsp olive oil

6 scallions & 1 medium leek, minced or chopped (to make 1½ cups)

2 stalks celery, diced (about 1 cup)

3½ cups non-GM corn, fresh or frozen (a 500-g [just over 1-lb] bag)

2 cups filtered water or vegetable stock (see page 164)

1 tbsp minced fresh basil leaves (or 1 tsp dried)

1 tsp sea salt

1 cup organic non-dairy milk

This recipe is adapted from a children's cookbook by the legendary cookbook author Mollie Katzen—it's no wonder that its mild taste is always a hit with kids.

Heat the oil in a soup pot on medium. Add the scallions, leek, and celery and sauté for about 8 minutes, stirring occasionally. Add the corn, stock or water, basil, and salt, and stir to combine.

Increase heat to bring to a boil. Once boiling, reduce heat to low, cover, and simmer for about 5 minutes.

Remove from heat. Purée soup with a hand blender (be careful of hot liquid) while slowly adding milk (otherwise transfer to a food processor or blender to purée and add the milk, then return to pot) for about 30 seconds or until smooth.

Re-heat for another 5 minutes, then ladle into soup bowls and be prepared to taste the most comforting food ever.

MAKES ABOUT 4 SERVINGS.   GF, SF, NF

SIMPLE DAL

Dal is a mainstay of Indian cuisine. I like it best served over chopped fresh organic spinach.

Combine the lentils, stock or water, chilies, turmeric, and salt in a soup pot on high heat. Bring to a boil, then reduce heat to simmer for about 30 minutes, until lentils are tender, stirring continually. You may add up to an additional cup of water or stock to adjust to desired consistency.

Heat the oil in a small skillet on medium-high. Add the cumin seeds and sauté for about 15–30 seconds, until seeds are fragrant but not burning, then stir in the onions, garlic, and ginger. Reduce heat to medium and sauté for about 5 minutes, until onions begin to brown. Add tomato and sauté for another 7 minutes.

Discard chilies once lentils are tender. Stir in the onion mixture, lemon juice, garam masala, and additional salt if desired.

MAKES ABOUT 6 SERVINGS.   GF, SF, NF (if omitting tomatoes)

1½ cups dry red lentils (hulled or unhulled), rinsed

4 cups vegetable stock (see page 164) or filtered water

2 whole dried chilies or ½ tsp crushed chilies

2 tsp turmeric

1 tsp sea salt

2 tbsp non-hydrogenated coconut oil or olive oil

1 tsp cumin seeds

1 medium onion, chopped

2 cloves garlic, minced or grated

1 tbsp grated fresh ginger root (or an additional clove of garlic)

1 cup chopped tomato (optional)

1 tbsp fresh lemon juice

1 tsp garam masala (see below)

GARAM MASALA

It's better to make your own spice blends rather than purchasing pre-made brands – you can be sure they'll be more potent if they're freshly ground, and you can customize the blend to suit your own taste. This garam masala recipe's from my friend Dan Olsen, who also created the Mango Salad (page 151).

Grind each item separately in a spice grinder (or a clean coffee grinder), except for the cayenne and nutmeg, then place all ingredients in a small jar, cover, and shake until well combined.

MAKES ABOUT ⅔ CUP.   GF, SF, NF

3 tbsp black peppercorns

Seeds from 2 tbsp green cardamom pods

2 tbsp coriander seeds

2 tbsp cumin seeds

2 cinnamon sticks

1 tsp whole cloves

1–2 tsp cayenne pepper

1 tsp grated nutmeg

⟶ GREEN PEA SOUP ⟶

1 tbsp olive oil

1 medium onion, diced

3–4 medium cloves garlic, minced or grated

1 large fist-sized potato (organic Yukon gold), peeled & diced (about 1½ cups)

4 cups vegetable stock (see page 164) or filtered water

1 tsp sea salt

4 cups peas, fresh or frozen (a 500-g [just over 1-lb] bag)

½ cup minced fresh parsley leaves

¼ cup pumpkin seed butter

freshly ground black pepper to taste (a few generous twists)

This soup has such a great color that reminds me of spring. This rarely celebrated legume is a good source of protein, B vitamins, vitamins C and K, and carotenes, and plenty of minerals, like phosphorus, manganese, magnesium, potassium, and iron. The pumpkin seed butter adds a smokey richness; Omega Nutrition makes a particularly tasty one.

Heat the oil in a soup pot on medium heat. Add the onions and garlic and sauté for about 8 minutes, until onions are translucent. Add the potato, stock or water, and salt.

Increase heat to bring to a boil. Once boiling, reduce heat to simmer for about 8–10 minutes, until potato is cooked. Stir in the peas and parsley and cook for another 2–3 minutes.

Remove from heat. Add the pumpkin seed butter. Purée soup with a hand blender (be careful of hot liquid) for about 30 seconds or until smooth (or transfer to a food processor or blender to purée then return to pot).

Add additional salt and pepper to taste and re-heat, if needed, before serving.

MAKES ABOUT 4 SERVINGS. GF, SF

Fresh is best
Canned peas have only 5% of the nutritional value of fresh peas. What a drag, hey? (Frozen peas are your next best bet.)

LEEK AND POTATO SOUP

A classic from my mum – now dairy-free! Leeks are grown in sandy soil, so the trick is to slice them lengthwise and rinse well between the layers of the stalks before putting them on the cutting board.

Heat the oil and 2 tbsp water in a soup pot on medium. Add the leeks and sauté for 10 minutes, until soft, being careful not to let them brown.

Add the potatoes, stock or water, salt, nutmeg, and pepper. Cover and simmer for 20–25 minutes, until potatoes are soft.

Remove from heat and mash; for smoother texture, give it a quick whirl with a hand blender (or in a food processor or blender, then return to pot).

Add the milk and stir while heating gently for 5 minutes. Adjust seasonings to taste. Serve garnished with chives.

MAKES 6 SERVINGS.　GF

3 tbsp olive oil + 2 tbsp filtered water

3 large or 6 small leeks, roots & green tops removed, then chopped (about 5 cups)

4–5 fist-sized potatoes (about 2¼ lb/1 kg), peeled & sliced ¼-in (²/₃-cm) thick

2½ cups vegetable stock (see page 164) or filtered water

1 tsp sea salt (or more to taste)

½ tsp nutmeg

freshly ground black or white pepper (a few generous twists)

2 cups organic non-dairy milk (unsweetened soymilk preferred; it's creemier)

¼ cup minced chives (for garnish)

2 tbsp olive oil

1 large onion, halved & sliced in thin half-moons

2 medium carrots, scrubbed (or peeled if not organic) & sliced*

up to 1 lb (454 g) tofu, cut in ½-in (1-cm) cubes

4–8 medium shiitake mushrooms, sliced

4 cloves garlic, minced

1 tbsp grated fresh ginger root

2 cups chopped kale, chopped bok choy, &/or halved snow peas

1 (6-in/15-cm) piece wakame

6 cups filtered water

2–3 tbsp tamari or shoyu soy sauce, or more to taste

2–3 scallions, thinly sliced

3 tbsp miso paste,** or more to taste

* Carrots look nice in this soup when they are sliced on an angle or julienned.

** Select high-quality miso paste that contains good-for-you enzymes from your grocer's fridge instead of the non-refrigerated brands that are far less nutritious.

Miso, a paste made with fermented soybeans and sometimes a grain, like rice or barley, has wonderful healing properties, so this is a great alternative to chicken soup when you or someone else is ill. And unlike the basic miso soups in many Japanese restaurants, this one is packed with tasty vegetables (and doesn't have any fish powder)! Be careful, though, as miso loses its nutritional properties when heated at too high a temperature – add it last and certainly don't let it boil.

Heat the oil in a soup pot on medium-high. Add the onion and sauté for about 8 minutes, until translucent. Add the carrots and sauté for another 6 minutes, until carrots begin to soften.

Add the tofu, mushrooms, garlic, and ginger, stir, and cook for 5 minutes more, stirring continually (add a small amount of water to prevent sticking if needed).

Toss in the kale, and/or boy choy, and/or snow peas, and wakame, and pour in the water and tamari or shoyu. Reduce heat to simmer for about 10 minutes. Throw in the scallions.

Turn off heat. Use a mug to scoop out some liquid to mix with the miso, then pour back into soup and stir to combine. Remove wakame and serve.

MAKES ABOUT 6 SERVINGS.   GF, NF

More minerals!
Make this soup even more mineral-rich with the addition of extra sea vegetables. When you add the water, also add ¼–½ cup arame, a couple of sheets of ripped-up nori, or a teaspoon of dulse flakes. These ingredients can be found in an Asian market or the Japanese food section at the grocer's or health food store.

MOROCCAN GARBANZO BEAN SOUP

It seems that Alison (a long-time friend and the food stylist for the photographs in this book) believes this is the only thing she makes that I can eat. Fine by me! I look forward to it every time I'm invited to dinner chez elle.

Heat the oil in a large soup pot on medium heat. Add the onion and sauté for about 6 minutes, until soft. Add the garlic, cumin, cinnamon, and saffron, and sauté for 1 minute.

Add the stock or water, tomatoes, squash, and potato, and stir. Increase heat to bring to a boil. Once boiling, reduce heat, cover, and simmer for about 20–25 minutes, until vegetables are very tender.

Stir in the chickpeas. Simmer for 10 minutes more, stirring occasionally.

Add the salt and pepper (and remove cinnamon stick if used). Serve hot, garnished with cilantro.

MAKES ABOUT 6 SERVINGS.   GF, SF

1 tbsp olive oil

1 medium-large onion, chopped

2 large cloves garlic, minced

2 tsp ground cumin

1 tsp cinnamon (or 1 stick)

½ tsp saffron threads (optional, but recommended)

5 cups vegetable stock (see page 164) or filtered water

3 cups diced fresh tomatoes (or 1 [28-oz/796-mL] can diced tomatoes in juice)

2½ lb (1 kg) butternut squash, peeled & cubed ½– ¾-in (1–2-cm) thick (about 5 cups)

12–14 oz (340–397 g) russet or Yukon Gold potato, cubed ½-in (1-cm) thick (about 2½ cups)

2 cups cooked chickpeas (garbanzo beans) (or 1 [19-oz/540-mL] can)

1½ tsp sea salt (or to taste)

freshly ground black pepper to taste

½ cup chopped fresh cilantro leaves (for garnish)

⟿ PORTOBELLO SOUP ⟿

2 tbsp olive oil

2 medium onions, chopped

½ lb (227 g) Portobello mushrooms, cleaned & thinly sliced (about 4½ cups)

2 tbsp whole grain flour

4 cups vegetable stock (see page 164) or filtered water

1 bay leaf

1½ tsp sea salt (or to taste)

freshly ground black pepper to taste

2 tbsp watercress or minced fresh parsley (for garnish)

Picture this: I've just returned from an autumn of organic farming and am having Christmas dinner with my family. I've only been vegan for a few weeks and am already used to the idea of not fitting in at any place where food is served. Sheila, my Scottish step-grandmother, says she has just the thing for me – a beautiful mushroom soup. Everyone else tucks in to plates of turkey and gravy, and I hungrily polish off three bowls of soup before asking Sheila for the recipe.

She begins to describe it: "You start with some chicken stock...."

I'm horrified, but accept the recipe nonetheless, planning to make my own still very flavorful but truly animal-free version at home.

Heat the oil in a soup pot on medium. Add the onions and sauté for about 6 minutes, until soft. Toss in the mushrooms and sauté for another 5 minutes. Stir in the flour, then add the stock or water, bay leaf, salt, and pepper.

Increase heat to bring to a boil. Once boiling, reduce heat, cover, and simmer for 15–20 minutes. Remove bay leaf, adjust seasoning to taste, then garnish with the watercress before serving.

MAKES 4 SERVINGS.   GF (if using GF flour), SF, NF

ADZUKI~SQUASH SOUP WITH CHIPOTLE AND RED PEPPERS

Small red adzuki beans are among the easiest legumes to digest (as well as being faster to cook than chickpeas or black beans), but people in the West rarely use 'em.

Serve this soup hot, garnished with a sprig or two of fresh cilantro. It's also nice alongside Molasses Cornbread (page 134) and a salad or steamed greens for a satisfying meal.

Heat the oil in a soup pot on medium. Add the cinnamon, coriander, and chipotle and sauté for about 2 minutes, until aromatic. Add the onions and sauté for another 8 minutes, until translucent (add a splash of water to prevent sticking if needed). Add the garlic and squash, stir, and then pour in stock or water.

Increase heat to bring to a boil. Once boiling, reduce heat, cover, and simmer for about 6 minutes, until squash begins to soften.

Go in there with a potato masher and start breaking up the squash a bit. Add red peppers and salt, and cook for 6 minutes more before adding the beans and cooking for 5 minutes more, until hot. Serve hot, garnished with cilantro.

MAKES ABOUT 8 SERVINGS. **GF, SF**

2 tbsp olive oil

1 tsp cinnamon

1 tsp ground coriander

1–2 tsp finely chopped chipotle pepper (or ¼ tsp cayenne pepper, but not nearly as good)

2 medium-large onions, minced

6 cloves garlic, minced

4 cups peeled and diced squash (I like to use butternut)

5 cups vegetable stock (see page 164) or filtered water

1 large or 2 medium red bell peppers, diced

2 tsp sea salt

4 cups cooked or canned adzuki beans, rinsed

a few sprigs fresh cilantro (for garnish)

SWEET POTATO and COCONUT MILK SOUP

4 cups vegetable stock (see page 164) or filtered water

2¼ lb (1 kg) orange-fleshed sweet potatoes (about 2–3 large ones), peeled & diced (about 6 cups)

1 tbsp turmeric

2 tsp sea salt

2 tbsp non-hydrogenated coconut oil or olive oil

2 tsp ground coriander

2 tsp ground cumin

½ tsp ground cinnamon

1 medium onion, diced

1½ tbsp grated fresh ginger root

2 cloves garlic, minced

⅔ cup coconut milk (canned, non-light version, or see page 108)

⅛ tsp cayenne pepper (or to taste)

a few sprigs fresh cilantro (for garnish)

I love this soup. Truth be told, I make it for people I want to impress ... but there's nothing complicated about it, it just tastes so good! Serve hot, perhaps with a swirl of hot sauce, like Sambal Olek, in the middle.

Pour the stock or water into a soup pot on high heat. Add the sweet potatoes, turmeric, and salt, and bring to a boil. Once boiling, reduce heat to medium, cover, and cook for about 8–10 minutes, until potatoes are soft, stirring occasionally. Remove from heat and set aside (do not drain!).

Heat the oil in a medium skillet on medium-high. Add the coriander, cumin, and cinnamon, and sauté for about 30 seconds, until fragrant but not browning. Add the onions and sauté for about 7 minutes. Add the ginger and garlic (and a splash of water if needed to prevent sticking), stir, and continue to sauté for another 5 minutes, until onions are translucent and soft.

Transfer onion mixture into the soup pot and stir in the coconut milk and cayenne. Remove from heat and purée with a hand blender (or transfer to a food processor or blender to purée then return to pot) until smooth. Reheat if necessary before serving, garnished with cilantro.

MAKES ABOUT 6 SERVINGS. GF, SF, NF (if omitting cayenne)

CHAPTER 18

MAIN DISH BOWLS AND ADDITIONAL ENTRÉES

Andrew's Butternut Risotto • Southern Bowl • Mushroom Quinoa Pilaf

Maple Roasted Roots • Coconut Cauliflower Chana

Barbecue-Baked Tofu with Mushrooms & Bell Peppers

Spaghetti Squash with Pinenut Parm • Fettuccini No-Fredo

Pesto White Bean Bowl • Green Coconut Milk Curry

Sesame Kale Soba • Chili Non-Carné with Pan-Seared Polenta

Portobello Burgers with Sunchoke Oven Fries & Homemade Ketchup

Millet-Stuffed Bell Peppers • Pinto's Refried Bean Burritos

The Good Shepherd's Pie • Luscious Lasagne • Millet & Mushroom Tourtière

If it weren't for my complete certainty that it wouldn't sell, I might have written a book called "Where Are the Vegetables?" It's what I often ask myself when I look at clients' diet diaries.

The precise quantities for optimum daily intake of vegetables varies depending on whom you're talking to: holistic nutritionists, naturopathic doctors, other foodie experts, or more allopathically-trained practitioners. One might say that 75% of your daily diet should be vegetables; another would encourage you to eat 3 cups of salad and 2 cups of cooked veg.

Never having been a big numbers person, when I prepare a plate of food I make sure at least two-thirds of it is covered in vegetables. For the most part, these entrées are vegetable-packed, or can be paired beautifully with raw or cooked veggies (just check the recipes' intros for suggestions). Also be sure to look up the Mouth-Watering Menu Ideas at the back of the book (starting on page 253) for complete meals, for nutritional balance, and for delicious flavor combinations.

ANDREW'S BUTTERNUT RISOTTO

Challenge convention with a dairy-free brown rice risotto that's rich and delicious. The brown rice takes longer to cook than white Arborio rice traditionally used in risotto, so be sure to use a lid and give it more time. And including a bit of margarine and soymilk with the smooth, roasted squash helps to give it a creamy deliciousness – you may roast the squash and garlic a day in advance if desired.

To prepare squash & garlic:

Drizzle the oil over top of garlic bulb. Place beside the squash in a baking pan and roast according to directions on page 90, removing garlic after 30 minutes.

Peel the garlic when cool enough to handle and transfer cloves to a small bowl. Mash with a fork until smooth and set aside.

Scoop out the flesh of squash when squash is done and cool enough to handle and transfer to a medium bowl. Mash with a fork or potato masher until smooth and set aside.

To prepare risotto:

Heat the stock in a small saucepan on a back burner on medium-high. Once warm, reduce heat to low so that it stays warm but won't evaporate as quickly. Heat the oil in a separate, heavy-bottomed saucepan or medium skillet on medium. Add the onions and allow them to sweat for 8 minutes, until translucent, taking care not to brown them. Add the rice and toast for 5 minutes.

Increase heat to medium-high and ladle enough stock over rice so rice is just covered. Adjust heat if necessary to continue simmering, stirring occasionally; do not let it boil or allow rice to stick.

Add another ladle of stock every few minutes, so there's always just enough liquid to cook rice. Once half of stock has been added to rice, add another 1–2 ladles stock, stir, cover, and reduce heat to low, allowing rice to cook for 15–25 minutes, until nearly done.

Increase heat to medium-low, uncover, stir in the non-dairy milk, and let most liquid simmer off (you don't want it runny) as you stir continually, then return heat to low.

Fold in the roasted garlic and squash (the suggested amounts are flexible – if you have additional roasted squash, you may add it according to taste). Gently stir in remaining ingredients (adding a small amount of salt to start as vegetable stock may be salty enough). Remove from heat, cover, and let stand for 5 minutes before serving.

MAKES ABOUT 6 SERVINGS. **GF, NF**

Roasted squash & garlic

2 tsp olive oil (plus extra [about 1 tbsp] for the squash)

1 bulb (about 6 large cloves) garlic, top sliced off

1 small (about 2¼ lb/1 kg) butternut squash, washed well, halved & seeded

Risotto

4 cups vegetable stock (see page 164)

1–2 tbsp olive oil

1 medium onion, diced

1½ cups sweet brown rice*

¼–½ cup organic non-dairy milk (unsweetened soymilk preferred)

1 bulb, mashed roasted garlic (from above)

1½–2 cups mashed roasted butternut squash (from above)

2 tsp fresh thyme leaves (or 1 tsp dried)

½–1 tsp sea salt, to taste

freshly ground black pepper to taste

1/3 cup chopped fresh parsley (flat-leaf Italian variety preferred)

1–2 tbsp non-dairy, non-GM margarine (I use Earth Balance Organic Whipped Buttery Spread)

* Sweet brown rice is best for this recipe as the grains' husks are removed and they will therefore cook faster and produce a creamier dish. But if sweet brown rice is unavailable, use short brown rice.

SOUTHERN BOWL: CHIPOTLE BLACK-EYED PEAS WITH MAPLE MASHED SWEET POTATOES AND COLLARD GREENS

How often do we hear black-eyed peas being talked about when it's not in reference to the pop group? This cute-looking legume is great because you can cook it from dry pretty quickly (relatively speaking). But it's the chipotle flavor that really makes the dish memorable. For a real Southern meal, serve this with Molasses Cornbread (page 134), yum!

1 cup dried black-eyed peas

2 tbsp olive oil

1 medium onion, diced

1 stalk celery, diced

1 small-medium zucchini, diced (about 1 cup)

3–4 medium cloves garlic, minced

2 bay leaves

1–2 minced chipotle peppers* or ½–1 tsp chipotle powder, to taste

¼ tsp ground allspice

1½–2 cups vegetable stock (see page 164) or filtered water

1 tsp sea salt

* If using whole peppers (I use organic dried peppers, but canned ones are also available), you can either cook them whole with the option of removing them later to reduce spiciness or mince 'em up to cook as directed.

CHIPOTLE BLACK-EYED PEAS

Soak the peas overnight in cold water or in just-boiled water for 1 hour.

Heat the oil in a 3-qt/L saucepan on medium or medium-high. Add the onions, celery, and zucchini, and sauté for 6 minutes, until onions begin to soften, stirring occasionally to prevent sticking.

Add the garlic and sauté for another 4 minutes. Stir in the bay leaves, chipotles, and allspice.

Drain and rinse soaked peas and add them to saucepan, along with stock or water.

Increase heat to bring to a boil. Once boiling, lower heat, cover partially, and simmer for 40 minutes, stirring occasionally. Add the salt, stir, and continue to cook for another 10–15 minutes, until peas are soft.

MAPLE MASHED SWEET POTATOES

Place a large pot of cold water on high heat to boil. Once boiling, add the sweet potatoes and ½ tsp salt and cook for about 12 minutes, until tender.

Remove from heat and drain. Return potatoes to pot and mash 'em real good, adding the milk, syrup, oil, remaining ¼ tsp salt, and pepper.

4 fist-sized orange-fleshed sweet potatoes, peeled & diced (about 5 cups)

¾ tsp sea salt

¼ cup organic non-dairy milk

2 tbsp maple syrup

2 tbsp non-hydrogenated coconut oil or olive oil

freshly ground black pepper to taste

COLLARD GREENS

Steam according to directions on page 89.

Distribute cooked greens evenly into 4 good-sized dinner bowls, followed by Mashed Sweet Potatoes, then Chipotle Black-Eyed Peas (recipes above).

1 bunch collard greens

MAKES ABOUT 4 SERVINGS.   GF, SF

MUSHROOM QUINOA PILAF

1 tbsp olive oil

1 small-medium onion, diced small

1 medium clove garlic, grated or minced

4 oz (114 g) cremini (brown) mushrooms, sliced (may substitute with oyster or white mushrooms)

1 cup quinoa, rinsed

1½ cups vegetable stock (see page 164)

1 tbsp minced fresh sage leaves (or 2 tsp dried)

1 tsp sea salt

½ cup sliced scallions or chives

This is another grain dish I got help from Andrew in creating. Embarrassingly, whenever I say pilaf it always comes out as "piaf," like the legendary French singer. Serve warm on a bed of greens. If you want this dish to have a fancier presentation, garnish with some cute little Enoki mushrooms.

Heat the oil in a medium-large skillet on medium-low. Add the onions and allow them to sweat for 5 minutes, being careful not to let them brown.

Add the garlic and cook for another 2 minutes. Add the mushrooms and cook for 4 minutes, stirring mixture, and allowing mushrooms to soften and release some of their liquid. Stir in the quinoa, stock, sage, and salt.

Increase heat to bring to a boil. Then reduce heat, cover, and simmer for about 15 minutes, until all liquid is absorbed. Remove from heat and let stand for 5 minutes before fluffing with a fork, then fold in scallions, and serve.

MAKES 4 SERVINGS. GF, SF, NF

◄— Maple Roasted Roots —►

This dish is a favorite on my blog, Domestic Affair, and a great way to enjoy grounding winter vegetables. For a simple weeknight supper, prep the veg in the morning (or the night before). When you get home from work, just preheat the oven, toss 'em with the glaze, and slide in the oven, preparing some greens and a simple grain or legume dish while the roots are roasting. If you have lots of roots left over, purée them for a roasted veg pasta sauce. Yum!

Preheat oven to 400°F (205°C). Toss the vegetables with the syrup, oil, vinegar, and thyme in a large bowl to disperse seasonings evenly.

Transfer onto 2 large, lightly-oiled baking pans, distributing evenly into one layer in each pan.

Roast for about 1 hour, removing pans from oven every 12 minutes or so to stir; halfway through the cooking time, toss roots with the salt and pepper. Roasting is complete when veggies are nice and tender. Serve hot.

MAKES ABOUT 8 SERVINGS.   GF, SF, NF (if omitting white potatoes)

16 cups chopped or cubed root vegetables*

½ cup maple syrup

⅓ cup olive oil (plus extra to coat pan)

2 tbsp balsamic vinegar (optional)

2 tsp fresh thyme leaves (or 1 tsp dried thyme)

1 tsp sea salt (or more to taste)

freshly ground black pepper to taste

For goodness sake, use organic produce so you don't have to fret about pesticides. Just scrub and rinse the organic veggies instead of peeling 'em (with the exception of squash, which you should peel); as for the garlic, use a bulb or two, and peel the cloves, but roast 'em whole.

**Root veggies can include winter squash, onions, garlic, beets (they add great color!), parsnips, carrots, potato, sweet potato, Jerusalem artichokes (see note on page 195), turnips, and/or celery root).*

COCONUT CAULIFLOWER CHANA

2 tbsp non-hydrogenated coconut oil or olive oil

2 medium-large onions, chopped

2 large carrots, chopped

3 large or 5 medium cloves garlic, minced

1 tbsp grated fresh ginger root

1–2 tbsp curry powder,* or to taste

¼ tsp cayenne pepper, or to taste

2 tsp sea salt

2 fist-sized orange-fleshed sweet potatoes (may substitute with regular potatoes), diced

3 cups diced cauliflower

1 red bell pepper, chopped

2½ cups cooked chickpeas (garbanzo beans) (or 2 [14-oz/398-mL] cans, drained & rinsed)

1 (14-oz/398-mL) can good quality coconut milk (not light version; also see recipe, page 108)

¼–½ cup filtered water (or more to thin sauce as desired)

¼ cup shredded unsweetened coconut

1 handful of chopped fresh cilantro leaves (for garnish)

Not all curry powder blends are created equal, so find one that you really like – it should include coriander, turmeric, cumin, cinnamon, black pepper, and maybe even cardamom.

I was inspired to create this recipe when I got home after a snowy, wet, and dreary mid-January day. This curry is rich and warming with coconut milk and all those spices. The sweet potatoes, red bell peppers, and coconut make it pleasantly sweet. Serve over brown basmati rice and fresh spinach.

Heat the oil in a soup pot on medium. Add the onions and sauté for about 5 minutes.

Add the carrots, garlic, ginger, curry powder, cayenne, and salt, and sauté for another 5 minutes. Stir in the sweet potatoes, cauliflower, red pepper, chickpeas, coconut milk, water, and shredded coconut, cover, and cook for about 15 minutes, stirring occasionally, until sweet potatoes are soft.

Remove from heat, garnish with cilantro, and serve hot.

MAKES 6–8 SERVINGS.　**GF, SF**

If your vegetables are organic, scrub them really well before chopping and don't bother to peel them, as there are lots of nutrients in the skin. If you are using conventional produce, you're better off peeling it to reduce pesticide exposure.

BARBECUE~BAKED TOFU WITH MUSHROOMS AND BELL PEPPERS

Whoever says tofu is boring hasn't tried this dish. I eat it for dinner with a fresh salad and some steamed grains, but it's also nice as a cold lunch the next day in a pita with fresh veggies. This barbecue sauce can spice up many different vegetables – use it in place of an overly-sugary store-bought sauce any time!

Place the tofu in a large bowl with green pepper, onions, and mushrooms, and gently toss with the tamari and oil using a silicone spatula. Allow to marinate for at least 30 minutes, or up to 4 hours.

Mix together all sauce ingredients in a small bowl. Set aside to allow all those flavors to get to know each other.

Preheat oven to 450°F (230°C).

Transfer marinated tofu and vegetables with marinade into a 9x13-in (23x30-cm) baking dish, or a similarly large, shallow baking dish, big enough for everything to rest in 1 layer.

Bake for 15 minutes.

Remove from oven, spoon on sauce, and gently toss to coat evenly. Return to oven and bake for another 15 minutes, or until lightly browned.

Remove from oven and let sit a few minutes to serve warm, not hot.

MAKES ABOUT 3 SERVINGS. GF

1 lb (454 g) firm (or extra firm) tofu, cut into ¾–in (2-cm) cubes & patted dry

1 green bell pepper, cut into bite-sized triangles

2 small onions, quartered lengthwise, then halved widthwise

4 oz (115 g) cremini (brown) or white mushrooms, halved or quartered (depending on size)

¼ cup tamari soy sauce

1 tbsp olive oil

Sauce

3 tbsp tomato paste

1 tbsp organic natural peanut butter

1 tbsp apple cider vinegar

2 tsp chili powder

1 tsp prepared mustard

1 tsp organic blackstrap molasses

2 medium cloves garlic, pressed or grated

$\frac{1}{8}$ tsp cayenne pepper (or to taste)

freshly ground black pepper to taste

⤙ SPAGHETTI SQUASH WITH PINENUT PARM ⤚

2¼ lb (1 kg) spaghetti squash

Mum's Vegetable Tomato Sauce

3 tbsp olive oil

2 medium or 1 large onion, chopped

2 medium cloves garlic, minced or pressed

8 oz (230 g) mushrooms, sliced (cremini [brown], Portobello, or white)

1 bell pepper, chopped (any color)

1 medium zucchini, chopped

1 (28-oz/796-mL) can crushed tomatoes

1 tbsp fresh oregano leaves (or 2 tsp dried), minced

1 tbsp fresh basil leaves (or 1 tsp dried), minced

1 tbsp fresh rosemary leaves (or 1 tsp dried), minced

1 tsp sea salt

Pinenut Parm

¼ cup pine nuts

1 tbsp nutritional yeast

¼ tsp sea salt

Squash that's been baked up to resemble spaghetti noodles is a nice change from the real thing – and more nutrient-dense than pasta, too. This tomato sauce (which can certainly be made a day or two in advance) is the one my mum's been making my whole life – it's delicious, and vegetable-packed.

Serve with a fresh salad, or steamed rapini (or broccoli) tossed with olive oil and crushed garlic.

Roast the squash according to directions on page 90 (and make the tomato sauce as it's roasting [see below]). Once squash is done and just cool enough to handle, scoop flesh into colander, cover with a pot lid or a plate (to keep warm), and allow to drain into a large bowl.

To prepare sauce:
Heat the oil in a 3-qt/L saucepan on medium heat. Add the onions and sauté for about 8 minutes, until softened. Add the garlic and mushrooms and sauté for another 5 minutes. Add the bell pepper and zucchini and sauté for another 5 minutes.

Pour in crushed tomatoes and reduce heat if necessary to simmer for 10 minutes. Stir in the oregano, basil, rosemary, and salt, cover, and simmer on low heat for another 20–60 minutes (the longer the better).

To prepare parm:
Toast pine nuts in a small skillet for about 5 minutes, until golden (or not, toasting is optional). Set aside to cool for 5–10 minutes, then grind with nutritional yeast and salt in a clean coffee grinder just until it's a coarse meal, not a paste. (Any leftovers can be stored in an airtight container in fridge for up to 3 weeks.)

To assemble:
Portion drained squash into bowls (or onto plates). Pour sauce on top and garnish with parm.

MAKES 4–5 SERVINGS.   GF, SF

⬤ FETTUCCINI NO~FREDO ⬤

*You want pasta with a rich alfredo-like sauce but without the dairy? No problem!
I'm glad to say I've figured it out. If you're avoiding soy, filtered water or rice milk
can replace the soymilk, but be a bit more generous with the tahini.*

Place a large pot of cold water on high heat to boil. Once boiling, add the noodles and a few shakes of salt and cook pasta according to package directions, until *al dente*, then drain and set aside.

Meanwhile, heat oil in a large saucepan on medium-high. Add the onion and garlic and sauté for about 8 minutes, stirring often to prevent browning.

Combine the soymilk, tahini, salt, and nutmeg in a small bowl, then pour the mixture into the skillet. Grind in the pepper.

Reduce heat to medium and cook for another 5 minutes.

Stir in the parsley and lemon juice, and heat for another minute.

Transfer pasta in a large bowl and pour sauce over top, to desired sauciness (there may be some sauce leftover – use it as a veggie dip if you like), and toss.

Serve hot, garnished with additional parsley.

MAKES ABOUT 3 SERVINGS. GF, NF

½ lb (227 g) brown rice fettuccini (or kamut/spelt soba noodles for the wheat-freebies, or whole wheat fettuccini for those who can tolerate it)

1 tbsp olive oil

¾ cup puréed onion (about 1 small-medium onion)

3 cloves garlic, grated or pressed

1½ cups organic unsweetened soymilk

¾ cup tahini (raw preferred)

1½ tsp sea salt

¼ tsp nutmeg

freshly ground black pepper to taste

¼ cup minced fresh parsley (plus extra for garnish)

2 tbsp fresh lemon juice

— PESTO WHITE BEAN BOWL —

1½ cups cooked cannollini (white kidney) or navy beans (or 1 [14-oz/398-mL] can, drained & rinsed)

¼ cup basil or cilantro pesto (see pages 156 or 157; or a non-dairy store-bought brand)

¼ tsp sea salt

freshly ground black pepper to taste

4 small bunches baby bok choy, chopped (or 4 cups organic baby spinach)

2 cups cooked quinoa* (or another grain like brown rice or millet) (see page 91)

2 tbsp flax seed oil or olive oil (optional, depending on oiliness of pesto)

If you don't already have quinoa cooked (yay, leftovers!), you'll want to start cooking it first.

This meal in a bowl is quick to put together and tastes great at room temperature for lunch or dinner out of the house. Both white beans and quinoa are great sources of protein, calcium, magnesium, and fiber. The bok choy and pesto add a fresh taste to the meal. Feel free to add a grated clove of garlic, if that's your kind of thing, or any other vegetables you may have on hand (like grated carrots or sliced red bell peppers). Garnish with hulled hemp seeds if you've got them on hand.

Gently combine the beans, pesto, salt, and pepper in a medium bowl.

Portion the cooked quinoa equally between two dinner bowls (or travel containers). Top with the bok choy, then the pestoed beans, and drizzle with the oil and season with additional salt and pepper if desired.

MAKES 2 SERVINGS.   GF, SF, NF

GREEN COCONUT MILK CURRY

My mum's partner, David, is one of the best cooks I know. He is inspired by many Asian culinary traditions and seems to be able to prepare entire feasts effortlessly. In fact, he's such a good cook that after almost 25 years together my mother gets a bit flustered when she is responsible for the dinner prep. It was a bit of a struggle to get David to write down a recipe with actual measurements because he's an intuitive cook, but eventually it worked out.

Serve this over steamed brown rice or another grain (see page 91) and marinated and grilled tempeh (page 122).

Heat the oil in a 3-qt/L saucepan on medium. Add the onion and sauté for about 8 minutes, until softened.

Bruise the lemongrass stalk with side of chef's knife.

Add the garlic, ginger, chili, turmeric, and salt, and sauté for just 15 seconds before adding the coconut milk, water, bruised lemongrass, green pepper, leek, zucchini, green beans, snow peas, and salt. Reduce heat to simmer for about 15 minutes, until veggies are cooked. Don't cover or allow to boil, as coconut milk will separate.

Remove lemongrass, stir in lime juice, and serve, garnished with cilantro or green onion.

MAKES 4–5 SERVINGS. GF, SF

1 tbsp non-hydrogenated co-conut oil

1 medium onion, cut in wedges

2 stalks fresh lemongrass, outer leaves & upper green stalks removed

2 medium cloves garlic, pressed

2 tsp grated or minced fresh ginger root

1 green chili (or to taste), chopped

¼ tsp turmeric

½ tsp sea salt

1 (14-oz/398-mL) can good-quality coconut milk (not light version)

1 cup filtered water

1 green bell pepper, cut in triangles

1 medium leek, chopped (tough upper stalks removed)

1 medium zucchini, cubed

1 cup green beans

½ cup snow peas

¾ tsp sea salt

juice of ½ a lime

chopped fresh cilantro leaves or green onion (for garnish)

⟶ SESAME KALE SOBA ⟵

1 large bunch green or black kale (about 8 oz/227 g)

1 (8-oz/227 g) pkg soba noodles (or spaghetti noodles if unavailable – preferably wheat-free)

3 tbsp tamari or shoyu soy sauce

3 tbsp toasted sesame oil

1 large clove garlic,* grated or pressed

½ tsp dulse powder (optional)

freshly ground black pepper* to taste (a few generous twists)

¼ cup arame (a dark sea veggie), soaked for 5 minutes until soft, then drained (optional)

3 tbsp unhulled sesame seeds

* You can mix it up a little by using 1 tsp grated fresh ginger in lieu of garlic or replace a touch of wasabi paste for black pepper.

Have you heard? You are supposed to have at least four servings of dark leafy greens each week – that includes spinach, kale, and Swiss chard. This leafy green used here is high in calcium (more so when it's been cooked), iron, folic acid, and vitamins C and A. This recipe's great because it's satisfying and flavorful, and it's so darn quick and simple to make! It's also a dish that will incorporate nutritious sea vegetables (i.e. seaweeds) into your diet. Can be eaten hot or cold (makes a great out-of-the-house meal).

Place a large pot of water on high heat to boil. Meanwhile, wash the kale thoroughly, remove the ends of the stems and discard, then chop kale to preferred size.

Add the noodles to boiling water and cook for 4 minutes.

Stir in the kale, and continue cooking until noodles are *al dente*, then drain and transfer noodles and kale to a large bowl and set aside.

Combine the tamari or shoyu, oil, garlic, dulse, and pepper in a small bowl, mix well, then pour on top of noodles and kale.

Toss gently with the arame and sesame seeds, and serve.

MAKES ABOUT 3 SERVINGS.   GF, NF

Sesame Kale Soba (page 192)

jae's All-Out Daily Deluxe salad (page 147)
and Green Pea Soup (page 172)

Portobello Burger with Sunchoke Oven Fries
& Homemade Ketchup (pages 194-195)

CHILI NON~CARNÉ WITH PAN~SEARED POLENTA

Kidney beans have the most fiber of any legume (15 g per cup), so why not throw on a pot of chili tonight? I like to eat my chili on a bed of chopped organic romaine lettuce or spinach, with cubes of avocado and chopped fresh cilantro leaves on top. Like many stews, this dish tastes better on the second day.

Heat the oil in a large pot on medium-high. Add the onions and sauté for about 8 minutes, until translucent. Toss in the garlic, bell pepper, chili powder, cumin, coriander, cayenne or chipotle pepper, cinnamon, and oregano, and sauté for another few minutes, adding a splash of water if necessary to avoid sticking.

Add the remaining ingredients and stir occasionally until heated through, about 10 minutes.

To prepare polenta:
Mix the cornmeal and 1½ cups water in a small bowl.

Bring the remaining 1½ cups water to a boil in a 3-qt/L saucepan. Add the salt and garlic. Once boiling, slowly stir in soaked cornmeal mixture.

Cook uncovered on medium-low heat for 20–30 minutes, stirring frequently to prevent scorching, until thick and smooth. It's done when you can jam a spoon into it and it'll stand on its own.

Stir in the oil and remove from heat. Using a silicone spatula, transfer polenta to a parchment-lined baking pan, smoothing it evenly, and allowing to set for 30–45 minutes.

Once set, cut polenta into squares or triangles (or with cookie cutters or the rim of a mug or glass).

Lightly oil a skillet and place on medium-high heat. Carefully place polenta pieces in skillet (you'll need to do this in batches) and fry for 3–4 minutes on each side until golden and brown at edges. Repeat until all polenta pieces are fried. Serve alongside the Chili Non-Carné.

MAKES 4–6 SERVINGS.   GF, SF

1 tbsp olive oil

2 medium onions, chopped

3–4 medium cloves garlic, minced

1 medium-large bell pepper, diced (any color)

1 tbsp chili powder

1 tbsp ground cumin

1 tbsp ground coriander

¼–½ tsp cayenne pepper or chipotle pepper powder

½ tsp cinnamon

½ tsp dried oregano

3 cups cooked kidney beans (or ½ kidney & ½ black or pinto beans)

1 cup frozen organic, non-GM corn kernels, thawed

1 (28-oz/796-mL) can organic tomatoes (diced or crushed, in juices)

2 tsp sea salt (or more to taste)

If you opt not to make the polenta, serve the chili with a handful of organic tortilla chips.

Polenta

1 cup non-GM cornmeal

3 cups filtered water (cold or room temperature)

1 tsp sea salt

1–2 cloves garlic, pressed or grated (optional)

1 tbsp olive oil (plus extra for frying)

PORTOBELLO BURGERS WITH SUNCHOKE OVEN FRIES AND HOMEMADE KETCHUP

It was my friend Paul who first served me Portobello mushrooms like this – no need to mess around with crumbly patties to get something burgerish.

4 Portobello mushrooms, 4–5 in (10–12½ cm) diameter (or 6 at 3–3½ in [7½–8 cm] diameter)

¼ cup tamari or shoyu soy sauce

3 large or 5 medium cloves garlic, pressed or grated

4 tsp olive oil (plus extra for frying)

2 tsp balsamic or apple cider vinegar

several dashes of your favorite hot sauce or ¼ tsp cayenne pepper (optional)

4 mini or 2 regular-sized fresh whole-grain pitas (in lieu of buns)

Possible burger toppings

additional grilled marinated vegetables, fresh greens, sliced tomato, caramelized onions, fresh sprouts, pickles, tahini or pumpkin seed butter, pesto, Homemade Ketchup (next page), mustard....

PORTOBELLO BURGERS

Gently slice or break off the mushroom stems and rinse caps quickly. Whisk together the tamari or shoyu, garlic, oil, vinegar, and hot sauce or cayenne in a bowl to make marinade.

Brush the mushroom caps with marinade and place them, tops down, in a shallow dish. Pour the remaining marinade evenly over mushrooms, ensuring each gets its share of garlic. Allow to sit, covered, for 30 minutes to 2 hours.

Lightly oil a skillet or barbecue set at medium-high heat. Place mushrooms, tops down, in a skillet or on a grill, brushing on any marinade that's dripped off. Cook for about 5 minutes, then flip to other side and cook for another 4 minutes until they're tender when you poke them. (Extra marinade can be stored in an airtight container in fridge for up to 1 week and used to flavor veggies, tempeh, or tofu.)

Toast the pitas if desired and cut in half. Place each mushroom cap in each mini-pita or pita-half and serve, stuffed with any topping combination that inspires you.

MAKES 2–4 SERVINGS.

GF (if using GF pitas), NF (if omitting cayenne & ketchup)

SUNCHOKE OVEN FRIES

What a treat. These fries fit nicely into the good-tasting and good-for-you categories. You can put them raw in salads, but here's how I like 'em best. Serve alongside Portobello Burgers, with or without ketchup (see below).

Preheat oven to 375°F (190°C). Cut the sunchokes into wedges (as best you can as they're irregularly shaped). Toss with the oil, salt, thyme, and garlic or chipotle powder in a large bowl to evenly coat with seasonings.

Transfer to a baking sheet, distributing them evenly, and bake for about 30 minutes (turning once at 15 minutes), until golden brown and crisp on edges and soft inside.

MAKES 2 SERVINGS.

* Jerusalem artichokes, also called sunchokes, have nothing to do with regular artichokes, nor do they come from Jerusalem (they are native of North America). They look like a cross between a small potato and ginger root and have a sweet flavor, but here's why you're gonna love 'em: they're said to be good for diabetics (as they're an amazing source of inulin, a natural fructose that's medicinal for those with diabetes), lung conditions (like asthma), and contain vitamins A, B-complex, potassium, iron, calcium, and magnesium, and, unlike other root vegetables, they contain no starch!

4 cups sunchokes,* scrubbed (not peeled)

2 tbsp olive oil

½ tsp sea salt

1 tsp fresh thyme (or ½ tsp dried)

1 clove garlic, minced, or 1 pinch chipotle pepper powder (optional)

HOMEMADE KETCHUP

Make this with organic tomato paste and you've got yourself a much higher quality condiment than the conventional stuff at the grocery store, which typically contains too much sugar.

Place all the ingredients but the tomato paste in a small saucepan on high heat to bring to a boil. Once boiling, reduce heat to low, stir in the paste, cover, and cook for about 8 minutes.

Stores in a jar in fridge for up to 2 weeks, or in freezer for up to 3 months.

MAKES 1 CUP.

¼ cup apple cider vinegar

¼ cup filtered water

1 tsp maple syrup, brown rice syrup, or barley malt

½ tsp sea salt

½ tsp ground cumin

½ tsp dried oregano

¼ tsp mustard powder

¼ tsp nutmeg

freshly ground pepper to taste

1 clove garlic, grated or pressed

1 (5½-oz/156-mL) can tomato paste

⟐ MILLET~STUFFED BELL PEPPERS ⟐

1 tbsp olive oil

2 medium onions, finely chopped

2–3 cloves garlic, minced

2 tbsp tamari soy sauce

2 tsp dried thyme (or 1 tbsp fresh)

1 tsp dried rosemary (or 2 tsp fresh)

½ tsp celery seed

freshly ground black pepper to taste

4 cups cooked millet (may substitute with quinoa or brown rice)

¾ cup tahini

¾ cup ground raw pumpkin or sunflower seeds

up to ¼ cup filtered water or vegetable stock (see page 164)

½ cup minced fresh parsley leaves

6–8 organic medium-large bell peppers

This tasty dish is wonderful for vegetarians at winter feasts. The millet, tahini, and raw seeds provide an impressive amount of protein, and serving it along-side beans will make the protein complete. Personally, I love its rich taste so much that I don't just wait for Thanksgiving and Christmas; I make it as often as I think of it. Mmmmm!

Serve with gravy (see pages 159–160), Maple Roasted Roots (page 185), Maple Mashed Sweet Potatoes (page 183), The Good Shepherd's Pie (page 198), or Beet & Green Bean Toss (page 154).

Preheat oven to 375°F (190°C).

Heat the oil in a 3-qt/L saucepan on medium-high. Add the onions and sauté for 8 minutes, until they begin to soften. Add the garlic, tamari, thyme, rosemary, celery seed, and pepper, and sauté for another 5 minutes.

Combine the millet, tahini, and seeds in a large bowl and mix well. Transfer to saucepan and cook until well heated, stirring occasionally; you'll likely want to add a few splashes of water or stock to prevent sticking.

Turn off heat and stir in the parsley. Adjust seasonings to taste (sometimes I add some extra thyme and rosemary).

Slice tops off the bell peppers, remove the core, seeds, and veins, and stuff peppers with millet mixture. Discard or compost bell pepper tops (or enjoy as a raw snack).

Place 1-in (2½-cm) water in a baking pan. Place peppers upright (they must stay upright to keep stuffing from getting soggy) in pan and bake for 25–30 minutes, until peppers are soft.

MAKES 6–8 SERVINGS.   GF

⟡ PINTO'S REFRIED BEAN BURRITOS ⟡

My former Peterborough housemate Derek Pinto used to make refried beans, and though he jotted down the recipe for me, I unfortunately lost it after I moved. Here's what I came up with on his behalf.

Heat the oil in a large pot on medium. Add the onions, chili powder, cumin, and coriander and sauté for about 5 minutes. Add the garlic and chili flakes or cayenne and continue to sauté until onions are soft and translucent (add a few splashes of water if needed to prevent sticking).

Stir in the beans, stock or water, and salt and cook for a few minutes until heated through.

Remove from heat, allow to cool slightly, then mash (using a potato masher, or a hand blender if you want a very smooth consistency) to desired consistency.

Stir in the lime juice and re-heat for another few minutes.

Evenly portion fillings down center of each tortilla, leaving about a 1-in (2 ½-cm) space on top and bottom. Fold the top and bottom edges over filling and roll up. Repeat until all tortillas and fillings are used. Enjoy immediately.

MAKES 8 MEDIUM BURRITOS (OR 6 LARGER BURRITOS).
 GF (if using GF tortillas), SF

**Refried beans
(makes 4 cups)**

2 tbsp olive oil

1 medium onion, minced

1 tsp chili powder

1 tsp ground cumin

½ tsp ground coriander

3–4 cloves garlic, minced

½ tsp chili flakes or ¼ tsp cayenne pepper, to taste

4 cups cooked pinto beans (may substitute with black beans)

½ cup (or more) vegetable stock (see page 164) or filtered water

2 tsp sea salt

juice of ½ a lime

Additional fillings

2 ⅔ cups cooked brown rice or quinoa

2–4 cups shredded lettuce

1 bell pepper, cored & sliced

½ cup chopped fresh cilantro leaves

Fresh Summer Salsa (page 144)

Great Guacamole (page 142) or 2 ripe avocados, sliced

8 large whole grain tortillas,* lightly warmed or at room temperature

* I like using Food for Life's Ezekiel 4:9 brand of organic sprouted grain tortillas for burritos and wraps. Defrost them and then toast quickly in a skillet to avoid making them too tough to wrap.

The Good Shepherd's Pie

I'll let you in on a little secret—shepherd's pie was traditionally made with left-over lamb. I used to make a version with grated tofu, but in the interest of not overloading our systems with soy products and getting more high-fiber, blood-sugar-balancing lentils in our diets, I came up with this even more virtuous shepherd's pie. Serve with steamed greens and roasted squash (see page 90).

Potatoes

4 fist-sized organic/non-GM potatoes (Yukon Gold preferred) (about 2¼ lb/1 kg), peeled & chopped

½ cup organic non-dairy milk

3 tbsp olive oil

3/4 tsp sea salt

Lentils

1¼ cup uncooked green lentils

2½ cups vegetable stock (see page 164) or filtered water

Vegetable filling

1–2 tbsp olive oil (plus extra to coat dish & finish casserole)

2 medium onions, diced

3 medium carrots, (peeled if not organic) diced

5 cremini (brown) mushrooms, sliced

6-in (15-cm) long zucchini or 2 stalks celery, diced

3 medium-large cloves garlic, minced or pressed

1½ tsp dried thyme

1 tsp ground coriander

1 tsp sea salt

freshly ground black pepper to taste

3 tbsp tomato paste

To prepare potatoes:

Place a large pot of cold, lightly-salted water with potatoes on high heat. Once boiling, reduce heat to simmer and cook for 10–15 minutes, until potatoes are soft, but not falling apart. Drain, then mash potatoes with milk, oil, and salt. Set aside.

To prepare lentils (can be simultaneous with potatoes):

Combine lentils with stock or water in a saucepan on high heat. Once boiling, reduce heat to simmer, cover, and cook for 35–45 minutes, stirring occasionally, until lentils are soft but not falling apart.

To prepare vegetable filling & pie:

Preheat oven to 350°F (180°C).

Heat the oil in a large skillet or medium saucepan on medium. Add the onions and sauté for about 7 minutes. Add carrots and sauté for another 5 minutes. Add the zucchini or celery, mushrooms, garlic, thyme, coriander, salt, and pepper and sauté for another 5 minutes, until everything is soft.

Stir in the tomato paste (a splash of water may be needed to prevent sticking) and cooked lentils and stir to combine. Transfer the lentil-veg mixture into a 3-qt/L lightly-oiled casserole dish (or two 1½-qt/L dishes), distributing mixture evenly, then top with the mashed potatoes, smoothing into an even layer.

Drizzle additional oil on top of casserole.

Bake for 20–25 minutes, until heated through – you'll want to turn on broiler for the remaining 5 minutes to brown the top, but watch that it doesn't burn!

Remove from oven and allow to stand for 5 minutes before serving.

MAKES ABOUT 8 SERVINGS.   GF, SF

⟵ LUSCIOUS LASAGNE ⟶

I don't know if I'd ever had a lasagne so jam-packed with vegetables before this recipe came along. Preparation of this dish requires some time, but it's well worth it. It can be prepared (unbaked) a day in advance and stored in the fridge – the next day, just slide it straight into the oven and increase the baking time to 1 hour and 15 minutes. Serve it up with a fresh green salad and maybe some garlic bread.

Preheat oven to 375°F (190°C).

Toss the eggplants in the 2 tbsp oil and the 1 tsp salt. Transfer to 2 parchment-lined lightly oiled baking sheets, laying rounds in 1 layer, and roast for 30 minutes, turning after 15 minutes. Separate out the largest and prettiest 8 rounds for the top layer of the dish.

Meanwhile, to make the sauce, heat the 1 tbsp oil in a 3-qt/L skillet on medium-high. Add the onions and sauté for about 8 minutes, until softened (add a splash of water if needed to prevent sticking). Toss in the mushrooms and garlic, and sauté for another 6 minutes. Add the tomatoes, water or stock, basil, marjoram, rosemary, and salt, and stir to combine. Cover and reduce heat to low to simmer, stirring occasionally, for 30 minutes.

To make "ricotta," add the tofu, soymilk, and salt to a food processor or blender and give it a whirl for about 1 minute, until it reaches a smooth, uniform consistency (similar to ricotta cheese).

Layer it all up in a lightly oiled 9x13-in (23x33-cm) glass baking dish: To begin, lay down enough noodles to sit flat on the bottom of the dish. Lay down half the eggplant rounds (not counting the 8 you reserved earlier) on the noodles. Spread 1½ cups tomato sauce evenly over the eggplant, then lay down half the zucchini over sauce, spread half the ricotta over zucchini, and lay down half the spinach over ricotta. Repeat the layering: noodles, eggplant, then 2 cups sauce, rest of zucchini, rest of ricotta, and other half of spinach. Put down one final layer of noodles, the 8 reserved eggplant rounds, and finally, the remaining 1½ cups sauce. Cover the top with aluminum foil. (At this point you could slide the dish in the fridge and wait to bake it up until tomorrow or the next day.)

Bake for about 55 minutes (1 hour and 15 minutes if stored in fridge), until heated through and zucchinis are soft. Uncover and bake for another 10 minutes to brown top.

Remove from oven and allow to stand for at least 5 minutes before serving.

MAKES 8–12 SERVINGS.   **GF**

2 large eggplants (about 2 lb [908 g]), sliced in ¼-in (1-cm) thick rounds

2 tbsp olive oil (plus extra to coat pan)

1 tsp sea salt

Sauce

1 tbsp olive oil

1 medium onion, chopped

8 oz (227 g) mushrooms, sliced (optional)

3–4 medium cloves garlic, minced

1 (28-oz/796-mL) can crushed tomatoes

¼–½ cup filtered water or vegetable stock (see page 164)

2 tsp dried basil (or 2 tbsp fresh)

1 tsp dried marjoram

1 tsp dried rosemary

1 tsp sea salt

"Ricotta"

1 lb (454 g) firm tofu, crumbled

1 cup organic soymilk (unsweetened preferred)

1 tsp sea salt

10 oz (280 g) brown rice lasagna noodles, cooked for about 10–12 minutes

4 – 5-in (13-cm) long zucchinis (about ¾ lb/340 g), sliced lengthwise ⅛-in (¼-cm) thick (an optional layer)

2 cups spinach leaves, rinsed

MILLET AND MUSHROOM TOURTIÈRE

Crust

3 cups whole spelt flour (or 2½ cups light spelt flour & ½ cup oat bran)

1 tsp sea salt

1 cup cold non-hydrogenated coconut oil, or olive or sunflower oil

2–4 tbsp cold organic non-dairy milk or ice water

Filling

1 tbsp olive oil

1 large or 2 medium onions, diced small

½ lb (227 g) mushrooms, sliced

3 medium cloves garlic, minced or pressed

3 tbsp tamari soy sauce

½ tsp dried sage (or 1 tsp minced fresh leaves)

½ tsp dried savory

½ tsp ground cloves

¼ tsp cinnamon

¼ tsp dried rosemary (or ½ tsp minced fresh leaves)

¼ tsp dried thyme (or ½ tsp minced fresh leaves)

freshly ground black pepper to taste (a few generous twists)

¼ cup chopped fresh parsley leaves (Italian, flat-leaf preferred)

2½ cups cooked millet (see page 91)

A traditional Québecois dish served at Christmas or New Year's, turned vegan. I was introduced to this delicious recipe when I worked in the kitchen at the restaurant Aux Vivres in Montreal. Serve with gravy (see pages 159–160) and steamed vegetables or a fresh salad.

To prepare crust:

Pulse the flour and salt in a food processor or blender to combine. Add the oil and pulse until the mixture looks like coarse cornmeal. Continue pulsing and slowly add the soymilk or water, until a ball of dough is formed.

Remove from processor and divide the dough into 2 even pieces. Roll out 1 piece on a clean, floured surface (or between 2 pieces of parchment paper) and gently fit into a 9-in (23-cm) pie plate. Trim off edges, prick the bottom and sides with a fork, and cover with plastic wrap or wax or parchment paper. Roll out second piece the same way and set on a flat plate, covered with plastic wrap or wax or parchment paper. Place both pieces of dough in fridge until needed.

To prepare filling:

Heat the oil in a large skillet on medium. Add the onions and cook slowly to caramelize, stirring continually for about 20–30 minutes, until soft and caramel in color but not crispy. Add the mushrooms and garlic and cook for another 10 minutes, stirring occasionally. Stir in remaining ingredients and cook until warmed through. Adjust tamari to taste.

To assemble pie:

Preheat oven to 350°F (180°C). Remove the dough from fridge and uncover. Transfer filling into the pie shell. Smooth top into a slight dome. Gently place the other piece of dough on top, trimming off any excess at edges, and press edges down with a fork to seal. Prick top a few times with a fork or cut in some pretty holes with a sharp paring knife.

Bake for 20 minutes, until top crust is set and begins to brown. Allow to cool slightly (about 10 minutes) before serving.

MAKES 6 SERVINGS.   NF

CHAPTER

19

CAKES, PIES AND CRUMBLES

TIPS FOR CAKE BAKING & DECORATING

Baking

To start, be sure to read through the general baking guidelines in chapter ten.

• Prep your pans first (so the batter doesn't sit around) with the baking powder and/or soda activated, before it goes in the oven.

• Line the bottom of pans with parchment paper (cut to fit) to reduce the likelihood of breaking the baked cakes as they are removed from pans.

• Whisk, or better yet, sift the dry ingredients before adding the wet ingredients. This will thoroughly combine all the dry ingredients and break up any clumps.

• Gently combine wet and dry ingredients with a silicone spatula – the cakes will be lighter and have a nicer texture.

• Avoid over-mixing the batter; otherwise, gluten develops and cakes won't rise as well.

• Do not open the oven door until cakes are done, or they will likely deflate, losing their cute domed tops.

• Use an oven thermometer to make sure your oven temperature is accurate, and adjust dial if it's not. (Most ovens are, in fact, off by anywhere from 5–30°F [5–20°C].)

• Allow the baked cakes to cool for 10 minutes before removing from pans. This will allow them enough time to shrink away from the sides of the pans a bit (but don't leave them in the pan for too long or they will be harder to remove).

• To remove each cake, place an inverted plate on top of the pan, turn pan with the plate upside down onto the countertop. Give pan a firm tap (or even a good shake), then lift off pan and replace with another plate (a flat one – if plate is concaved, the cake will cave in) on top of the now bottom-up cake. Flip plates with cake (sandwiched in between) over again (so cake is now right-side up) removing plate that is now on top – this is far less complicated that it sounds.

Frosting

• Allow the cake to cool completely before frosting.

• Use a metal or silicone spatula or a dinner knife to apply the icing.

• Spread a very thin layer of icing over cake, and then refrigerate cake for 10 minutes (this is called a "crumb coat": because it should seal in any crumbs so they don't poke through the final layer of icing). Remove cake from fridge and apply rest of icing, starting from center top and working your way out to and down the sides.

• For a smoother finish, dip a spatula in hot water and then shake any excess water off before frosting.

- Use the back of a spoon to create wavy peaks in the icing if you wish.
- Be creative! Garnish cake however you'd like (see below for ideas).
- Cakes are best stored (covered) in the fridge, and served at room temperature.

To cut the cake
- Use a sharp (non-serrated) knife.
- Wipe off any excess icing and dip in warm water between cuts for extra smoothness and ease.

Tools every cake baker should have
- Thin, metal offset spatula (not the wide kind for flipping pancakes)
- Lazy susan (for frosting)
- Piping bag, or a sandwich bag (with a small corner piece cut off to pipe on icing)

Decorations to try
- Cocoa powder or powdered sugar (organic and fair trade preferred) passed through a fine mesh strainer
- Fresh or dried fruit, sliced
- Unsweetened shredded coconut, shaved non-dairy chocolate (organic and fair trade preferred)
- Slivered and/or whole almonds, or other nuts and/or seeds
- Well-washed small plastic toys (not to be eaten – with supervision or for adults only!)
- Well-washed Scrabble pieces to spell words (again, for adults only – this is an idea I got from *Vegan Cupcakes Take Over the World*)

THE NEW CLASSIC CHOCOLATE CAKE

Cakes

3 cups light spelt flour

2 cups organic sugar*

²⁄₃ cup cocoa powder* (Dutch-processed if possible) (plus extra to dust pans)

2 tsp baking soda

1 tsp sea salt

2 cups organic non-dairy milk, strong-brewed coffee (cold),* or filtered water

1 (scant) cup softened non-hydrogenated coconut oil or sunflower oil (plus extra to coat pans)

1 tbsp pure vanilla extract

3 tbsp apple cider vinegar

Chocolate ganache

16 oz (454 g) non-dairy bitter- or semi-sweet chocolate,* finely chopped

1½ cups good-quality coconut milk (canned, non-light version, or see page 108) or organic soymilk

2 tbsp agave nectar

1 tsp pure vanilla extract

You'd be hard-pressed to find a two-layer chocolate cake as simple and satisfying as this one. Remember that elementary school volcano project? The one where you made a hollow, volcano-looking structure, shook some baking soda inside, then poured in red-colored vinegar, and it all came bubbling out? The science in this recipe is similar: adding vinegar to the batter creates a noticeable baking soda reaction which gives the cake its lightness – or buoyancy, if you will. No eggs required. See pages 202–203 for cake baking tips.

To prepare cakes:

Preheat oven to 375°F (190°C). Prepare two 9-in (23-cm) cake pans with a light coating of oil and a dusting of cocoa (instead of flour). If you wanna be guaranteed easy release of cakes from pans, oil them, then line with a circle of parchment paper, which you should oil before dusting with cocoa.

Whisk together the flour, sugar, cocoa, baking soda, and salt in a large bowl. Pour in the milk, coffee, or water, and oil and vanilla. Mix with a silicone spatula just until all flour is absorbed. Add the vinegar and stir quickly – you'll see pale swirls as it reacts with baking soda. Stir just until vinegar is evenly distributed throughout batter, and immediately pour batter evenly into pans.

Bake for about 30 minutes, until a toothpick inserted in center come out clean.

Remove from oven and allow to cool in pans for 10 minutes before transferring to a rack to cool. Peel parchment paper lining off the bottoms.

To prepare chocolate ganache:

Place the chocolate in a heatproof bowl (no plastic!) and set aside.

Pour the coconut milk or soymilk and agave nectar into a small saucepan on medium or medium-high to bring to a simmer. Once milk is hot but not boiling, pour it over chocolate and allow to sit for a few minutes to melt, then gently whisk until smooth. Stir in the vanilla.

Chill in the fridge for about 1 hour, stirring every 15 minutes, until it is set to a spreadable consistency. Remove from fridge and set aside.

To assemble:

Select one of your cakes as the bottom layer (I always pick one whose top is the least beautifully domed). Saw off its domed top very gently using a serrated knife (bread knife) to create a flat surface, and discard the sliced-off top. Place this bottom layer on a serving platter. Smoothly spread about ⅔ cup ganache on top. Carefully place second cake on top, ensuring edges are aligned.

Gently frost with remaining ganache – starting from center top and then working out to and down the sides, preferably using a metal offset spatula. Decorate cake as desired.

MAKES ONE 2-LAYER CAKE, 12–16 SERVINGS.   SF, NF

* FAIR TRADE & ORGANIC

It's best to use fair trade and organic sugar, coffee, chocolate, and cocoa products whenever possible (see page 103 for more info).

⤙ CAROB CHAI CAKE WITH CARDAMOM ICING ⤚

1¼ cups light spelt flour

⅓ cup carob powder (plus extra to dust pan)

1 tsp ground cardamom

1 tsp cinnamon

1 tsp ground ginger

1 tsp nutmeg

½ tsp ground cloves

4–5 twists of the black pepper mill

1 tsp baking soda

½ tsp sea salt

1 cup maple syrup

⅔ cup organic non-dairy milk

½ cup softened non-hydrogenated coconut oil or sunflower oil (plus extra to coat pan)

2 tsp pure vanilla extract

2 tbsp apple cider vinegar

For a two-layer cake, double the recipe and divide the batter evenly between two cake pans. You'll want to double the frosting recipe, too. Follow assembly directions on page 205.

The first time I made this cake I used strongly steeped chai in lieu of milk. Now with the addition of ground spices, there's no need to brew any tea. See pages 202–203 for tips on baking and frosting cakes.

Preheat oven to 350°F (180°C). Lightly oil a 9-in (23-cm) cake pan and dust with carob (yup, carob powder, not flour).

Whisk together the flour, carob, cardamom, cinnamon, ginger, nutmeg, cloves, pepper, baking soda, and salt in a large bowl.

Pour in the syrup, milk, oil, and vanilla, and mix with a silicone spatula just until all flour is absorbed. Add the vinegar and stir quickly – you'll see pale swirls as vinegar reacts with baking soda. Stir just until vinegar is evenly distributed throughout the batter, and immediately pour batter evenly into pan.

Bake for 25–30 minutes, until top is domed, edges have begun to pull away from sides, and a toothpick inserted in center comes out clean. Remove from oven and allow to cool in pan for 10 minutes before transferring to a rack or serving plate.

Serve warm, simply dusted with powdered sugar and pinch of ground cardamom, or let it cool completely before frosting it.

I think carob gets a bad rap because everyone's hoping for chocolate in a dessert, and assumes carob is a second-rate substitution. I say, let carob be its own fine self! It's an excellent source of vitamins A, B2, B3, and B6 as well as the minerals copper, calcium, magnesium, manganese, and potassium. It's relatively low in calories and high in fiber, and compared to cocoa powder, it's stimulant-free and low in fat. If you've still got a hate-on for the stuff though, substitute it with the same amount of cocoa powder.

CARDAMOM ICING

Combine all ingredients (except almonds) in a medium bowl or food processor. Mix until smooth, adjusting measurements slightly if necessary for a spreadable texture. Spread a very thin layer of icing over top of cake (this is called a "crumb coat"), and then refrigerate the cake for 10 minutes to set.

Remove from fridge and frost with the remaining icing, starting in the center and working out to and down the sides. Garnish with a combination of chopped and whole raw almonds if desired.

MAKES ABOUT 8 SERVINGS.   **SF, NF**

1¾ cups powdered organic sugar (fair trade if possible), sifted

¼ cup arrowroot powder, non-GM cornstarch, or tapioca flour, sifted

½ cup softened non-hydrogenated coconut oil or non-dairy, non-GM margarine

¼ cup good-quality coconut milk (canned, non-light version, or see page 108) or organic soymilk

2 tsp ground cardamom

1 tsp pure vanilla extract

⅛ tsp sea salt (omit if using margarine)

5–13 raw almonds (for garnish)

MOCHA FUDGE PUDDING CAKE

1 cup spelt flour

1¼ cup organic sugar*

½ cup cocoa powder* (Dutch-processed if possible)

1 tbsp ground espresso beans*

1 tbsp baking powder

¼ tsp sea salt

½ cup softened non-hydrogenated coconut oil or sunflower oil (plus extra to coat baking dish)

½ cup organic non-dairy milk

1 tsp pure vanilla extract

2 cups freshly brewed, hot coffee*

FAIR TRADE & ORGANIC

It's best to use fair trade and organic sugar, coffee, chocolate, and cocoa products whenever possible (see page 103 for more info).

I love this dessert. It's great for clumsy bakers. You can create the swirls of fudgey pudding in the cake effortlessly, and when you serve it at a dinner party, everyone will be impressed and ask, "How did you do that?!"

I'm not a coffee drinker (it makes me a little loopy), but I love the taste and smell of the stuff; putting it in baked goods adds another dimension of flavor to the chocolatey goodness (while allowing me to stay level-headed).

Serve with organic non-dairy ice cream if desired.

Preheat oven to 350°F (180°C). Lightly oil a 2½-qt/L baking dish.

Whisk together the flour, ½ cup sugar and ¼ cup cocoa, and the ground espresso, baking powder, and salt. Add the oil, milk, and vanilla, and mix just until all flour is absorbed. Spread evenly into the baking dish and set aside.

Combine the remaining ¾ cup sugar and ¼ cup cocoa in a small bowl, and sprinkle over batter.

Carefully pour the hot (yes, hot) coffee over top. *Don't you dare mix this in!* It will do its own thing in the oven.

Bake for about 45 minutes, until a toothpick inserted in center comes out clean (but be sure you're poking into a cakey bit and not a pudding bit).

Remove from oven and to serve, scoop out portions into small bowls.

MAKES 8–10 SERVINGS (OR 12 IF SERVED WITH NON-DAIRY ICE CREAM). SF, NF

SPICE SWIRL BUNDT CAKE WITH BUTTAHMILK GLAZE

I love the way this cake looks! It tastes great too, of course, and can turn an afternoon tea into a celebratory affair. This recipe requires a 2½-qt/L donut-shaped Bundt cake pan. Be sure to read the directions once or twice before making cake so you can "swirl" the batter with confidence.

Preheat oven to 350°F (180°C). Lightly oil and flour a 2½-qt/L Bundt pan – ensure all interior surface is coated to prevent cake from sticking.

To prepare vanilla batter:
Whisk together the flour, sugar, baking soda, and salt in a large bowl.

Add the milk or water, oil, and vanilla and mix just until all flour is absorbed.

To prepare spice batter:
Whisk together the flour, Sucanat or sugar, cinnamon, nutmeg, ginger, baking soda, and salt in a separate large bowl.

Add the milk or water, oil, and molasses and mix just until all flour is absorbed.

Add the vinegar to each of the bowls and quickly mix one then the other, just until vinegar is evenly distributed through batter in each bowl.

Pour the vanilla batter into the Bundt pan first, tilting pan at a bit of an angle so batter fills one side of pan (it will still flow to other side, but the objective is to have the batter mostly on one side). Place pan on a table or counter top and immediately pour the spice batter in other side (the two batters will mix but won't completely combine).

Gently draw a snake-like swiggle with a toothpick, skewer, or knife once through batter to help that swirl happen (don't over-swiggle, as batters will lose their swirl and begin to blend – we don't want that!).

Bake for 45–50 minutes, until cake begins to pull away from sides of pan and a toothpick inserted into center comes out clean.

Remove from oven and allow to cool in pan for at least 30 minutes before inverting cake onto a serving plate and removing pan.

Once cake is completely cooled, combine all ingredients for glaze in a liquid measuring cup and mix until smooth. Gently pour over cake (don't worry about the glaze being distributed perfectly).

Vanilla batter

2 cups light spelt flour (plus extra to dust pan)

1 cup organic sugar (fair trade if possible)

1 tsp baking soda

½ tsp sea salt

1 cup organic non-dairy milk or filtered water

½ cup softened non-hydrogenated coconut oil or sunflower oil

1 tbsp pure vanilla extract

1 tbsp apple cider vinegar

Spice batter

2 cups light spelt flour

¾ cup Sucanat or organic sugar (fair trade if possible)

1 tbsp cinnamon

1 tsp nutmeg

1 tsp ground ginger

1 tsp baking soda

½ tsp sea salt

¾ cup organic non-dairy milk

½ cup softened non-hydrogenated coconut oil or sunflower oil

¼ cup organic blackstrap molasses

1 tbsp apple cider vinegar

Buttahmilk glaze

2 cups powdered organic sugar (fair trade if possible)

¼ tsp nutmeg (optional)

3–4 tbsp organic non-dairy milk

2 tbsp fresh lemon juice

MAKES 12–16 SERVINGS.   SF, NF

LIME COCONUT CAKE WITH LIME COCONUT BUTTAHCREEM ICING

2¼ cups light spelt flour (plus extra for dusting)

1 cup organic sugar (fair trade if possible)

1/3 cup unsweetened shredded coconut

1 tsp baking soda

½ tsp sea salt

1 cup coconut milk*

¼ cup softened non-hydrogenated coconut oil (plus extra to coat pan)

zest of 2 organic limes

1 tsp pure vanilla extract

¼ cup freshly squeezed lime juice

powdered organic sugar (fair trade if possible) (for garnish)

Use a good quality, organic brand of canned coconut milk, like Earth's Choice, Thai Kitchen, or Native Forest; ensure that it is a regular, non-light version. If you prefer to make your own fresh coconut milk, see the recipe on page 108.

I was really pleased with myself when I created this recipe for my 24th birthday party. Try it and you'll see why – the flavor's excellent.

Serve warm, simply dusted with powdered organic sugar, or let it cool completely before frosting with Lime Coconut Buttahcreem (below) (or cover with the Buttahmilk Glaze, on page 209, replacing lemon juice with lime juice).

Preheat oven to 350°F (180°C). Lightly oil a 9-in (23-cm) cake pan and dust with flour.

Whisk together the flour, sugar, coconut, baking soda, and salt in a large bowl.

Add the coconut milk, oil, zest, and vanilla, and mix with a silicone spatula just until all flour is absorbed. Add the lime juice, stir quickly, just until juice is evenly distributed throughout batter, and immediately pour into pan.

Bake for 25–30 minutes, until top is domed, edges have begun to pull away from sides, and a toothpick inserted into center comes out clean.

Remove from oven and allow to cool in pan for 10 minutes, before transferring it to a rack or serving plate. Serve warm, dusted with powdered organic sugar, or allow to cool completely before frosting or glazing.

For a two-layer cake, double the recipe and divide the batter evenly between two cake pans. You'll want to double the frosting recipe, too. Follow assembly directions on page 205.

LIME COCONUT BUTTAHCREEM ICING

Toss the coconut into a food processor and give it a whirl for about 1 minute to make a fine powder. Add the sugar, oil, lime juice, coconut milk, vanilla, and salt, and blend until smooth, slightly adjusting measurements if needed for a spreadable texture. (If you don't have a food processor, you can powder coconut in a blender or a clean coffee grinder and then transfer to a bowl and mix rest of icing by hand.) Scrape all the icing into a bowl using a silicone spatula and fold in the zest.

Spread a very thin layer of icing over the cake (to create a "crumb coat"), then refrigerate cake for 10 minutes to set.

Remove cake from fridge and frost with remaining icing, starting from center top and working out to and down the sides. Garnish with the lime slices and additional shredded coconut.

MAKES ABOUT 8 SERVINGS.   SF, NF

1 cup unsweetened shredded coconut (plus extra for garnish)

1 cup powdered organic sugar (fair trade if possible), sifted

½ cup softened non-hydrogenated coconut oil

3 tbsp fresh lime juice

2 tbsp good-quality coconut milk (canned, non-light version, or see recipe on page 108)

½ tsp pure vanilla extract

⅛ tsp sea salt

1 tsp finely grated lime zest

1 fresh lime, thinly sliced (for garnish)

GLAZED LEMON POPPY SEED CAKE

2 cups spelt flour (plus extra to dust pan)

1 tsp baking soda

½ tsp baking powder

½ tsp sea salt

¼ cup poppy seeds

⅔ cup maple syrup or agave nectar

½ cup organic non-dairy milk

½ cup softened non-hydrogenated coconut oil or sunflower oil (plus extra to coat pan)

finely grated zest of 1 organic lemon* (about 1½ tsp)

⅓ cup fresh lemon juice

1 tsp pure vanilla extract (omit if using vanilla non-dairy milk)

Lovely Lemon Glaze

⅓ cup agave nectar or organic sugar (fair trade if possible)

¼ cup fresh lemon juice

½ tsp finely grated organic lemon zest*

Use an organic lemon to avoid pesticide residues on the citrus skin.

The first time I made a lemon poppy seed cake was the day my friend Roco (of granola fame, see page 115) and I arrived for a visit at the Emma Goldman Cooperative House in Madison, Wisconsin. Soon after our arrival, I offered to help, and the woman on kitchen duty asked me to make lemon poppy seed cake while she prepared dinner. Referring to my own cookzine, Vegan Freegan, I measured out four times the recipe for the 17 co-op members and guests, but I accidentally put in 12 times the baking powder! I quickly adjusted the ingredients to compensate for the baking powder, making 12 cakes-worth of batter in two huge roasting pans – we ate cake for days afterward.

Preheat oven to 350°F (180°C). Lightly oil a 9-in (23-cm) cake pan or a 1¾-qt/L Bundt pan and dust with flour.

Whisk together the flour, baking soda and powder, salt, and poppy seeds in a large bowl. Add the syrup or nectar, milk, oil, zest, lemon juice, and vanilla, and stir just until all flour is absorbed.

Pour the batter evenly into the cake pan, and bake for about 30 minutes, until a toothpick inserted into center comes out clean.

Remove from oven and allow to cool in pan for 10 minutes before releasing and transferring it to a rack to cool completely before glazing.

Combine the ingredients for the glaze in a small saucepan on high heat and bring to a boil. Once boiling, reduce heat to a simmer, stir, and cook for 5 minutes.

Remove from heat and allow to cool for at least 10 minutes before using a spoon to dribble the glaze over top of the cake, allowing it to drip down sides.

MAKES ABOUT 8 SERVINGS. SF, NF

APPLEYEST SPICE CAKE

This cake is a nice dessert to complete a savory autumn harvest dinner.

Preheat oven to 350°F (180°C). Lightly oil a 9-in (23-cm) cake pan and dust with flour.

To prepare walnut streusel topping:
Combine the walnuts, flour, sugar, cinnamon, and salt in a small bowl, cut in the oil, and set aside.

To prepare cake:
Lay down as many apple slices in pan that will fit in 1 layer, without overlapping.

Whisk together the flour, sugar, baking powder and soda, cinnamon, nutmeg, cloves, and salt in a large bowl, and set aside.

Add the applesauce, milk, and oil and stir just until all flour is absorbed. Add the vinegar and stir just until they are evenly distributed throughout the batter, then quickly pour batter into the cake pan over sliced apples, and sprinkle with the streusel topping.

Bake for about 30 minutes, until a toothpick inserted in center comes out clean.

Remove from heat and allow to cool in pan for 10 minutes before transferring to a serving platter. Drizzle with syrup or malt and serve.

MAKES 8–10 SERVINGS. SF, NF

Walnut streusel topping

1/3 cup chopped walnuts

1/3 cup spelt flour

1/4 cup Sucanat or organic sugar (fair trade if possible)

1 tsp cinnamon

1/4 tsp sea salt

2 tbsp non-hydrogenated coconut oil or non-dairy, non-GM margarine

Cake

1 medium apple, peeled, cored & thinly sliced

1 2/3 cups spelt flour (plus extra for dusting)

1/2 cup Sucanat or organic sugar (fair trade if possible)

1 tsp baking powder

1 tsp baking soda

1 tsp cinnamon

1 tsp nutmeg

1/4 tsp ground cloves

1/2 tsp sea salt

3/4 cup applesauce (see page 114)

1/2 cup organic non-dairy milk

1/4 cup softened non-hydrogenated coconut oil or sunflower oil (plus extra to coat pan)

2 tsp apple cider vinegar

brown rice syrup or barley malt (to drizzle on top)

SWEET ALMOND CUPCAKES

¼ cup almond meal

½ cup brown rice flour

¼ cup quinoa or millet flour

¼ cup tapioca flour or non-GM corn flour

2 tbsp flax seeds, freshly ground

1 tsp baking powder

½ tsp baking soda

¼ tsp sea salt

¾ cup maple syrup or agave nectar

⅔ cup organic non-dairy milk

⅓ cup softened non-hydrogenated coconut oil or sunflower oil

1 tsp pure almond extract

1 tsp pure vanilla extract

1 tsp apple cider vinegar

* If you over-fill the muffin cups with batter, the cupcakes won't rise as they should.

** A dinner knife (or, better yet, a grapefruit knife) can help remove the cupcakes from the tray.

As I said in chapter thirteen, I used to insist that you could have vegan baked goods or gluten-free baked goods, but it was next to impossible to make a vegan, gluten-free baked good and not wind up with a big disappointment. But how could I deny a cakey dessert from those who steer clear of gluten? These babies are sweet and delicate (not at all dense). The trick is to use a blend of flours.

Preheat oven to 350°F (180°C). Prepare a 12-cup muffin tray with paper liners (may need an extra tray or just make 2 batches; pour a small amount of water into each unused cup to maintain adequate humidity in oven).

Whisk together the almond meal, flours, flax seeds, baking powder and soda, and salt in a large bowl.

Add the syrup or nectar, milk, oil, and extracts, and stir just until all flour is absorbed. Stir in the vinegar just until it's evenly distributed (the batter will seem too thin, but don't worry) and immediately portion batter into muffin cups (filling them no more than ¾ full*).

Bake for 22–24 minutes, until a toothpick inserted in center comes out clean.

Remove from oven and allow to cool in pan for 5 minutes, then transfer** the cupcakes to a cooling rack.

ALMOND BUTTAHCREEM ICING

Combine all ingredients (except the almonds) in a medium bowl or a food processor, and mix until smooth, adjusting measurements slightly if needed for a spreadable texture.

Transfer the icing into a piping bag (or a sandwich bag, then cut off a small piece of corner), and pipe on icing in a spiral motion, starting at the outer edge of the cupcake and working into center. Alternately, you can frost using the back of a spoon. Garnish with the almonds.

MAKES 12–14 CUPCAKES.   **GF, SF, NF**

3¼ cups powdered organic sugar (fair trade if possible), sifted

¼ cup non-GM cornstarch or arrowroot powder, sifted

1 cup non-hydrogenated coconut oil (or ½ coconut & ½ non-dairy, non-GM margarine)

¼ cup almond milk (or another organic non-dairy milk)

1 tsp pure almond extract

1 tsp pure vanilla extract

⅛ tsp sea salt

12–24 whole almonds or ¼ cup slivered almonds (for garnish)

TIPS FOR PIE BAKING

I admire people who are queens or kings of pie baking. When I first started, I was so nervous about ruining pie crusts, making them too crumbly, rolling them too thin, or under- or over-baking them. Even now that I've learned more about baking pies, it's not the first dessert I leap up to make. I usually leave it to my mum.

Through my trials and errors, I've accumulated enough experience to provide you the basics that every aspiring pie royal should know:

Making pie dough

• Use a food processor to pulse the dry ingredients (flour and salt, sugar if using), then gradually add the oil in small amounts, pulsing again until the texture is like coarse cornmeal. If you want to do this by hand, sift together the dry ingredients and slowly drizzle in the oil, mixing with a fork until the texture of coarse cornmeal is achieved.

• Add the water (and maple syrup if using) and blend to combine, or transfer to a bowl and mix, using a silicone spatula. It's better to have too much water than not enough – pie crusts that are too dry won't roll out, whereas sticky crusts can be worked on a floured surface, with a floured rolling pin and your floured hands.

Rolling out dough

• Roll the pie dough when it's room temperature, not cold, for maximum malleability.

• Roll dough evenly by turning it and rolling, turning it and rolling, etc. (your work surface may need re-flouring), until dough measures about 9 in (23 cm).

• Carefully pick up dough (use a spatula to transfer it by rolling onto rolling pin), re-flour your work surface, then lay it down on the other side to roll out to about 4 in (10 cm) wider than diameter of pie plate. Carefully transfer dough by rolling it onto the pin again, and drape it evenly over pie plate, gently moving it to fit into creases of pan. Press lightly to make sure it sticks.

• An alternative to working on a floured surface is to roll dough between two pieces of parchment paper, peeling top one off before laying it upside down in pie plate, and then peeling other piece off. (This is my preferred method.)

• Keep your pie plate prepared with dough in fridge until you're ready to fill it and bake.

Cutting a clean edge

• Trim excess pie crust with a pair of clean scissors, allowing a short overhang which will shrink as it bakes.

• Press down the edges evenly with tines of a fork to make a decorative pattern.

◆— ALMOND CHOCOLATE CREEM PIE —◆

This one's a real winner! It's smooth and rich with chocolate. The nut butter acts as a waterproof barrier from the tofu, keeping the crust crisp. Sometimes I just make the filling and enjoy it as a mousse.

To prepare crust:

Preheat oven to 350°F (180°C). Lightly oil a 9-in (23-cm) pie plate.

Pulse the oat cakes (if using) in a food processor or blender. Transfer to a large bowl, add other ingredients, and mix well (the crumbs should hold together when pinched). Press firmly into bottom and sides of the pie plate. Pre-bake for 10 minutes. (If you ever use this crust recipe to make a pie that will be baked anyway, unlike this pie, there is no need to pre-bake.)

Remove from oven and allow to cool completely.

To prepare filling:

Fill bottom of a double-boiler** with 1–2 in (2½–5 cm) of hot water, place second pot on top, making sure that the water in bottom pot isn't touching the bottom of the top pot, and place double-boiler on stove element.

Add the chocolate to top pot and turn heat on to medium (or medium-high, depending on your stove) so that steam from water in bottom pot will melt chocolate. Stir continually with a heat-proof silicone spatula to prevent burning or hardening. Once chocolate has melted into a dreamy liquid, about 5 minutes, remove double-boiler from heat. Scrape the melted chocolate into a food processor or blender, add the tofu, and blend until no tofu pieces remain. Add the syrup or sugar, and vanilla, and blend again, until velvety smooth.

Gently spread the nut butter on bottom of pie crust. Pour the filling into crust, smooth out the surface, then cover and chill in fridge for 1–2 hours. Garnish with chopped almonds.

MAKES 8 SERVINGS.   NF

*** If you have a double boiler – a set up of 2 pots of the same diameter in which one fits into the other, leaving a few inches of space between the bottom and top pots – you probably already know that the set is called a double boiler and you are a lucky duck when it comes to heating temperature-sensitive things like chocolate that need a gentler heat from hot water vapor. If you don't have one, not to worry – use a heat-proof bowl (ideally metal, but also Pyrex-type glass) that can fit over a saucepan like a double-boiler.*

Crust

1½ cups crumbled oat cakes or graham cracker crumbs (for those who tolerate wheat)

¼ cup softened non-hydrogenated coconut oil or sunflower oil

2 tbsp maple syrup or organic sugar*

2 tbsp filtered water

¼ tsp sea salt

Filling

12 oz (340 g) non-dairy semi-sweet chocolate, chopped small, or 2 cups non-dairy chocolate chips*

24½ oz (698 mL) silken tofu

3 tbsp maple syrup or organic sugar*

1 tsp pure vanilla extract

1 cup organic almond butter (or natural peanut butter), softened

chopped almonds (for garnish)

* FAIR TRADE & ORGANIC

It's best to use fair trade and organic sugar, coffee, chocolate, and cocoa products whenever possible (see page 103 for more info).

PUMPKIN PIE WITH CASHEW CREEM

1 – 9-in (23-cm) pie crust (see recipe on next page)

1 tbsp non-GM cornstarch or arrowroot powder

¾ cup coconut milk (canned, non-light version, or see page 108) (plus extra for finishing)

¼ cup filtered water (or ½ cup if using a drier squash like acorn or kombucha)

½ cup non-GM silken tofu

⅔ cup maple syrup

1½ tsp cinnamon

1 tsp grated fresh ginger root (or ½ tsp ground)

½ tsp nutmeg

¼ tsp ground cloves

¼ tsp sea salt

2 cups cooked pumpkin or other orange-fleshed squash (see page 90 for baking directions)

Cashew Creem (see recipe on next page)

My mum is the Pumpkin Pie Queen – though her recipe isn't vegan, she uses organic eggs. Creating a vegan recipe that was worthy of a space at my family's Thanksgiving Day dinner table was something I was determined to do!

If you don't feel up for making a pie crust, you can simply make the filling (as noted below) for pumpkin custard.

Preheat oven to 350°F (180°C).

Combine the cornstarch and water in a small bowl and whisk until smooth. Transfer mixture, along with the coconut milk, water, tofu, syrup, cinnamon, ginger, nutmeg, cloves, and salt in a blender or food processor and blend until smooth. Add the pumpkin or squash and blend until there are no large chunks, but do not over-purée.

Pour into a prepared pie crust or a lightly oiled baking dish and bake for about 45 minutes, until somewhat firm in middle.

Remove from oven and allow to cool for 30 minutes before serving with Cashew Creem on the side or drizzled with coconut milk, if desired.

PIE CRUST

Lightly oil a 9-in (23-cm) pie plate.

Pulse the flour, salt, and cinnamon in a food processor or mix by hand (see making pie dough, page 216). Add the oil, syrup, and milk or water as needed to mix and form into a ball of dough.

Roll out dough onto a clean, floured surface to fit into pie plate. Trim edges. Cover with plastic wrap and chill in fridge until ready to use.

1½ cups spelt flour (or 1¼ cups light spelt flour & ¼ cup oat bran)

½ tsp sea salt

½ tsp cinnamon (optional)

½ cup cold non-hydrogenated coconut oil, diced (if unavailable, may use sunflower oil) (plus extra to coat pan)

1 tbsp maple syrup (optional)

1–2 tbsp cold organic non-dairy milk or ice water

CASHEW CREEM

Caroline Dupont, my friend and author of Enlightened Eating, *said I could share this raw recipe with you here. It can also be served over Apple Crumble (page 220), Strawberry Rhubarb Crumble (page 221), or Blueberry Breakfast Polenta (page 121).*

Drain the water off the soaked cashews.

Transfer drained cashews and remaining ingredients (starting with ¾ cup water) to a food processor or blender and process for about 2 minutes, until smooth, adding extra water if necessary.

Keep in an airtight container in fridge until ready to serve. Store any leftovers in fridge for up to 3 days. Or in freezer for up to 2 months.

1 cup raw cashews, soaked in enough water to cover for 4 hours or overnight

$^3/_4$–1 cup filtered water

2 tbsp maple syrup, brown rice syrup, or raw agave nectar

1 tsp pure vanilla extract

$^1/_8$ tsp sea salt

MAKES 1¾ CUPS (ENOUGH FOR 2 PIES).
 NF (Pumpkin Pie); GF, SF, NF, R (Cashew Creem)

APPLE CRUMBLE

Fruit bottom

5 largish apples, peeled, cored & sliced

1 tbsp Sucanat or organic sugar (fair trade if possible)

2 tbsp whole grain flour (can be gluten-free)

½ tsp cinnamon

Crumble top

⅓ cup non-hydrogenated coconut oil or non-dairy, non-GM margarine

⅔ cup rolled oats

½ cup whole grain flour (e.g,. kamut, millet, or spelt)

½ cup Sucanat or organic sugar (fair trade if possible)

1 tsp cinnamon

½ tsp sea salt (use only ¼ tsp if using margarine)

I've never tasted an apple crumble better than the one my mum makes. She puts it together by feel, but I managed to get some measurements out of her! Serve warm on its own, or with a side of Cashew Creem (page 219). It's also nice for breakfast.

Preheat oven to 350°F (180°C). Lightly oil a 2–2½-qt/L baking dish.

To prepare fruit bottom:
Toss apples with sugar, flour, and cinnamon in baking dish and spread out evenly.

To prepare crumble top:
Combine oil or margarine in a separate bowl and add oats, flour, sugar, cinnamon, and salt, and mix to combine – it should be kind of clumpy.

Spread crumble over fruit and bake for 35–45 minutes, until fruit crumble is golden and soft (use a knife to check).

MAKES ABOUT 6 SERVINGS.   SF, NF

STRAWBERRY RHUBARB CRUMBLE

An early to mid-summer treat. I freeze freshly picked rhubarb for baked goods when it's not in season locally. Serve warm on its own, or with a side of Cashew Creem (page 219). It's also nice for breakfast.

Preheat oven to 350°F (180°C). Lightly oil a 2–2½-qt/L baking dish.

To prepare fruit bottom:
Toss the rhubarb and strawberries with arrowroot, kudzu, tapioca flour, or cornstarch in a baking dish and spread out evenly.

To prepare crumble top:
Place the oil or margarine in a separate bowl and add the oats, flour, sugar, salt, and zest, and mix to combine – it should be kind of clumpy.

Spread crumble over fruit and bake for 35–45 minutes, until fruit is soft (use a knife to check).

MAKES ABOUT 6 SERVINGS.   SF, NF

Fruit bottom

5 cups chopped rhubarb stalks (just less than 1½ lb/680 g)

1½ cups sliced organic strawberries (about 10)

¾–1 cup organic sugar (fair trade if possible)

2 tbsp arrowroot powder, kudzu, tapioca flour, or non-GM cornstarch

Crumble top

½ cup non-hydrogenated coconut oil or non-dairy, non-GM margarine

1 cup rolled oats

¾ cup whole grain flour

¾ cup organic sugar (fair trade if possible)

½ tsp sea salt (or ¼ tsp if using margarine)

finely grated zest of organic orange or lemon* (optional)

* Use an organic orange or lemon to avoid pesticide residues on the skin. You may consider omitting zest from recipe if you only have conventional, non-organic citrus.

CHAPTER
20

COOKIES, PUDDINGS AND OTHER SWEET TREATS

FLAX MAPLE COOKIES

Thanks to my blog, Domestic Affair, these cookies are now known and loved world-wide. Try 'em and you'll see why – they only take a moment to whip up, and they're simply delicious.

Preheat oven to 350°F (180°C). Prepare a baking sheet (or two) with a sheet of parchment paper or a light coating of oil.

Whisk together the flour, flax seeds, cinnamon, and salt in a large bowl. Pour in the syrup and oil and mix just until all flour is absorbed.

Roll the dough into walnut-sized balls and place them, evenly spaced apart, on baking sheet(s). Press down on each ball gently with your index and middle fingers (slightly apart, like a peace sign) to flatten, making a nice wavy impression on each cookie.

Bake for about 12 minutes, until the bottoms are golden brown.

Eat 'em warm, or allow to cool completely on a rack before storing in an airtight container.

MAKES ABOUT 20 COOKIES. SF, NF

2 cups spelt flour

¼ cup flax seeds

1 tsp cinnamon

½ tsp sea salt

½ cup maple syrup

½ cup sunflower or olive oil
(plus extra for coating pan)

SHORTBREAD COOKIES

½ cup organic sugar (fair trade if possible)

½ tsp sea salt

2¼ cups brown rice flour (may substitute half with white rice flour)

1 tsp baking powder

1 cup cold non-hydrogenated coconut oil, diced

¼ cup room-temperature applesauce (see page 114)

Being raised by Brits, simple light-colored shortbread was a staple in our house, especially around the Christmas holidays. But butter- and gluten-free shortbread cookies that are actually tasty?! These lovelies are made with rice flour – a traditional ingredient in Scottish shortbread, may I add, which imparts a unique nutty flavor.

Preheat oven to 275°F (135°C).

Place the sugar and salt in a food processor or blender and give it a whirl for about 30 seconds to give it a finer texture.

Add the flour and baking powder, and whirl again to combine. Add the oil and applesauce and process until combined, but don't allow mixture to form a ball.

Scrape the dough onto a clean surface with a silicone spatula, and gently knead with your clean hands to form a ball. Divide dough in half and roll out each half to ½-in (1-cm) thick.

Cut dough into rounds using a 2-in (5-cm) cookie cutter (or if you'd like to defy convention, any shape you'd like – I'm partial to hearts and stars).

Place the cookies on unoiled baking sheets (you may use parchment paper, but it's not necessary) and prick each cookie with a fork (again, this is conventional, and therefore, defiable).

Bake for 25–35 minutes, until they turn a creamy color. The shortbread will not be firm, but it will harden as it cools.

Remove from oven and allow to cool on baking sheets before storing in an air-tight container for up to a month.

MAKES ABOUT 30 COOKIES. **GF, SF, NF**

Mind the temperature
Unless specified, keep all ingredients at room temperature. The temperature of the oil is especially important for baking cookies, if the oil is too warm the cookies will spread.

Mushroom Quinoa Pilaf (page 184)
with Beet & Green Bean Toss (page 154)

Spice Swirl Bundt Cake
with Buttahmilk Glace (page 209)

Coconut Sticky Rice with Mangoes (page 239)

(Left to right:) Tahini Thumbprint Cookies (page 232), Fig & Anise Biscotti (page 233), Double Trouble Chocolate Cookies (page 227), and Flax Maple Cookies (page 223)

COWGRRRL COOKIES

It's hard to find a good vegan chocolate chip cookie recipe that isn't too oily or too dry. These ones are just right. The raisins, walnuts, and cinnamon are optional ingredients, but highly recommended. Guaranteed to cure sweet lovin' cowgrrrls of the blues!

Preheat oven to 350°F (180°C).

Whisk together the flour, oats, baking powder and soda, and salt in a large bowl. Toss in the chocolate chips, raisins, nuts, and cinnamon. Stir to combine, then set aside.

Mix the oil and sugar or Sucanat thoroughly in a separate bowl (use an electric mixer if you have it, and the energy to clean it off afterward). Add the apple-sauce and vanilla and mix again until well combined.

Add the dry ingredients to wet, and mix just until all flour is absorbed. Drop heaping tablespoons of the dough onto an unoiled baking sheet (you may use parchment paper, but it's not necessary), spacing them about 2-in (5-cm) apart.

Bake for 13 minutes, until golden.

Eat 'em warm, or allow to cool completely on a rack before storing in an airtight container.

MAKES ABOUT 3 DOZEN COOKIES.   SF, NF

2 cups spelt flour

2 cups rolled oats

½ tsp baking powder

1 tsp baking soda

½ tsp sea salt

1¼ cups non-dairy chocolate chips (organic & fair trade if possible)

½ cup organic raisins (optional, or an additional ¼ cup non-dairy chocolate chips)

½ cup coarsely chopped walnuts or pecans (optional)

½ tsp cinnamon (optional)

1 (scant) cup* softened non-hydrogenated coconut oil or sunflower oil

1 cup organic sugar or Sucanat (fair trade if possible)

⅓ cup room-temperature apple-sauce (see page 114)

1 tsp pure vanilla extract

* In this recipe, the oil should measure 1 cup less 2 tbsp (or, ¾ cup plus 2 tbsp).

Freezing cookie dough

Sometimes you don't need to bake all the cookie dough that your recipe produces: make balls of dough as you would if you were baking them and place them on parchment paper on a baking tray; place the tray in the freezer for an hour or two; and when they are frozen, transfer them into a freezer bag. This way, you can bake them, even one or two at a time, when you want them. And you don't have to thaw them before baking, just cook them for a couple of minutes longer.

DATE COCONUT COOKIES

2½ cups spelt flour

2 cups rolled oats

1½ tsp baking soda

1 tsp cinnamon

1 tsp sea salt

1 cup chopped pitted dates

1 cup unsweetened shredded coconut

1 cup maple syrup

¾ cup softened non-hydrogenated coconut oil or sunflower oil (plus extra if using to coat pan)

zest of an organic lemon or orange

1 tsp pure vanilla extract

This is one of my favorite flavor combinations – date, coconut, and citrus zest – yes!

Preheat oven to 350°F (180°C). Prepare a baking sheet (or two) with a sheet of parchment paper or a light coating of oil.

Whisk together the flour, oats, baking soda, cinnamon, and salt in a large bowl. Toss in the dates and coconut and stir to combine. Add the syrup, oil, zest, and vanilla and mix just until all flour is absorbed.

Drop heaping tablespoonfuls of the dough onto the baking sheet(s), spacing them 2-in (5-cm) apart.

Bake for about 12 minutes, until golden.

Eat 'em warm, or allow to cool completely on a rack before storing in an airtight container.

MAKES ABOUT 3 DOZEN COOKIES. SF, NF

Zesting tip
When zesting lemon or orange rind, lightly grate one area of the peel then rotate to the next. Grate, rotate, grate, rotate. Do not grate down to the white pith – it's bitter. My favorite tool for this is a Microplane Rasp, available at kitchen stores or online.

ꝺOUBLE TROUBLE Chocolate Cookies

Chocolate lovers beware – these are indeed a decadent treat! The banana flavor is there, but it's subtle.

Preheat oven to 350°F (180°C). Prepare a baking sheet (or two) with a sheet of parchment paper or a light coating of oil.

Whisk together the flour, cocoa, baking soda, and salt in a large bowl and set aside.

Cream together the oil and sugar in a separate bowl, or preferably with an electric mixer, for about 1 minute. Beat in the banana and vanilla until well combined.

Add wet ingredients to dry and mix just until all flour is incorporated. Fold in chocolate and nuts until they are evenly dispersed throughout dough.

Roll dough into walnut-sized balls with clean hands and place them, spaced 2-in (5-cm) apart, on the baking sheet(s). Press each ball gently to flatten to ½-in (1-cm) thick.

Bake for about 13 minutes, until crusty on top but still soft.

Eat 'em warm, or allow to cool completely on a rack before storing in an airtight container.

MAKES ABOUT 30 COOKIES.   **SF, NF**

Crumbly dough solution

If you ever find your cookie dough is crumbly, there's no need to fight with it. It could be that your measuring technique (see pages 85–86) or measuring cups are inaccurate, but sometimes it's just a particular bag of flour that's drier than normal. Feel free to add filtered water or organic non-dairy milk, 2 tbsp at a time, until your dough is a smooth (but not sticky) consistency.

2½ cups light spelt flour

½ cup Dutch-processed cocoa powder*

1 tsp baking soda

¼ tsp sea salt

1 (scant) cup** softened non-hydrogenated coconut oil or sunflower oil (plus extra if using to coat pan)

1¼ cups organic sugar*

1 ripe medium banana, mashed (about 1/3–½ cup)

1 tsp pure vanilla extract

1¼ cups non-dairy chocolate chunks or chips*

1 cup chopped pecans (optional)

FAIR TRADE & ORGANIC

It's best to use fair trade and organic sugar, coffee, chocolate, and cocoa products whenever possible (see page 103 for more info).

*** In this recipe, the oil should measure 1 cup less 2 tbsp (or, ¾ cup plus 2 tbsp).*

— DOUBLE~WHAMMY GINGER COOKIES —

2 ⅔ cups spelt flour

1 tsp baking powder

1 tsp baking soda

1 tsp ground ginger

½ tsp sea salt

⅔ cup maple syrup

⅓ cup organic blackstrap molasses

½ cup softened non-hydrogenated coconut oil or sunflower oil (plus extra if using to coat pan)

⅓ cup minced or grated* fresh ginger root

organic sugar (fair trade if possible) (for coating cookies; optional)

* I often make a double batch of these, so I roughly chop the ginger and then toss it in my food processor for 20–30 seconds until it's minced. If you're going to grate it, use the widest teeth on a box grater; do not use something as fine as a Microplane zester, which will produce a paste that makes the cookie dough too wet.

Although ginger root is very warming and these cookies often make me think of December festivities, they can be enjoyed at any time of year.

Preheat oven to 350°F (180°C). Prepare a baking sheet (or two) with a sheet of parchment paper or a light coating of oil.

Whisk together the flour, baking powder and soda, ground ginger, and salt in a large bowl. Add the syrup, molasses, and oil, and stir to combine. With clean hands, first squeeze in juice from the fresh ginger root before adding (this provides more gingery flavor). Mix just until all flour has been absorbed.

Place the sugar in a small bowl or on a saucer. Roll the dough with clean hands into walnut-sized balls (smaller balls are okay too, just make them a consistent size) – the dough can be quite sticky, so lightly coating your hands with oil first can help – then roll each ball around in sugar before placing on baking sheet.

Bake for 10–12 minutes, until crusty on top but still soft.

Eat 'em warm, or allow to cool completely on a rack before storing in an airtight container.

MAKES ABOUT 3 DOZEN LARGE COOKIES (OR 4 DOZEN SMALL COOKIES).
SF, NF

❧ CHEWY PEANUT BUTTAH COOKIES ❧

Anywhere you find them, peanut butter cookies can be identified by their criss-cross pattern on top. Believe it or not, this decorative tradition apparently goes back to the 1930s, when a Pillsbury recipe specified for the baker to press the cookies using fork tines. Does this particular peanut butter cookie-making tradition exist because the dough is dense and needs to be pressed to cook evenly, or is there another secret reason?

I modified this recipe from an older version that included sugar. I hope it still meets your expectations for this classic cookie.

Preheat oven to 350°F (180°C).

Whisk together the flour, baking soda, and salt. Mix in the peanut butter, syrup, oil, and vanilla just until all flour is absorbed. Fold in the peanuts and chocolate chips.

Drop heaping tablespoonfuls of dough onto an unoiled cookie sheet, spacing them a good 2-in (5-cm) apart (they tend to spread out more than most cookies), and press down gently on each one with back of a fork.

Bake only for 12 minutes – even if they don't look entirely done, they will harden as they cool.

Eat 'em warm, or allow to cool completely on a rack before storing in an airtight container.

MAKES ABOUT 3 DOZEN COOKIES.　**SF, NF**

2 cups spelt flour

1 tsp baking soda

½ tsp sea salt

1 cup organic natural peanut butter

1 cup maple syrup

⅓ cup sunflower or olive oil

1 tsp pure vanilla extract

⅓ cup chopped organic peanuts (optional; may not be necessary if using chunky peanut butter)

½ cup non-dairy chocolate chips (organic & fair trade if possible) (optional)

⟞ RAW CAROB ALMOND COOKIES ⟝

1¼ cups pitted dates with just enough room-temperature filtered water to cover (about ¾ cup)

½ cup unsweetened shredded coconut

1½ cups carob powder

1½ cups raw nut or seed butter (almond or cashew butter &/or tahini)

whole almonds or pecans (about 16)

It's nice to be able to make raw "cookies" without the need for a dehydrator. This rich treat is an adapted version of a recipe from my baker-friend Bryn. If you're looking for a good brand, MaraNatha makes amazing raw almond butter and tahini.

Allow the dates to soak for 30 minutes to 1 hour, until soft.

Transfer the soaked dates, along with the soaking water, into a food processor or blender and give it a whirl for 30–60 seconds. Scrape down the sides with a silicone spatula, add the coconut, and process again until well combined and there are no date chunks left.

Transfer into a large bowl, scraping it all out with spatula, and mix in the carob powder. Add the nut butter and mix again until a uniform dough is achieved.

Roll the dough into walnut-sized balls with clean hands. Flatten each ball between your palms to form a ½-in (1-cm) thick disc and place on serving plate. Press an almond or pecan into the center of each cookie.

Enjoy at room temperature, or store in an airtight container in fridge for up to 5 days.

MAKES ABOUT 16 COOKIES.   GF, SF, NF, R

STEVIA 'N' SPICE COOKIES

These babies are completely sugar-free – perfect for kids, diabetics, candida-sufferers, or anyone who just wants a healthier dessert option. I recommend that you make the cookies into a narrow biscotti shape, but that's just for something different. They can be enjoyed as round cookies too.

Preheat oven to 350°F (180°C). Prepare a baking sheet (or two) with a sheet of parchment paper or a light coating of oil.

Whisk together the flour(s), stevia, cinnamon, cardamom, ginger, cloves, baking soda, and salt in a large bowl.

Add the oil, milk, and applesauce, and mix just until all flour is absorbed.

Form the dough with clean hands into a rectangle about 1-in (2½-cm) thick and 4-in (10-cm) wide, then slice widthwise, about ¼-in (⅔-cm) thick (may also form into conventional 1-tbsp balls flattened to ½-in (1-cm) thick).

Lay the cookies flat and evenly spaced apart on baking sheet(s) and bake for 8 minutes.

Eat 'em warm, or allow to cool completely on a rack before storing in an airtight container.

MAKES ABOUT 3 DOZEN BISCOTTI-SHAPED COOKIES (OR 28 ROUND COOKIES). **SF, NF**

2½ cups spelt flour (or 2 cups spelt & ½ cup rye flour)

1 tbsp green stevia powder*

3 tbsp poppy, sesame, or flax seeds (optional)

1 tbsp cinnamon

2 tsp ground cardamom

1 tsp ground ginger

½ tsp ground cloves

1 tsp baking soda

½ tsp sea salt

⅔ cup softened non-hydrogenated coconut oil or sunflower oil (plus extra if using to coat pan)

½ cup organic vanilla non-dairy milk**

¼ cup room-temperature applesauce (see page 114)

1 tsp pure vanilla extract (non-alcoholic variety preferred)

* Stevia is a herb sometimes referred to as sweetleaf. You might say it's like a herbal version of aspartame, only without the scary side effects or the disgusting taste! Like other sugar-free sweeteners, it's often far more concentrated than conventional white sugar, so you use significantly less. It's available at your local food co-op or health food store.

** Yü brand's vanilla rice milk has no added sugar! Or for unsweetened vanilla almond milk, look for Pacific Natural Foods and Almond Breeze brands.

— TAHINI THUMBPRINT COOKIES —

Filling*

1 cup chopped pitted dates

²/₃ cup filtered water

2 cups spelt flour (other flours
will make cookies too crumbly)

1 cup tahini (may use another
seed or nut butter)

½ cup maple syrup

¼ cup sunflower or olive oil

½ tsp sea salt

** This filling can be substituted
with apple butter or jam if you're
in a rush, or if you're not a fan of
dates.*

*Given to me by my dear friend Cheendana, this was the first vegan cookie recipe
I ever made. It was she who introduced me to whole foods when I worked with
her in her rural Nova Scotia garden one autumn and had my dairy-lovin' self
vegan-bound by the time I was on a plane back to Toronto.*

*These cookies are as simple to make as the ever-popular Flax Maple Cookies (page 223). Although we usually think of tahini as a savory ingredient, it can
be deliciously paired with maple syrup for a sweet treat. These are also a great
calcium-rich substitute for peanut butter cookies.*

Preheat oven to 350°F (180°C).

Combine the dates and water in a small pot on medium or medium-low heat to
simmer for 5–10 minutes, until softened. Mash with a fork into a paste.

Mix the remaining ingredients in a large bowl just until all flour is absorbed.

Roll the dough into walnut-sized balls with your clean hands and space 2 in (5 cm)
apart on an unoiled cookie sheet. Make an indent in each ball with your thumb
(or index finger) and fill that space with about 1 tsp date mush.

Bake for 10–12 minutes, until lightly brown on bottom.

Eat 'em warm, or allow to cool completely on a rack before storing in an airtight
container.

MAKES ABOUT 30 COOKIES.   SF, NF

FIG ᴀɴᴅ ANISE BISCOTTI

This flavor combination was my friend Ryan's idea one Christmas when we wanted to make food gifts for people. He wanted to make cranberry and white pepper biscotti too, but this version seemed less risky – better than that, they were a hit!

Whisk together the flour, sugar, anise, baking powder, and salt in a large bowl. Add the flax goop, oil, and vanilla, and mix just until all flour is absorbed. Fold in the figs.

Form into a large ball with clean hands, cover with plastic wrap, and refrigerate for 1 hour.

Preheat oven to 300°F (150°C). Line a baking sheet with parchment paper. Remove the dough from fridge, place on the lined baking sheet, and form into two 13x2-in (33x5-cm) loaves.

Bake for 30 minutes, until top is domed.

Remove loaves from oven and allow to cool on a rack for 5–10 minutes. Reduce oven temperature to 275°F (135°C).

Transfer to a cutting board and carefully cut each loaf diagonally with a serrated knife into ½-in (1-cm) thick slices, then return to the baking sheet, laying the pieces flat and evenly spaced apart.

Bake for 20 minutes, then remove from oven, flip to other side, and bake for another 10 minutes, until dry but not rock hard.

Remove from oven and transfer to a rack to cool completely before serving or storing in an airtight container for up to a month.

MAKES ABOUT 32 PIECES.   SF, NF

4½ cups light spelt flour

2 cups organic sugar (fair trade if possible)

2 tbsp anise seeds, ground if desired

2 tsp baking powder

½ tsp sea salt

1 cup flax goop, version 2 (see page 101)

½ cup softened non-hydrogenated coconut oil or sunflower oil

1 tsp pure vanilla extract

1½ cups chopped dried figs (dry stems removed)

CHOCOLATE~DIPPED BISCOTTI

3¾ cups light spelt flour

2 cups organic sugar*

½ cup Dutch-processed cocoa powder*

2 tsp baking powder

½ tsp sea salt

1 cup flax goop, version 2 (see page 101)

½ cup softened non-hydrogenated coconut oil or sunflower oil

1 tsp pure vanilla extract

3 cups non-dairy bitter- or semi-sweet chocolate chips*

FAIR TRADE & ORGANIC

It's best to use fair trade and organic sugar, coffee, chocolate, and cocoa products whenever possible (see page 103 for more info).

*** See note on double-boilers on page 217.*

A perfect treat with chai (see page 244) or a cup of fair trade coffee.

Whisk together the flour, sugar, cocoa, baking powder, and salt in a large bowl. Add the flax goop, oil, and vanilla, and mix just until all flour is absorbed. Form into a large ball, cover with plastic wrap, and refrigerate for 1 hour.

Preheat oven to 300°F (150°C). Line a baking sheet with parchment paper. Remove the dough from fridge, place on the lined baking sheet, and form into two 13x2-in (33x5-cm) loaves.

Bake for 30 minutes, until tops are domed.

Remove the loaves from oven and allow to cool on baking sheet for 5–10 minutes. Reduce oven temperature to 275°F (135°C).

Transfer to a cutting board and carefully cut each loaf diagonally with a serrated knife into ½-in (1-cm) thick slices, then return to baking sheet, laying the pieces flat and evenly spaced apart.

Bake for 20 minutes, then remove from oven, flip to other side, and bake for another 10 minutes until dry but not rock hard. Remove from oven and transfer biscotti to a rack to cool completely.

Fill bottom of a double-boiler** with 1–2 in (2½–5 cm) of hot water, place second pot on top, making sure that water in bottom pot isn't touching the bottom of top pot, and place double-boiler on stove element.

Add chocolate into top pot and turn heat on to medium (or medium-high, depending on your stove) so that steam from water in bottom pot will melt chocolate. Stir continually with a silicone spatula to prevent burning or hardening, until chocolate has melted into a dreamy liquid, about 5 minutes.

Remove double-boiler from stove, but keep top pot over the hot water-filled bottom pot so chocolate doesn't cool down too fast. Dip ½–⅔ of each (completely cooled) biscotti in chocolate for a thin coating (but you shouldn't see the biscotti beneath chocolate coating)—you may need the help of a silicone spatula to paint on the chocolate coating (as prettily as you can).

Place the chocolate-coated biscotti back on the parchment-lined baking sheet (making sure any cookie crumbs have been knocked off) and allow chocolate to set completely before serving or storing in an airtight container for up to a month.

MAKES ABOUT 32 PIECES. SF, NF

GREAT DATE SQUARES

I love date squares. They're a substantial dessert, great for road trips, picnics, and even for breakfast on the odd occasion!

Preheat oven to 350°F (180°C). Line a 9x13-in (23x33-cm) baking pan with parchment paper or lightly oil and dust with flour.

To prepare date filling:
Bring the water to boil in a small saucepan on high heat. Add the dates and salt, stir, and reduce heat to simmer for 5–10 minutes, until dates are soft and mashable. Remove from heat and mix in lemon juice.

To prepare crust:
Whisk together the oats, flour, Sucanat or sugar, cinnamon, salt, and baking powder in a large bowl. Add the zest, oil, and ¼ cup water and mix into an even meal. If crust is too dry add the remaining ¼ cup water or an additional 1–2 tbsp oil.

To assemble:
Press half of the crust mixture evenly into bottom of the pan. Lay down the apples in one layer. Evenly smear the date filling over apples, and sprinkle with remaining crust mixture.

Bake for 30–45 minutes, until the top is lightly browned.

Remove from oven and allow to cool in pan for about 30 minutes before cutting into squares (2 cuts lengthwise, 4 cuts widthwise). Serve, or store in an airtight container, using wax or parchment paper to separate layers.

MAKES 15 SQUARES. SF, NF

Date filling

1 cup filtered water

2 cups packed pitted dates

½ tsp sea salt

1 tbsp fresh lemon juice

Crust

4 cups rolled oats

2 cups spelt flour

½ cup Sucanat or organic sugar (fair trade if possible)

1 tsp cinnamon

½ tsp sea salt

1 tsp baking powder

zest of an organic lemon or orange*

1 cup softened non-hydrogenated coconut oil or sunflower oil (plus extra if needed for additional moisture &/or to coat pan)

¼–½ cup filtered water

2 apples, peeled, cored & thinly sliced

* Use an organic lemon or orange to avoid pesticide residues on the citrus skin. You may consider omitting zest from recipe if you only have conventional, non-organic citrus.

❧ Brownies with Wings (Triple Chocolate Chipotle Brownies) ❧

4 oz (114 g) non-dairy semi-sweet chocolate,* chopped

3 oz (86 g) non-dairy unsweetened chocolate,* chopped

¼ cup cocoa powder* (Dutch-processed if possible) (plus extra for dusting)

1¼ cup organic sugar* (or ½ sugar & ½ Sucanat)

1 cup blended non-GM silken tofu

½ cup softened non-hydrogenated coconut oil or sunflower oil (plus extra for coating pan)

2 tsp pure vanilla extract

¾ cup light spelt flour

1 tsp chipotle pepper powder (optional; may be substituted with ½–1 tsp cayenne pepper)

½ tsp baking powder

½ tsp sea salt

FAIR TRADE & ORGANIC

It's best to use fair trade and organic sugar, coffee, chocolate, and cocoa products whenever possible (see page 103 for more info).

*** See note on double-boilers on page 217*

I first enjoyed a chewy brownie with chipotle pepper at the charming Swan Restaurant in Toronto. But alas, it wasn't vegan, nor was it wheat-free, so I set out to create a comparable dessert that suited all my basic baking requirements – with a heavenly decadence and a devilishly fiery kick. If you have an interest in traditional Chinese medicine, it's worth noting that both chocolate and chilies nourish the fire element.

Preheat the oven to 350°F (180°C). Lightly oil an 8-in (20-cm) square baking pan, then line with parchment paper and lightly coat with oil again and dust with cocoa (yep, that's right – cocoa, not flour, for dusting).

Fill bottom of a double-boiler** with 1–2 in (2½ –5 cm) of hot water, place second pot on top, making sure that water in bottom pot isn't touching the bottom of top pot and place double-boiler on stove element.

Add chocolate into top pot and turn heat on to medium (or medium-high, depending on your stove) so that steam from water in bottom pot will melt chocolate. Stir continually with a silicone spatula to prevent burning or hardening. Once chocolate has melted, about 5 minutes, mix in cocoa and remove double-boiler from heat.

Combine the sugar, tofu, oil, and vanilla in a large bowl using a silicone spatula. Stir in the chocolate, then the flour, chipotle, baking powder, and salt, and mix just until all flour is absorbed. Pour the batter into the pan, using the spatula to spread it into the corners and smooth it out.

Bake for 35 to 40 minutes, until slightly puffed and a toothpick inserted in center comes out with just a few crumbs on it.

Remove from oven and allow to cool completely in pan, for about 2 hours, before cutting into squares (5 cuts lengthwise and 5 cuts widthwise or 3 cuts in both directions for larger brownies). Store in an airtight container, using waxed or parchment paper to separate layers, in fridge for up to 5 days.

MAKES 36 SMALL BROWNIES (OR 16 LARGE BROWNIES).

SF, NF (if omitting pepper)

CREEMY RICE PUDDING

Puddings are one of the great comfort foods, and this one is an excellent way to use up leftover grains (just as long as you didn't initially cook them with seasonings other than a pinch of salt). This pudding can also be often enjoyed for breakfast.

Combine the syrup or malt and just 3½ cups milk in a 3-qt/L saucepan on medium-high heat. Once heated, add the rice, vanilla, and salt, and any or all optionals, if desired.

Dissolve the cornstarch in the remaining ½ cup milk, then slowly pour into saucepan, stirring continually. Reduce heat to medium if mixture starts to boil, stirring every 5 minutes, but it may take up to 40 minutes for noticeable thickening to occur; or, if you leave heat on medium-high, stir more often to prevent sticking or a skin forming on surface.

Once it's thickened and no longer runny, turn off heat (it should thicken more as it cools.)

Eat warm or cool. Stores in an airtight container in fridge for up to 3 days.

MAKES 8 SERVINGS.   GF, SF, NF

⅓ cup maple syrup, or ½ cup barley malt or brown rice syrup (or more to taste)

4 cups organic non-dairy milk

2 cups cooked brown rice (may substitute with millet)

3 tbsp non-GM cornstarch

2 tsp pure vanilla extract

⅛ tsp sea salt

Optionals

zest of 1 organic lemon or orange*

½ tsp cinnamon

¼ tsp nutmeg

½ cup organic raisins

½ cup pistachio nuts

* Use an organic lemon or orange to avoid pesticide residues on the citrus skin. You may consider omitting zest from recipe if you only have conventional, non-organic citrus.

❧ CARDAMOM TAPIOCA PUDDING ❧

¼ cup tapioca pearls

2 cups organic non-dairy milk

1 tsp green stevia powder*

½ tsp ground cardamom

½ tsp pure vanilla extract

⅛ tsp sea salt

* May substitute stevia with ¼ cup maple syrup or organic, fair trade sugar.

Tapioca pearls have such a fun texture! The recipe is gluten free as long as the non-dairy milk you use is gluten-free. Stevia is a herb used as a completely sugar-free sweetener (see page 102), and the cardamom flavor compliments the stevia nicely. This pudding can be topped with organic berries before serving.

Soak the tapioca pearls in milk for 1 hour.

Transfer tapioca and milk into a small saucepan, and heat on medium-high for 5 minutes, stirring continually to avoid clumps or mixture sticking to bottom of pot.

Whisk in the stevia, cardamom, and salt. Continue to stir for about 10 minutes until a noticeable thickening occurs.

Ladle the pudding into 4 custard bowls, ensuring tapioca is distributed equally. Set the bowls aside on counter to cool for 15 minutes, then transfer to fridge to set for 1 hour.

Eat cool, or allow to warm back up to room temperature before serving.

MAKES 4 SERVINGS.   GF, SF, NF

⌐ Coconut Sticky Rice with Mangoes ⌐

Another tasty dish from my step-father, David, and a beautiful end to an Asian-inspired meal. This recipe is simple to make and easy to present as a fancy dessert if you have a sharp knife and the creativity to play around with the mango slicing.

Combine the rice and water in a saucepan on high heat and bring to a boil. Once boiling, cover, and simmer on low heat for 20 minutes until cooked.

A few minutes before rice has finished simmering, dissolve the sugar or nectar and salt in the coconut milk in a small pan on medium heat.

Transfer the syrup mixture into the cooked rice, cover with a lid, remove from heat, and let sit for 30 minutes.

Fluff rice before serving warm, with the slices of fresh mango and raspberries.

MAKES 4–6 SERVINGS. GF, SF, NF

1 cup uncooked glutinous or "sticky" rice*

1½ cups filtered water

¼ cup organic sugar (fair trade if possible) or agave nectar

¼ tsp sea salt

½ cup coconut milk (canned, non-light version, or see page 108)

2 medium ripe mangoes, peeled & sliced

½–1 cup fresh organic raspberries (optional)

* Glutinous rice doesn't actually contain gluten, it's just sticker than other rices, so it's fine for folks who have Celiac's or are avoiding gluten for other reasons. This rice is easily found in Asian markets, but almost impossible to find anywhere else! Don't let a grocery clerk try to sell you white sushi rice instead; it's glutinous rice you want, and nothing else.

DARK CHOCOLATE PUDDING WITH CHIPOTLE

2¼ cups organic non-dairy milk

1½ cups coconut milk (canned non-light version, or see page 108)

⅔ cup maple syrup or agave nectar, or ½ cup organic sugar*

¼ tsp sea salt

⅔ cup Dutch-processed cocoa powder*

¼ cup non-GM cornstarch

¼–½ tsp chipotle pepper powder (or to taste)

FAIR TRADE & ORGANIC
It's best to use fair trade and organic sugar, coffee, chocolate, and cocoa products whenever possible (see page 103 for more info).

Smoky chipotle peppers are an enticing flavor combination with chocolate. Every time I make this pudding, I wish I had made a double batch – it's just so good.

Combine just 1½ cups non-dairy milk with the coconut milk and syrup, nectar, or sugar, and salt in a 2–3-qt/L saucepan on medium heat (or medium-high, depending on your stove). Stir occasionally, allowing mixture to heat.

Put the remaining 1 cup milk into a bowl and sift in the cocoa and cornstarch, whisking to combine. Pour this into the coconut milk mixture in a slow, steady stream, gently whisking all the while.

Stir in the chipotle (you may start with a smaller amount, taste after 10 minutes, and add more if desired, but try not to be a wuss).

Whisk continually for another 15–20 minutes to avoid clumping or burning the bottom. (Maybe you'll want to get something to read – you can hold the book in one hand and still stir with the other.) Once a noticeable thickening has occurred (although it will thicken more in fridge), transfer mixture to 5–6 custard cups or 1 medium glass or ceramic bowl (no plastic, please – never mix heat with plastic), cover, and set in fridge for at least 2 hours. Alternately, allow to cool on the counter if you're a warm-pudding kind of person.

MAKES 5–6 SERVINGS.   GF, SF, NF (if omitting chipotle)

~ COCOA AVOCADO MOUSSE ~

Oh-ho! Have I got a rich dessert for you! This creamy treat whips up in just a minute or two – all you need is patience to let it cool in the fridge.

Those of you who think of avocado as a vegetable may cringe at the thought of it being featured in a dessert, but I'm happy to point out that it is indeed a fruit (with a nutritional value closer to that of a nut). And with a fairly neutral flavor, avocados can be blended into savory or sweet treats. They're also a great source of B vitamins, folic acid, potassium, tryptophan, and zinc.

Toss all the ingredients into a food processor or blender and whirl for about 30 seconds, until smooth. (You may need to stop the processor, scrape down sides with a silicone spatula, and whirl again.)

Scrape the mousse into 2 small bowls using the spatula and place in fridge to set for 1–2 hours. (Alternately, if you used a ripe avocado that was already chilled in fridge, you can make the pudding and allow it to set in fridge for just half an hour.) Stores in an airtight container in fridge for up to 3 days.

MAKES 2 SERVINGS, BECAUSE IT'S SOOO RICH. THIS RECIPE CAN EASILY BE DOUBLED OR TRIPLED.   GF, SF, NF, R

1 ripe avocado (about size of a large fist), peeled & pitted

½ cup coconut milk (canned, non-light version)*

2 tbsp raw agave nectar (or maple syrup)

2 tbsp cocoa powder (organic, fair trade, Dutch-processed preferred)

* Technically, this recipe isn't completely raw if you're using canned coconut milk. But you can make your own raw coconut milk – see page 108.

ꓓECADENT TRUFFLES

½ cup cocoa powder* (Dutch-processed preferred)

6 oz (170 g) good-quality dark chocolate*,**

⅓ cup good-quality coconut milk (canned, non-light version)

⅛ tsp sea salt (optional)

* FAIR TRADE & ORGANIC
It's best to use fair trade and organic sugar, coffee, chocolate, and cocoa products whenever possible (see page 103 for more info).

** For this recipe, I recommend using Cocoa Camino Fair Trade 70% couverture. Callebaut dark chocolate will also do (although it's not organic or fairly traded).

*** See note on double-boilers on page 217.

These treats are killer (and they make great gifts)! It's easy to get addicted to them, but try to savor one at a time. This recipe can doubled, tripled, or quadrupled.

Line a baking tray or container with parchment paper.

Place the cocoa in a small bowl and set aside.

Chop the chocolate into small and somewhat uniform pieces.

Fill bottom of a double-boiler*** with 1–2 in (2½–5 cm) hot water, place second pot on top, making sure that water in bottom pot isn't touching the bottom of top pot and place double-boiler on stove element. Transfer chocolate into top pot and turn heat on to medium (or medium-high, depending on your stove) so that steam from water in bottom pot will melt chocolate. Stir continually with a silicone spatula to prevent burning or hardening.

Once chocolate has melted into a uniform consistency, about 5 minutes, remove double-boiler from heat. Scrape melted chocolate into a medium bowl, cover, and refrigerate for about 1 hour, until mixture is firm but not hard.

Scoop out 1 tbsp of mixture. (In an ideal world, you'd use a 1-tbsp [15-mL] cookie dough scoop with a release mechanism, but a nice round tablespoon will do.) Roll into a ball (do this quickly as chocolate melts fast – it helps to do this with cold hands), roll the ball in the cocoa to evenly coat, then place on the lined tray or in the lined container. Repeat until you run out of chocolate.

Cover and refrigerate to set, but serve at room temperature (this is very important). Stores in an airtight container in fridge for up to 2 weeks, or in freezer for up to a month.

MAKES ABOUT 12 TRUFFLES.   GF, SF, NF

CHOCOLATE~DIPPED CLEMENTINES

Chocolate with orange and cinnamon reminds me of Christmas time. I make these Clementines every year for my mum's mid-December Cookie Party.

Line a baking tray with parchment paper.

Fill bottom of a double-boiler* with 1–2 in (2½–5 cm) hot water, place second pot on top, making sure that water in bottom pot isn't touching the bottom of top pot and place double-boiler on stove element. Place chocolate in top pot and turn heat on to medium (or medium-high, depending on your stove) so that steam from water in bottom pot will melt chocolate. Stir continually with a silicone spatula to prevent burning or hardening. Once chocolate has melted into a uniform consistency, about 5 minutes, remove double-boiler from heat.

Dip ⅔ of one orange section in chocolate, then lay it gently down on lined tray. Repeat until all chocolate and/or fruit is used, spacing sections equally apart on tray.

Sprinkle with cinnamon then transfer tray to fridge to set for 30 minutes.

Remove from fridge and gently peel the treats off the parchment to arrange on a pretty plate, and serve.

Store in fridge for up to 2 days; otherwise, the Clementine skins will get too tough.

MAKES 5–10 SERVINGS. **GF, SF, NF**

1 cup bittersweet chocolate chips (or chopped chocolate; fair trade & organic if possible)

¼ cup organic non-dairy milk &/or filtered water

5 Clementine oranges, peeled & separated into sections

cinnamon (for finishing)

* See note on double-boilers on page 217.

⟋ After Dinner Rooibos Chai ⟍

4 cups filtered water

1 heaping tbsp loose rooibos/
red bush tea leaves (or 2 tea
bags)

1 thumb-sized piece fresh ginger
root, chopped

2 cinnamon sticks

3 star anise

3 cloves

6 green cardamom pods

6 black peppercorns

1 tsp fennel seeds

2 cups organic non-dairy milk
(may use vanilla-flavored)

2 tbsp maple syrup

I like to serve chai at the end of a dinner party. This hot, spiced beverage helps digestion and is nice to enjoy before dessert (or instead of dessert). Green tea, or even black tea, can be substituted for rooibos.

Combine the water, tea, ginger, cinnamon, star anise, cloves, cardamom, peppercorns, and fennel in a saucepan on high heat and bring to a boil. Once boiling, reduce heat to simmer, stir, cover, and simmer for 7 minutes.

Whisk in the milk and syrup, and reduce heat to low for another 3 minutes more (ensure heat is low, or milk will separate).

Adjust the spices or sweetness to taste, then carefully pour through a strainer into teacups or mugs.

MAKES 4–6 SERVINGS.   GF, SF, NF

⟋ Quick Rooibos Chai ⟍

1 rooibos/red bush tea bag

1 cinnamon stick

1 star anise

1 green cardamom pod

1 clove

1 black peppercorn

1 cup just-boiled water

½ cup organic non-dairy milk
(may use vanilla-flavored)

1 tsp maple syrup

Chai for one? I like to make a big mug for myself as an evening treat.

Place the tea bag, cinnamon stick, star anise, cardamom, and clove in a large mug.

Pour in the just-boiled water. Allow to steep for 5–8 minutes.

Remove tea bag, stir in the milk and syrup, and enjoy.

MAKES 1 SERVING.   GF, SF, NF

MULLED WINE

I based this recipe on one I found on a culinary website. For this drink, you do not need to splurge on expensive wine – a cheap, though preferably organic or local, wine will do just fine.

Pour the wine into a 3-qt/L saucepan. Add the cinnamon, cloves, allspice, anise, orange peel, and syrup or nectar. Stir, cover, and heat slowly on low for 10 minutes – do not allow to boil, or even simmer, it should just barely steam.

Remove from heat, stir in rum, and serve.

MAKES ABOUT 4 SERVINGS. RECIPE CAN EASILY BE DOUBLED OR TRIPLED. GF, SF, NF

1 (750 mL) bottle red wine

3 cinnamon sticks

5 whole cloves

4 whole allspice

2 whole star anise

peel of 1 large organic orange (white pith removed)

¼ cup maple syrup or agave nectar (or to taste)

½ cup dark rum (optional)

HOT CHOCOLATE

A cozy treat after a day of tobogganing. If you have vegan marshmallows, plunk one in each mug of hot chocolate before serving so you can indulge in this childhood treat once more.

Heat the milk in a saucepan on low, stirring occasionally.

Break or chop the chocolate into small pieces and add to heated milk. Stir continually until chocolate is melted. Stir in the cayenne or chipotle pepper if desired.

Pour into mugs, and sprinkle with the cinnamon or nutmeg.

MAKES 2 SERVINGS. GF, SF, NF

2 cups organic non-dairy milk

3 oz (85 g) semi-sweet chocolate (organic & fair trade if possible)

ground cinnamon or grated fresh nutmeg (optional)

For spicy hot chocolate:

¼ tsp cayenne or chipotle pepper powder

COFFEE SYRUP

3 cups filtered water

1 tsp pure vanilla extract

¾ cup sugar (organic & fair trade if possible)

1 cup or ¼ lb (113 g) coffee beans (organic & fair trade if possible)

This is a treat from my stepfather David, who makes a batch every summer as soon as it gets hot. For iced coffee, pour syrup into bottom ¼ of a glass. Add ice, fill with organic non-dairy milk, and stir. Coffee syrup can also be drizzled on organic non-dairy ice cream.

Combine the water, vanilla, and sugar in a large pot on high heat and bring to a boil. Boil for 5 minutes.

Grind the coffee beans (not too finely), then add to the boiling liquid, stir, and allow to boil for another 4 minutes.

Remove from heat and allow the syrup to cool. Once cool, strain into a sterilized bottle or jar and store in fridge.

MAKES ABOUT 2 CUPS (OR ENOUGH FOR ABOUT 8 ICED COFFEES).
GF, SF, NF

CHAPTER

21

CLEANSING AND DETOXIFICATION

I often meet people who are interested in a cleansing, or detoxification, program, but they don't have sufficient information to do one in a successful or healthy way. I've heard, "I was doing a juice fast last week, but then I went to a potluck and had a bowl of chili and a piece of chocolate cake." Or at a party, beer in hand: "I just finished a week of drinking only lemon water with cayenne and maple syrup." *Yikes.* People can make themselves sick in an attempt to get healthier because they're unaware that cleansing can have serious effects on their bodies and needs to be approached with care. And I'm sorry to say, doing a cleanse once a year doesn't give you a get-out-of-jail-free card to commit complete debauchery the rest of the time.

Beer in hand or not, many of us do have a general understanding that our world is not as clean as it once was – so no matter where we go, we're exposed to toxins. Cleansing is supposed to help reduce the exposure to and eliminate the accumulation of toxins in the body. It can also help pro-tect our bodies from developing allergies, arthritis, and cancer. I've limited the discussion to some very basic cleansing protocols, but if you want more extensive information, see the Resource List on page 256.

If you're new to cleansing, maybe a fast – meaning, a chunk of time where you eat no food and subsist only on liquids, like water, herb teas, fresh juices, and soup broths – isn't what you need straight off. It's better to start cleansing simply by cutting out the crap from your diet and focus on eating what will nourish you.

WHY CLEANSE?

It's generally understood in holistic health circles that our bodies are designed to function well, if we support them. One of the primary causes of disease is the accumulation of wastes (substances we don't need) that aren't eliminated from the body. Our bodies are designed to be a healing environment, but if our health is compromised or we are exposed to too many toxins, our bodies lose their ability to fight off disease and allergens.

Each person tolerates toxin exposure and exhibits symptoms of toxicity in different ways – two people with similar lifestyles can develop sickness or disease differently. When the body is overloaded with toxins, it may manifest as:

• Allergies (congestion, sinus inflammation, itchy eyes)

When talking about "toxins," I'm referring to things like:
- *Dirty air & water*
- *Pesticide, insecticide & hormone residues from conventionally-produced foods*
- *Stimulants like sugar, caffeine, alcohol, drugs (prescription & street), cigarettes*
- *Foods you're allergic to*
- *Synthetic chemicals from body care & household products (like cleaners & paints)*
- *Xenoestrogens from plastic products (see page 70)*
- *Stress & negative thoughts*

Let me remind you that I'm no doctor, and it would be wise to consult with your health care provider before changing your routine/health regime. Serious detoxing is not appropriate for women who are pregnant or breastfeeding and should be approached cautiously by people on meds or with a chronic condition like diabetes. Again, talk to a health professional that you respect and trust.

- Poor digestion (gas, bloating, constipation, diarrhea)
- Less-than-glowing skin (zits, rashes, eczema, psoriasis)
- Unhealthy body weight
- Fatigue, dizziness
- Inability to focus (lack of concentration, overactive mind, Attention Deficit Disorder)
- Anger, irritability, negative thoughts
- Headaches, migraines
- Muscle & joint pain
- Respiratory problems (coughing, wheezing, bronchitis, asthma, emphysema)
- Menstrual irregularities, infertility
- Chronic illness (irritable bowel syndrome, Crohn's, colitis, diverticulitis, diabetes, cardiovascular disease)
- Infection (bacterial, viral, fungal, parasitic – e.g., urinary tract infections, yeast infections, candida, dysbiosis)
- Mental illness (depression, anxiety, autism, Alzheimer's, Parkinson's, senility)
- Cancer, other major diseases

With toxin accumulation leading to all this unpleasantness, it's important to eliminate toxins and waste from our systems regularly.

I typically cleanse for 1–2 weeks at the change of the season in spring and fall, as less extreme temperatures put less stress on our bodies. You, however, should do what feels right for you and fits realistically into your lifestyle – a whole month of cleansing would be amazing, a week would be great, but a few days, or one day in a week would also be helpful.

The basics of cleansing the body of toxins are listed next. In general, I highly recommend these steps to people who are new to cleansing or want to regularly cleanse but have a busy schedule. If you want to do a more thorough detox program, it's best to consult your health care practitioner to find one that's best for your needs.

CLEANSING BASICS

Increase your daily consumption of clean (filtered) water. Carry a non-plastic water bottle filled with the stuff when you're out and about. Aim to drink a glass each hour. Room temperature water is better for your body (cold water can shock the system) and sipping is better than chugging. Avoid drinking liquids with meals as it dilutes your digestive juices.

Start your morning with lemon water (see page 105), first thing – before eating your breakfast, and especially before downing your cup of coffee. As you drink the Good Morning Elixir, imagine it reaching your liver and saying, "Good morning! Time to wake up and do your day's work!"

Improve the quality of your food. The foods you eat the most should be organic – other foods that should be organic are: any animal products (meat, dairy, eggs – if you're not vegan),

YOU MAY WANT TO DO A CLEANSE BECAUSE YOU:
- *Have headaches, skin problems, allergies, poor digestion*
- *Are struggling with infertility, mental health issues, or weight gain/loss*
- *Have a chronic health condition that's not improving*
- *Have irregular menstrual cycles, or yeast or urinary tract infections*
- *Want to get pregnant and avoid morning sickness, produce healthier children, and offer them cleaner breast milk*
- *Live in the world and for that reason alone are sadly exposed to far too many toxins*

* *Improves digestion*
* *Greater sense of calm & ease*
* *Clearer thinking & better focus*
* *Improves health*
* *Reduces reoccurrence of chronic conditions & diseases*

oils, leafy greens, and berries, as they have the highest exposure to pesticides when produced conventionally (see page 62). Organics can seem expensive, but sometimes it's a question of priority. When you're at a bar, order a juice instead of a beer and put the cash you saved toward more organics on your next grocery shop.

Eat a healthy serving of greens everyday (2–4 cups). Dark leafy greens, (like kale, collards, chard, spinach, dandelion greens, and parsley) contain many important minerals – lightly steaming them (2 minutes max, don't overcook) can make them easier to digest and makes their calcium more bioavailable than when they're raw. Alternatively, take a greens powder supplement like spirulina or chlorella.

Eat veggies from the cruciferous family at least every other day. These foods include broccoli, cauliflower, Brussels sprouts, cabbage, and kale. Crucifers contain sulforaphane, which has been found to increase the liver's ability to detoxify carcinogenic compounds and free radicals. (These veggies have also been proven to support complex chemical processes related to estrogen in the body that reduce risk of breast cancer.)

Fill up on fruit (2–6 pieces a day) – they're full of water, fiber, and vitamins that you need. When I cleanse, fruit is the primary component of my breakfast. (You may want to include protein too though to stay grounded – try making a smoothie with hemp or another good-quality protein powder.)

Incorporate more raw foods into your diet, especially in spring and summer.

Avoid flour products (baked goods, pastas) and eat whole grains instead. Non-glutinous grains, like brown rice, quinoa, millet, and buckwheat, are less congesting, or "cleaner-burning" in your system.

Increase fiber intake to help eliminate toxins and balance blood sugar levels. Try the "Apple Pie" Fiber Drink (page 106) – I drink it up to 4 times a day during a cleanse.

Eliminate all stimulants – sugar, caffeine, alcohol, drugs (prescription and street), and cigarettes. If you're addicted, do your darndest to cut down.

Reduce food additives like salt and excess oil (other than EFA-rich oils like flax seed, hemp seed, and olive). This is easier to do if you're eating home-cooked meals. Instead of salt, try using dulse powder.

Throw out conventional body care products. Drug-store shampoos made with synthetic perfumes and dyes? Antiperspirant made with aluminum? *Yech*. Not sweating is a bad idea anyway, as sweating is a primary way for our bodies to eliminate waste – sweating is good for you. Spending short periods of time in a sauna during a cleanse is helpful (consult a naturopathic doctor to guide you on a sauna detox program).

Exercise. You just don't have the time, right? If you do not already have a regular exercise program, start off with a small amount exercise everyday day (even if it's just for 2 minutes), and work your way up to 20–40 minutes a day. Aim to work yourself up into a good sweat at least twice a week. If you start with small goals, you'll likely to have more success in the long run.

Meditate for 5–20 minutes, once or twice a day; or do conscious breathing (observing your inhales and exhales). Think of your in-breaths as nourishing and your out-breaths as cleansing. Your mind will wander (it always does) – don't criticize yourself, just label the thoughts as "thinking," and return to the awareness of your breath.

Manifest happy, accepting, generous, and optimistic thoughts and feelings (with genuine sincerity, of course). Anger and negativity are toxic! You could be doing everything else on this list, but if you're walking around with the belief that the world has it in for you, you're never going to be truly healthy. (If you need help with this, pick up a copy of Louise Hay's bestseller *You Can Heal Your Life*.)

Turn off the TV.

Limit time spent at the computer.

Avoid stressful situations, or manage them as efficiently as you can.

Get a decent night's sleep. Try to get to bed before midnight (as your body best produces melatonin between 1 and 3 a.m. and you need to be sound asleep for that). Also allow yourself to have a period of rest during the day if you can.

DETOX SIDE EFFECTS

As your body begins to be cleansed of toxins, it's common for you to experience some side effects, as the toxins that have been deep in storage (often in your fat cells) in your body are being mobilized. Be sure to allow all that junk to be flushed out of your system – drink water, eat fiber, and sweat it out. At this time, it's important to listen to your body – be

HERBAL CLEANSING KITS

Health food stores offer herbal cleansing kits to supplement cleansing programs; follow their specific guidelines. Otherwise, you may also consult a naturopathic doctor, herbalist, or homeopath about creating a herbal cleansing program tailored to your needs. Milk thistle and dandelion tinctures are often recommended for liver support.

DRY SKIN BRUSHING

Skin, as the largest organ in the body, plays a huge role in detoxification. Dry skin brushing helps to keep your pores open, encouraging the elimination of toxins and other metabolic waste products. It also improves the surface circulation of your blood and lymphatic fluid, resulting in a stronger immune system and increased ability to bring much-needed oxygen and other nutrients to your skin.

Use a natural (non-synthetic) bristle brush or loofah. (I like the bristle area to be about the size of my hand and a long enough handle so that I can reach my middle back.) Brushing shouldn't scratch, but you should feel friction against your skin. Brushing dry skin is best – doing it before showering or bathing so you can then wash off any dead skin cells and you won't feel itchy.

The experts say to brush in circular strokes, but I often just do straight sweeps toward the direction of my heart. Start on the soles of your feet and moving up to your ankles, calves, thighs, butt, abdomen, breasts/chest, and back. Then brush palms of your hands, wrists, arms, and shoulders. If your face is too sensitive for brushing, you can skip it; ditto for the inner thighs. Give your brush a soap-and-water wash every few weeks to keep it clean.

patient and kind to yourself, and get lots of rest.

Although you probably won't experience extreme cases of the symptoms below, you may notice:

• Bad breath
• Stronger body odor
• Increased gas
• Itchy skin, break outs
• Irritability, higher emotions
• Fatigue, sleep routine changes
• Aches, headaches (especially in first 3 days)
• Symptoms from past illnesses

It's quite common for our bodies to exhibit heightened signs of toxicity as toxins become mobilized, though they should subside quickly as you flush them out.

DETOX TOOL KIT & SHOPPING LIST

Here is a list of equipment and groceries that will aid you in keeping your body clean and healthy, whether you are have daily cleansing practices or are following a time-limited detoxification regime.

Tool kit

☐ Water filter
☐ Non-plastic water bottle
☐ Lemon reamer
☐ Coffee grinder (not for coffee, silly – for flax seeds!)
☐ Yoga mat, running shoes
☐ Tongue scraper
☐ Dry skin brush
☐ Juicer

Shopping list

☐ Organic lemons (for lemon water, see page 105)
☐ Fresh whole flax seeds (to grind & sprinkle on foods for additional fiber)
☐ Fresh organic (& local) produce
☐ Greens powder (for juices & smoothies)
☐ Dulse powder (to replace salt)

CONGESTION & TOXICITY CHART

(This chart includes animal products for those of us who may not be vegan.)

Most Congresting/ More Potentially Toxic						Least Congesting/ More Detoxifying
drugs allergenic foods organ meats hydrogenated fats	fats fried foods refined flours meats	sweets milk eggs baked goods	nuts seeds beans pasta wheat	rice millet buckwheat oats potatoes	roots squash other veg	fruit greens herbs water

APPENDIX
Mouth-Watering Menu Ideas • Resource List

MOUTH-WATERING MENU IDEAS

I will never forget the embarrassing evening I served my then-boyfriend's family a meal with tofu in every dish. I was the stereotypical vegan wearing a cute apron. It taught me the value of menu planning – a chance to see the big picture before you hit the grocery store. Have a Choose-Your-Own-Adventure approach to these suggestions – I often find a soup and a salad is enough for a meal, but you may want to make most of the dishes in a particular menu if you're feeding a large brood of hungry guests.

Comfort foods I

Leek & Potato Soup (page 173)

Buttahmilk Biscuits (page 132)

Roasted veggies (e.g., Brussels sprouts, fennel bulb, onions) **or** steamed greens (e.g., broccoli, kale, Swiss Chard) (see page 89)

"Macaroni & cheese" – Red Star Sauce (page 158) on cooked brown rice pasta – **or** Andrew's Butternut Risotto (page 181)

Dark Chocolate Pudding with Chipotle (page 240)

Comfort foods II

Fresh salad (see pages 146–47) with Duma Dressing (page 149)

Creemy Corn Soup (page 170)

Almost Focaccia Bread (page 136) **or** Molasses Cornbread (page 134)

The Good Shepherd's Pie (page 198)

Maple Roasted Roots (page 185) **or** roasted squash (see page 90)

Apple Crumble (page 220) **or** Creemy Rice Pudding (page 237)

Easy Tea (page 110)

Simple weeknight dinner

Fresh salad with raw pumpkin seeds (see pages 146–47) and House Dressing (page 148)

Cannellini Kale Soup (page 168) **or** Sesame Kale Soba (page 192)

Maple Roasted Roots (page 185)

Decadent Date Smoothie (page 109) **or** Hot Chocolate (page 245) **or** Quick Rooibos Chai (page 244)

Summer barbecue

Fresh salad (see page 146–47) (including local organic strawberries & raw almonds) with Balsamic Vinaigrette (page 149)

Quinoa Tabouleh (page 153)

Portobello Burgers with Sunchoke Oven Fries & Homemade Ketchup (page 194) **or** marinated grilled veggies (e.g., bell peppers, eggplant, tomatoes, zucchini)

Almond Chocolate Creem Pie (page 217) **or** Glazed Lemon Poppy Seed Cake (page 212) **or** Coffee Syrup (page 246) over organic non-dairy ice cream

Indian supper I

Mango Salad (page 151)

Simple Dal (page 171) over chopped fresh spinach

Steamed broccoli &/or roasted cauliflower (see page 89) with Date Apple Chutney (page 157)

Creemy Rice Pudding (page 237) with cardamom & pistachios **or** Cardamom Tapioca Pudding (page 238)

After-Dinner Rooibos Chai (page 244)

Indian supper II

Red Lentil Hummus (page 139) with fresh carrots & bell peppers &/or store-bought papadums

Coconut Cauliflower Chana (page 186) over chopped fresh spinach

Date Coconut Cookies (page 226) **or** Carob Chai Cake with Cardamom Icing (page 206)

After-Dinner Rooibos Chai (page 244) **or** Turmeric Ginger Tea (page 111)

East Asian supper

Colorful Pressed Salad (page 151)

Mighty Miso Soup (page 174)

Sesame Kale Soba (page 192)

Coconut Sticky Rice with Mangoes (page 239)

Southeast Asian supper

Sweet Potato & Coconut Milk Soup (page 178) **or** Green Coconut Milk Curry (page 191)

Marinated & grilled tempeh (see page 182) with Perfect Peanut Sauce (page 158)

Beet & Green Bean Toss (page 154) with Simplest Salad Dressing (page 148)

Steamed brown rice (see page 90)

Fresh fruit salad (serve 30 minutes after dinner) with mangoes, bananas, pineapple, papaya & fresh lime juice (see page 113)

Italian feast

Fresh salad (see pages 146–47) with Balsamic Vinaigrette (page 149)

Almost Focaccia Bread (page 136)

Cannellini Kale Soup (page 168)

Spaghetti Squash with Pinenut Parm (page 188) **or** Luscious Lasagne (page 199) **or** Fettuccini No-Fredo (page 189) **or** Andrew's Butternut Risotto (page 181)

Fig & Anise Biscotti (page 233) **or** Chocolate-Dipped Biscotti (page 234) **or** Sweet Almond Cupcakes (page 214) **or** Mocha Fudge Pudding Cake (page 208)

Mediterranean dinner

Baba Ganouj (page 141) with chopped fresh veggies

Moroccan Garbanzo Bean Soup (page 175) over chopped fresh spinach or Swiss chard

Quinoa Tabouleh (page 153) **or** Millet-Stuffed Bell Peppers (page 196) **or** Mushroom Quinoa Pilaf (page 184)

Tahini Thumbprint Cookies (page 232) **or** Sweet Almond Cupcakes (page 214)

Mexican fiesta

Great Guacamole (page 142) & Fresh Summer Salsa (page 144) with non-GM tortilla chips

Adzuki-Squash Soup with Chipotle & Red Peppers (page 177)

Pinto's Refried Bean Burritos (page 197) **or** Chili Non-Carné with Pan-Seared Polenta (page 193) & chopped fresh lettuce

Brownies with Wings (page 236)

Weekend brunch

Fresh fruit salad (see page 113)

Immune Boost Juice (page 110)

Cinnamon Swirl Biscuits (page 133) **or** Blueberry Breakfast Polenta (page 121)

Fresh green salad with dressing of choice (see chapter 15)

Maple Tempeh Strips (page 122) **or** Tofu Scram (page 123) **or** Crispy-Fried Tofu (page 123)

Maple Roasted Roots (page 185) **or** Sunchoke Oven Fries with Homemade Ketchup (page 195)

Picnic lunch

Cilantro Black Bean Dip (page 140) with chopped veggies or flat bread

Colorful Pressed Salad (page 151) **or** fresh green salad with dressing of choice (see chapter 15)

Ginger Sesame Pasta Salad (page 152) **or** Chickpea Salad (page 153) **or** Pesto White Bean Bowl (page 190)

Chewy Peanut Buttah Cookies (page 229) **or** Cowgrrrl Cookies (page 225) **or** Great Date Squares (page 235)

Living foods feast

Fresh salad with sprouts (see pages 146–47) & Green Tahini Dressing (page 150)

Caroline's Raw Veggie Paté (page 144) on sweet potato rounds or store-bought raw crackers

Summer squash spaghetti – spiralized zucchini with Fresh Tomato Sauce (page 156) or Fresh Basil Pesto (page 156) & Pinenut Parm (page 188)

Cocoa Avocado Mousse (page 241) **or** Raw Carob Almond Cookies (page 230)

Thanksgiving feast

Apple Carrot Soup with Coriander (page 165) **or** Broccoli Creem Soup (page 167)

Spiced Squash Muffins (page 131)

The Good Shepherd's Pie (page 198)

Millet-Stuffed Bell Peppers (page 196) with Miso Gravy (page 160)

Maple Roasted Roots (page 185) **or** roasted veggies (e.g., , Brussels sprouts, fennel bulb, squash)

Steamed greens (see page 89)

Pumpkin Pie with Cashew Creem (page 218)

Winter holiday feast

Beautiful Borscht (page 166) **or** Leek & Potato Soup (page 173) **or** Portobello Soup (page 176)

Millet & Mushroom Tourtière (page 200) with Cashew Gravy (page 159)

Steamed greens (see page 89)

Roasted veggies (e.g., Brussels sprouts, fennel bulb, squash, sweet potatoes)

Spiced Swirl Bundt Cake with Buttahmilk Glaze (page 209) **or** Shortbread Cookies (page 224)

Chocolate-Dipped Clementines (page 243)

Mulled Wine (page 245)

RESOURCE LIST

Chapters noted in the brackets denote which sections of the book in which the resources are most applicable.

Barnard, Tanya, and Sarah Kramer. *How It All Vegan!* Vancouver: Arsenal Pulp Press, 1999. (Chapter 1)

Bateson-Koch, Carolee. *Allergies*. Burnaby, BC: Alive Books, 1994.

Brown, Ruth Tal, and Jennifer Houston. *Fresh at Home*. Toronto: Penguin, 2004.

Burros, Marian. "Is Organic Food More Nutritious?: Is Organic Food Provably Better?" *The New York Times* (July 16, 2003). (Chapter 4)

CarbonCounted (*carboncounted.com*) (Chapter 4)

Colbin, Annemarie. *Food and Healing*. New York: Ballantine Books, 1986. (Chapters 1 & 2)

Cook's Illustrated editors. *Baking Illustrated*. Brookline, Massachusetts: America's Test Kitchen, 2004. (Chapter 10)

Cook's Illustrated magazines (Chapters 7 & 8)

Coop Directory Service, The (*coopdirectory. org*) (Chapter 6)

Cousens, Gabriel. *Conscious Eating*. Berkeley: North Atlantic Books, 2000. (Chapter 2)

Davis, Brenda, and Vesanto Melina. *Becoming Vegan*. Summertown, TN: Book Publishing Company, 2000. (Chapter 2)

Duke, James A. *The Green Pharmacy Herbal Handbook*. New York: Rodale Inc., 2000.

Dupont, Caroline Marie. *Enlightened Eating*. Richmond Hill, ON: Health and Beyond Publishing, 2006.

Environmental Working Group (*ewg.org*) (Chapter 4)

Erasmus, Udo. *Fats that Heal, Fats that Kill*. Vancouver: Alive Books, 1993. (Chapter 3)

Galland, Leo. *Superimmunity for Kids*. New York: Dell, 1988.

Garcia, Deborah Koons. *The Future of Food* (film). Mill Valley, CA: Lily Films, 2005. (Chapter 4)

Green Living Now (*greenlivingnow.com/ column/irradiation.htm.*) (Chapter 4)

Haas, Elson M. *Staying Healthy with Nutrition*. Berkeley: Celestial Arts, 2006. (Chapter 3)

———. *Staying Healthy with the Seasons*. Berkeley: Celestial Arts, 1981. (Chapter 23)

———. *The New Detox Diet*. Berkeley: Celestial Arts, 2004. (Chapter 23)

———. *The Staying Healthy Shoppers' Guide*. Berkeley: Celestial Arts, 1999. (Chapter 6)

Happy Cow's Vegetarian Guide to Restaurants and Health Food Stores (*happycow.com*) (Chapter 2)

Hay, Louise L. *You Can Heal Your Life*. Carlsbad, CA: Hay House Publishing, 1984. (Chapters 2 & 23)

Hurd, Frank J., and Rosalie Hurd. *A Good Cook ...Ten Talents*. Collegedale, TN: The College Press, 1968.

Issenmen, Jo Ann. *To Love and Feed People*. Vancouver, BC: EarthWorks Publishing, 1993. (Chapter 10)

Katzen, Mollie. *Honest Pretzels*. Berkley: Tricycle Press, 1999.

———. *The New Moosewood Cookbook*. Berkley: Ten Speed Press, 2000.

Kaur, Sat Dharam, et al. *The Complete Natural Medicine Guide to Women's Health*. Toronto: Robert Rose, 2005. (Chapters 3 & 23)

Kingsolver, Barbara, et al. *Animal, Vegetable, Miracle*. New York: HarperCollins, 2007. (Chapter 4)

Lappé, Anna, and Bryant Terry. *Grub*. New York: Penguin, 2006.

Lee, Stella, et al. *The Supermarket Tour*. Hamilton, ON: OPIRG – McMaster University, 2001. (Chapter 6)

Local Food Plus (*localflavourplus.ca*) (Chapter 4)

Local Harvest.org (*localharvest.org/food-coops*) (Chapter 6)

Loux, Renée. *The Balanced Plate*. New York: Rodale Press, 2006.

Madison, Deborah. *Vegetarian Cooking for Everyone*. New York: Broadway Books, 1997.

Marieb, Elaine N. *Essentials of Human Anatomy and Physiology*. 8th ed. San Francisco: Pearson Education, 2006. (Chapter 3)

McEachern, Leslie. *The Angelica Home Kitchen*. Berkley: Ten Speed Press, 2003.

Mitrea, Lilieana Stadler. *Pathology and Nutrition*. Toronto: CSNN Publishing, 2005.

Moosewood Collective. *Moosewood Restaurant Book of Desserts*. New York: Clarkson N. Potter, 1997.

Moosewood Collective. *Sundays at Moosewood Restaurant*. New York: Simon & Schuster/Fireside, 1990.

Moskowitz, Isa Chandra, and Terry Hope Romero. *Vegan Cupcakes Take Over the World*. New York: Marlowe & Company, 2006.

Murray, Michael. *Diabetes and Hypoglycemia*. Roseville, CA: Prima Publishing, 1994.

———., et al. *The Encyclopedia of Healing Foods*. New York: Atria Books, 2005.

People's Potato Project Collective. *Vegan on a Shoestring*. Montreal: People's Potato, 2002.

PETA – People for the Ethical Treatment of Animals (*peta.org*) (Chapter 1)

Pfeiffer, Carl C. *Nutrition and Mental Illness*. Rochester, VT: Healing Arts Press, 1987. (Chapter 3)

Pitchford, Paul. *Healing with Whole Foods*. 3rd ed. Berkley: North Atlantic Books, 2002. (Chapters 2 & 23)

Porter, Jessica. *The Hip Chick's Guide to Macrobiotics*. New York: Avery, 2004.

Raw Family (*rawfamily.com*) (Chapter 2)

Raw School (*rawschool.com*) (Chapter 2)

Robertson, Laurel, et al. *The New Laurel's Kitchen*. Berkley: Ten Speed Press, 1986.

Sass, Lorna J. *Lorna Sass' Complete Vegetarian Kitchen*. New York: Hearst Books, 1992.

Shiva, Vandana. *Stolen Harvest*. Cambridge, MA: South End Press, 2000. (Chapter 4)

Smith, Alisa, and J. B. MacKinnon. *The 100-Mile Diet*. Toronto: Random House, 2007. (Chapter 4)

Stepaniak, Joanne. *The Vegan Sourcebook*. Los Angeles: Lowell House, 2000.

Underkoffler, Renee Loux. *Living Cuisine*. New York: Avery, 2003. (Chapters 2 & 5)

Water Filter Comparisons. (*waterfiltercomparisons.net*) (Chapter 5)

Wikipedia.org

Wood, Rebecca. *The New Whole Foods Encyclopedia*. New York: Penguin, 1999. (Chapter 5)

The World's Healthiest Foods (*whfoods.com*) (Chapters 3 & 5)

INDEX

Note: Page numbers that are italicized denote an informational reference about the entry.

jae steele is a registered holistic nutritionist who divides her time between Montreal and Toronto. She is the author of several vegan cookzines and features whole-foods recipes on her popular blog, *Domestic Affair* (*domesticaffair.ca*). jae has applied her passion for food to her work with children, on organic farms, and as a vegan baker and health workshop facilitator.